THE UNOFFICIAL HARRY POTTER COOKBOOK

FROM BUTTERBEER TO PUMPKIN PASTIES—
MORE THAN 80 MAGICAL RECIPES!

By
TOM GRIMM

With photos by
TOM GRIMM & DIMITRIE HARDER

Moseley Road Inc.

To my children,
who, after years full of darkness,
gave me the gift of once again believing
in wonder and magic.

Moseley Road Inc.

Copyright © 2020 Heel Verlag GmbH
Email: info@heel-verlag.de
www.heel-verlag.de

Originally published in German by HEEL Verlag GmbH, 53639 Koenigswinter,
Germany under the title: Das inoffizielle Kochbuch für Harry Potter Fans
All rights reserved.

Project Editor: Hannah Kwella
Text and Recipes: Tom Grimm, Grinning Cat Productions
Art Direction: Tom Grimm
Food Photography: Dimitrie Harder & Tom Grimm
Graphic Design: Roberts Urlovskis
Endpaper Illustrations: Angelos Tsirigotis

US Editor: Finn Moore
US Production: Adam Moore
Cover Design: Kate Stretton & Adam Moore
US Publisher: Sean Moore

Translated from the German by First Edition Translations Ltd

DISCLAIMER
Some words are trademarked and are the property of the trademark holder. They have been used for identification purposes only with no intention of infringement of the trademark. The book is not authorized or endorsed by J.K. Rowling, Pottermore Ltd., Wizarding World Digital LLC., Warner Bros. Entertainment Inc. or any other Harry Potter rights holder. All texts, graphic elements, and properties in this book are used exclusively within the framework of the right of quotation according the German Copyright Act (Urhebergesetz §5) and the Berne Convention; any aforementioned copyright holders and / or other Harry Potter Rights holders remain unaffected.

The recipes in this book are tried and tasted by the author. Every effort has been taken to review each recipe carefully. You may not always achieve the results desired due to various reasons like quality of products, variations in ingredients, individual cooking ability etc.The reader assumes full responsibility for using their best judgment when cooking with raw ingredients such as beef, poultry, or eggs, and seeking information from an official food safety authority if they are unsure. Readers should review all listed ingredients in a recipe before cooking to ensure that none of the ingredients may cause a potential adverse reaction to anyone eating the food based on recipes featured this book. This includes allergies, pregnancy-related diet restrictions, etc. This book and the recipes contained in it have been written to the best of our knowledge and belief. Neither the publisher nor the author bear responsibility for unintended reactions or adverse affects.

ISBN: 978-1-62669-209-1
Printed in China

10 9 8 7 6 5 4 3 2 1

Content

Magic for Muggles! 8

Fresh from *Honeydukes*
Cauldron cakes 12
Bertie Bott's Beans 14
Cockroach Clusters 16
Butterbeer Fudge 18
Drooble's Best Blowing Gum 20
Chocolate Frogs 22
Pumpkin Juice 24
Dumbledore's Favorite Lemon Drops 26
Ice Mice 28
Canary Creams 30
Jelly Slugs 32
Bat's Blood Soup 34

From the Menu of the *Leaky Cauldron*
Hot Chocolate 38
Elfwine 40
Chocolate Pudding 42
Butterbeer 44
Scotch Eggs 46
Black Pudding 48
Shepherd's Pie 50
Pea Soup 52

Privet Drive Delicacies
Aunt Petunia's Windtorte Pudding 56
Hearty Mulligatawny Curry Soup 58
Fruitcake 60
Lemon Meringue Tart 62
Poached Salmon with Honey Mustard Dill Sauce 64
Knickerbocker Glory 66
Pork Loin with Apple Glaze and Peach 68

From the "World's Best Cook"
Corned Beef Sandwich 72
Apple Cakes 74
Pumpkin Pasties 76

Ginger Snaps	78
Ginny Weasley's Pepperup Paprikash	80
Christmas Cakes	82
Meatballs in Onion Sauce	84
Chicken and Ham Pasty	86
Mince Pies	88
Eggnog	90

Hogwarts Culinary Delights

Beauxbatons Bouillabaisse	94
Dragon Meat Tartare	96
Stuffed Feast Day Turkey	98
Bread Pudding	100
Fluffy Mashed Potatoes and Gravy	102
Luna Lovegood's Radish Salad	104
Beef Goulash	106
Braised Lamb Cutlets with Green Beans	108
Golden Snitches	110
Harry's Gillyweed Salad	112
Syrup Torte	114
Scrambled Eggs with Bacon	116
Roast Beef with Yorkshire Pudding and Butter Peas	118
Baked Sweet Potatoes	120
Felix Felicis	122
Juicy Roasted Chicken Thighs	124
Vol-au-vents	126
Oatmeal with Fresh Fruit	128
Fried Green Tomatoes	130
Pheasant with Lentils and Grilled Corn on the Cob	132
Dumbledore's Favorite Tea	134
Hedwig Muffins	136

Hagrid's Attempts at Cooking

Harry's Birthday Cake	140
Rock Cookies	142
Spider Eggs	144
Raisin Buns	146

Dobby's House-Elf Cuisine

Dobby's Veggie Frittata	150
Dobby's Turkey Sloppy Joes	152

Dobby's Bowtie Pasta with Broccoli Sauce 154
Dobby's Spicy Pineapple Salad 156

Nearly-Headless Nick's Deathday Party
Maggoty Haggis 160
Rotten Fish 162
Coal-Black Charred Pastry and Moldy Cheese 164
Gravestone Cake with Tar Frosting 166

Magical Morsels from the Wizarding World
Magic Wands 170
Polyjuice Potion 172
Shortbread Howler 174
Baby Mandrakes 176
Enchanted Apple Strudel 178
Kreacher's Onion Soup 180

Classics from the *Three Broomsticks*
Gigglewater 184
Gillywater 186
Old Firewhisky 188
Hot Mulled Mead 190

Acknowledgments 192

Magic for Muggles!

On July 31, 1991, his 11th birthday, the orphan Harry Potter discovered not just a world of magic and wonder, but also a whole universe of culinary delights!

Since the death of his parents by the hand of He-Who-Shall-Not-Be-Named, Harry, the "Boy Who Survived," had languished, unwanted and unloved, in a tiny room under the stairs at the Dursleys' house. He hardly ever got the slightest morsel from their table. Now, he suddenly found himself surrounded by a veritable universe of delicacies and treats, wherever he went. In Diagon Alley, in the Hogwarts Express, at the Weasleys', in establishments like the *Three Broomsticks* and the *Leaky Cauldron*, in *Honeydukes*—and, of course, at the Hogwarts wizarding school itself, where at all mealtimes there were luxuriantly laid tables with the most wonderful dishes to delight the palates of the hungry pupils.

In J. K. Rowling's Harry Potter novels, eating and drinking play a fundamental role. During his first visit to the Burrow, the cozy home of his best friend Ron's family, "[b]ooks were stacked three deep on the mantelpiece"—and it's no coincidence that these were all cookbooks, with promising titles like *Charm Your Own Cheese*, *Enchantment in Baking*, and *One Minute Feasts - It's Magic!* For Harry, Mrs. Weasley was the best cook in the whole world, and he loved everything she prepared. But Ron's mother didn't conjure the delicious food that she served to her loved ones from nothing, as her son erroneously claimed. If Ron had paid a little bit better attention in school, he would have known that conjuring food was one of the five "Principal Exceptions to Gamp's Law of Elemental Transfiguration," as an exasperated Hermione explained to him in *Harry Potter and the Deathly Hallows* when he complained about her cooking: "It's impossible to make good food out of nothing! You can Summon it if you know where it is, you can transform it, you can increase the quantity if you've already got some..." But a banquet can't just be conjured out of thin air. Rather, a person summons existing food and drink from elsewhere, for example the school kitchen, a restaurant, or a pantry. Someone must have previously made it, with the necessary technique, following a recipe, and using the necessary ingredients—just like in real life!

Besides, one of the secrets for the phenomenal success of Harry Potter is that however fantastic the magical world of Harry, Ron, and company may seem, it is only superficially about magic. In fact, the Potterverse turns out to be, soberingly, downright normal. Aside from their magical abilities, Harry and his friends are normal teenagers, with the same worries and challenges as any other normal teenagers. They have to study for school, are bullied by classmates, have their first great loves and their first bitter losses—all the same things that we can all identify with.

Moreover, magic spells, potions, and other magic gimmicks aren't what lead to Dumbledore's Army triumphing in the end. Rather, it is friendship, courage, loyalty, and willingness to sacrifice: basic human virtues, which we Muggles wield like the magic in Harry's world. In other words: Apart from the talking hats, friendly giants with pink umbrellas who rumble around through the clouds on motorcycles, and all the other magical stuff, Harry and friends live in the exact same world as us, in familiar surroundings with familiar problems—and with familiar food and drink (for the most part, anyway).

In the Harry Potter books, believe it or not, 200 dishes are described: breakfast, lunch, and dinner, along with all kinds of snacks and sweets. Many are fantastical, but most are real, so we can make them even though we can't get our hands on exotic ingredients like dragon meat, gillyweed, or gillywater. More than 80 of these dishes and drinks are available in the following pages.

Some of these dishes are traditional British fare, and while the British unquestionably have many great accomplishments in their glorious history, some would say that the island's cuisine isn't one of them.

Accordingly, as I live in Germany, I have permitted myself to include a few recipes in this book with a little Teutonic twist. Anyhow, don't forget that everything you find in these pages are ultimately only food for thought, to stimulate *your* creativity. Because after all, the greatest thing about cooking—just like in brewing beverages or trying new spells—is to experiment! The same applies to Muggle cooking and the magical world: The only limits that apply to us are the limits of our own imaginations.

The greatest magic that we can do—Muggle or wizard—is to make others happy. And how better to do that than with a legendarily delicious feast-day turkey, braised lamb cutlets, fluffy mashed potatoes, an enchanted apple strudel, magic roast beef with Yorkshire pudding, or an exquisite veggie frittata, washed down with a hearty butterbeer? You'll see. You can conjure a smile on your loved ones' faces—and without any spells!

With this in mind: Have magical fun!

Tom Grimm

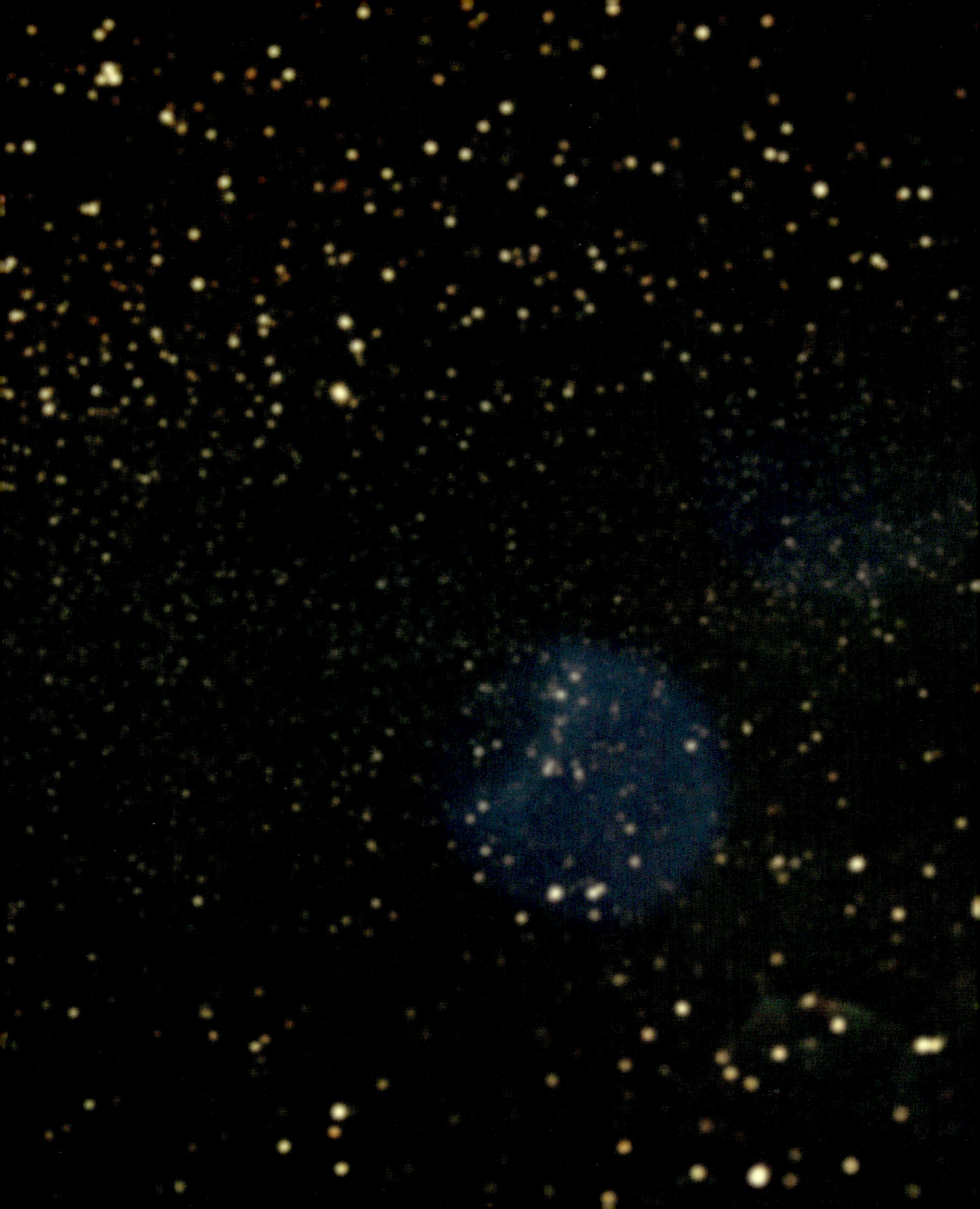

Fresh From Honeydukes

The sweet shop *Honeydukes* is one of the best-loved shops in the magical town of Hogsmeade, and it is often *ransacked* by pupils (and teachers!) from Hogwarts. No wonder. After all, the shelves are chock-full of everything that a sweet tooth like Ron (who has always spent quite a few sickles and knuts from his modest pocket money on Chocolate Frogs, Fizzing Whizzbees, Pepper Imps, and, naturally, Bertie Bott's Every Flavor Beans) could dream of. There is something for everyone here—even blood-flavored lollipops for vampires! Even the otherwise nutrition-conscious Hermione sometimes buys sweets there that her dentist parents would approve of: Toothflossing Stringmints! There's no question: *Honeydukes* is a paradise for anyone with a sweet tooth!

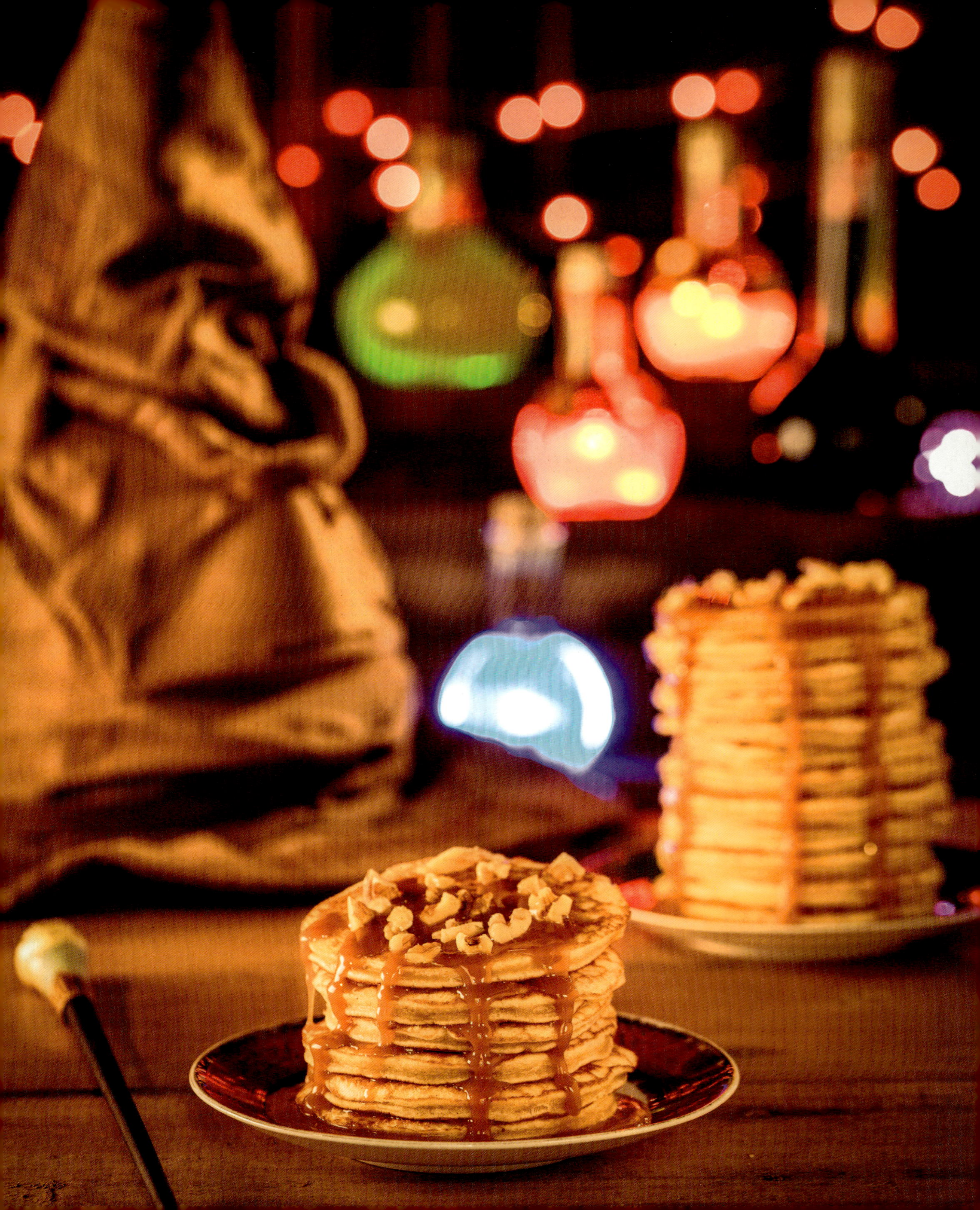

Cauldron cakes

INGREDIENTS FOR ABOUT 10 CAKES

3 eggs
⅓ cup buttermilk
⅔ ml plain yogurt
1½ cups flour
2 tbsp vanilla sugar
2 tsp baking powder
1 pinch salt
Olive oil

To serve:
Caramel sauce, coarsely chopped walnuts, whipped cream, seasonal fruit, etc.

1. In a bowl, whisk the eggs into a nice, light mousse. Stir in the buttermilk and plain yogurt. Then, a little at a time, add the flour, the vanilla sugar, the baking powder, and the salt. Stirring continuously, make a smooth batter that is thick but supple and can be poured. Let rest 15 minutes.

2. Preheat the oven to 175°F.

3. In the meantime, heat about 1 tsp olive oil on medium heat, in as large a coated frying pan as possible. With a ladle, add the desired amount of batter. To make smaller cauldron cakes, simply add less batter. Normally, 3 to 4 cauldron cakes should fit in a pan.

4. Cook the cakes about 2 to 3 minutes, until they are golden-brown on both sides; with a spatula, regularly turn them as soon as bubbles are visible on top. Here, it is important to use as little oil as possible and not to cook the cauldron cakes on too high a heat setting, so they can become nice and light!

5. When finished, put the cauldron cakes on a flat plate, loosely cover with aluminum foil, and keep warm by placing in a pre-warmed oven. As soon as all the cauldron cakes are done, serve. Top with caramel sauce, coarsely chopped walnuts, whipped cream, powdered sugar, or fresh seasonal fruit, for example.

DOBBY THE HOUSE-ELF'S TIP: To make savory cauldron cakes, just leave out the sugar and the vanilla sugar!

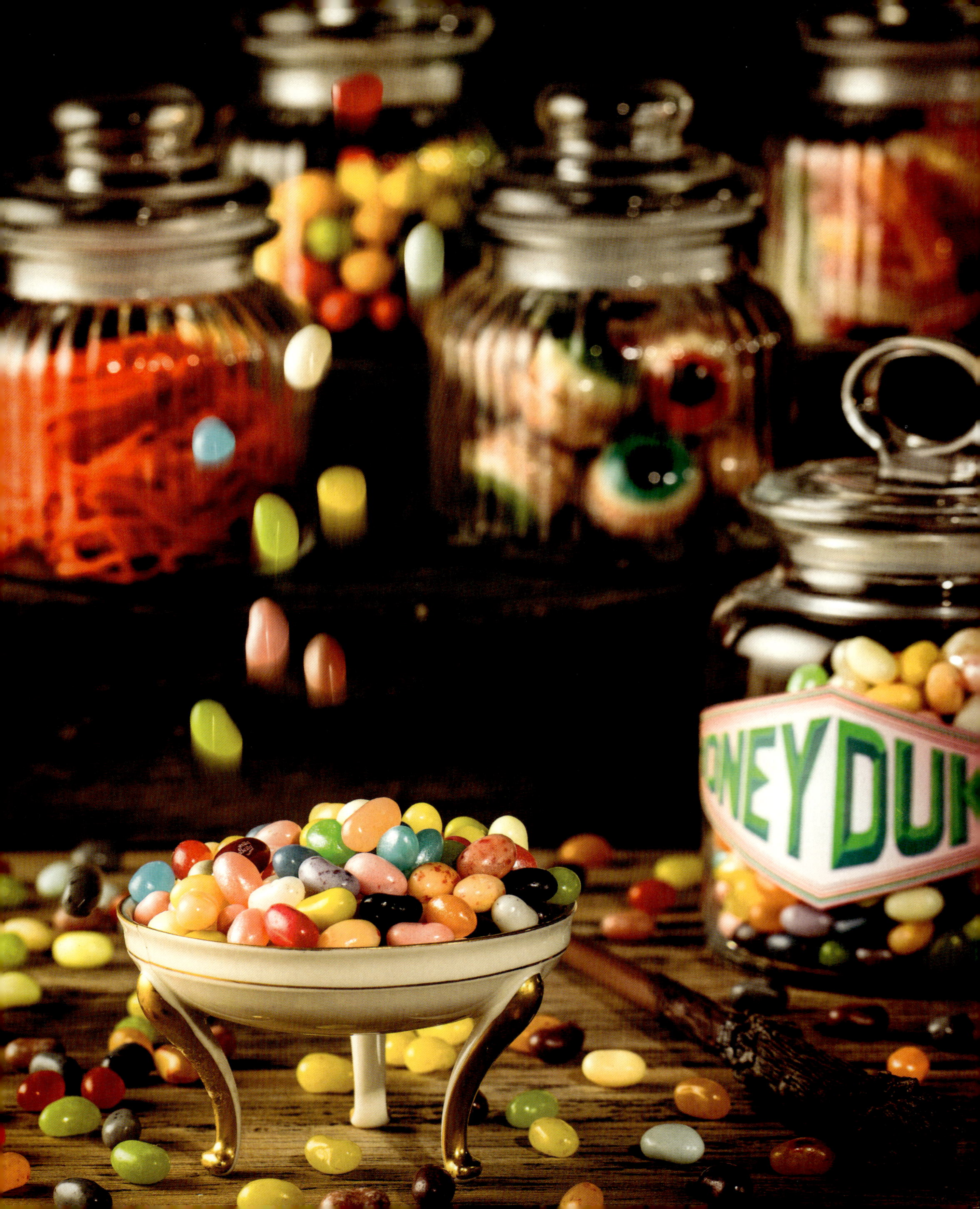

Bertie Bott's Beans

INGREDIENTS
FOR ABOUT 2½ CUPS EVERY
FLAVOR BEANS

⅓ cup water, plus 2 tbsp for the glaze
⅓ cup fruit syrup of your choice
1⅓ cups fine sugar
4 tsp powdered gelatin
5 drops food coloring of your choice
1 cup powdered sugar
Cooking spray

Also required:
2 mini Easter egg silicon molds,
sugar thermometer

1. Put ⅓ cup water, the fruit syrup, and the sugar in a saucepan, and warm on low heat while gently stirring until the sugar is totally dissolved. Then stir in the powdered gelatin.

2. Stirring constantly, heat until the sugar syrup reaches 230°F (about 20 minutes). Be very careful at this stage, because the syrup is very hot, and contact with skin can cause serious burns! Regularly check the temperature with a thermometer!

3. Spray the silicon molds liberally with cooking spray.

4. As soon as the syrup has reached the right temperature, stir in your choice of coloring and fill the silicon forms evenly. Smooth the tops with a spatula, cover with plastic wrap, and let dry overnight.

5. In a small bowl, stir the powdered sugar with 2 tbsp water until smooth. Remove the bean halves from the molds. Paint the flat surfaces of the bean halves with the glaze, stick together in pairs, and let dry 30 minutes.

DOBBY THE HOUSE-ELF'S TIP: With this recipe, you can make Bertie Bott's Beans in any color and flavor you like! All you have to change are the fruit syrup and the coloring!

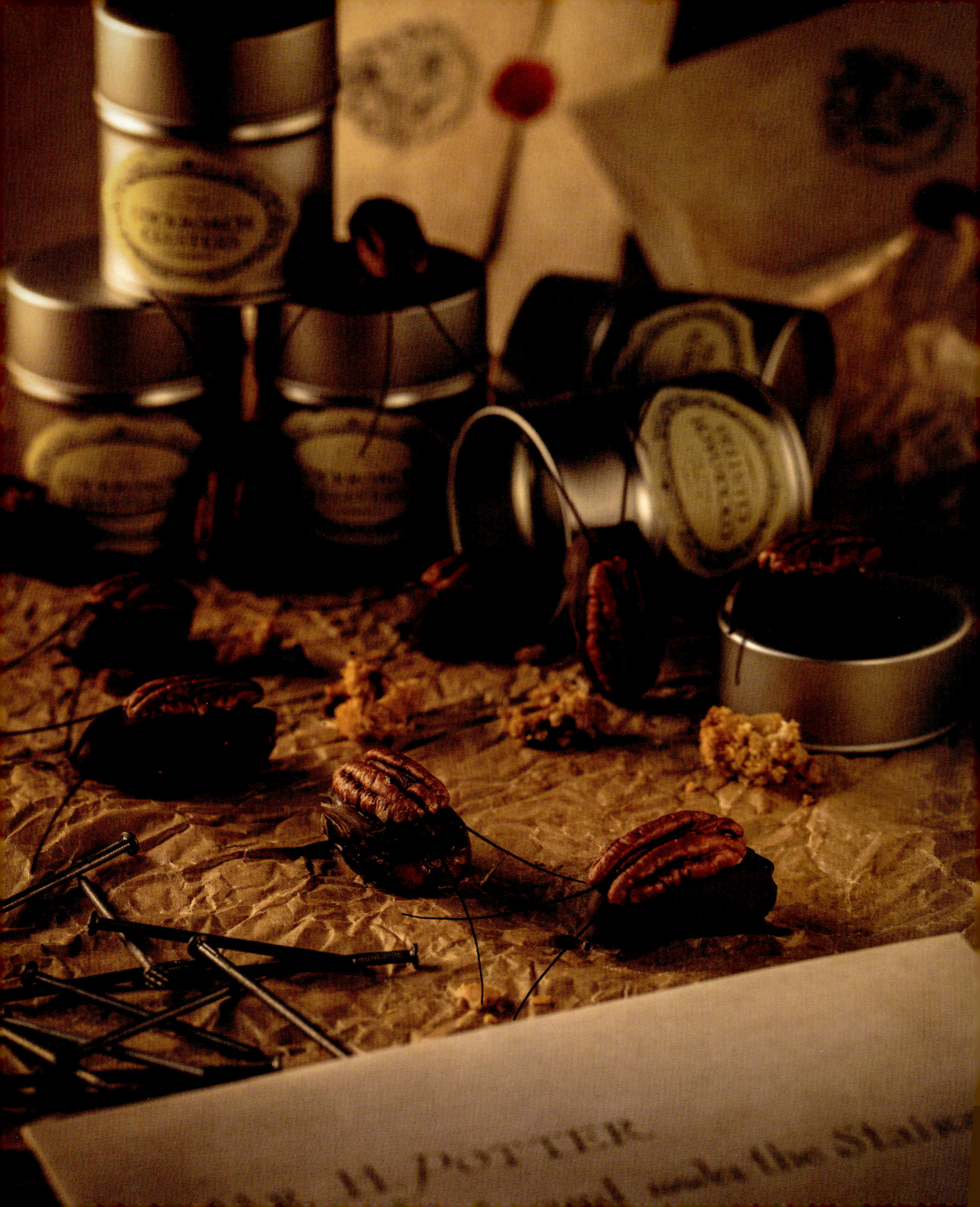
H. POTTER

Cockroach Clusters

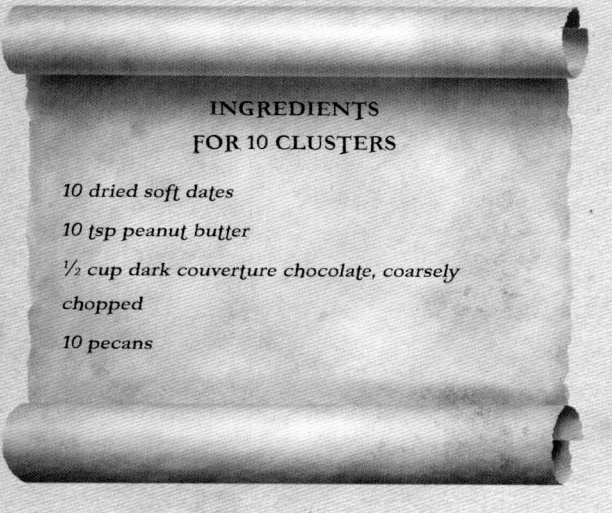

INGREDIENTS FOR 10 CLUSTERS

10 dried soft dates

10 tsp peanut butter

½ cup dark couverture chocolate, coarsely chopped

10 pecans

1. Carefully cut open the dried dates and remove the pits; make sure the underside of the fruit stays intact!
2. Put 1 tsp peanut butter in the middle of each date, and carefully squeeze the top of the fruit. Place in the refrigerator.
3. Melt the couverture chocolate in a small, heat-resistant bowl on top of a pan with simmering water. Take the filled dates from the refrigerator, and dip in the melted chocolate, so that the dates are covered all over. Place a pecan on each date, and place them back in the refrigerator until the chocolate has hardened (about 15 minutes). Keep cool until ready to eat.

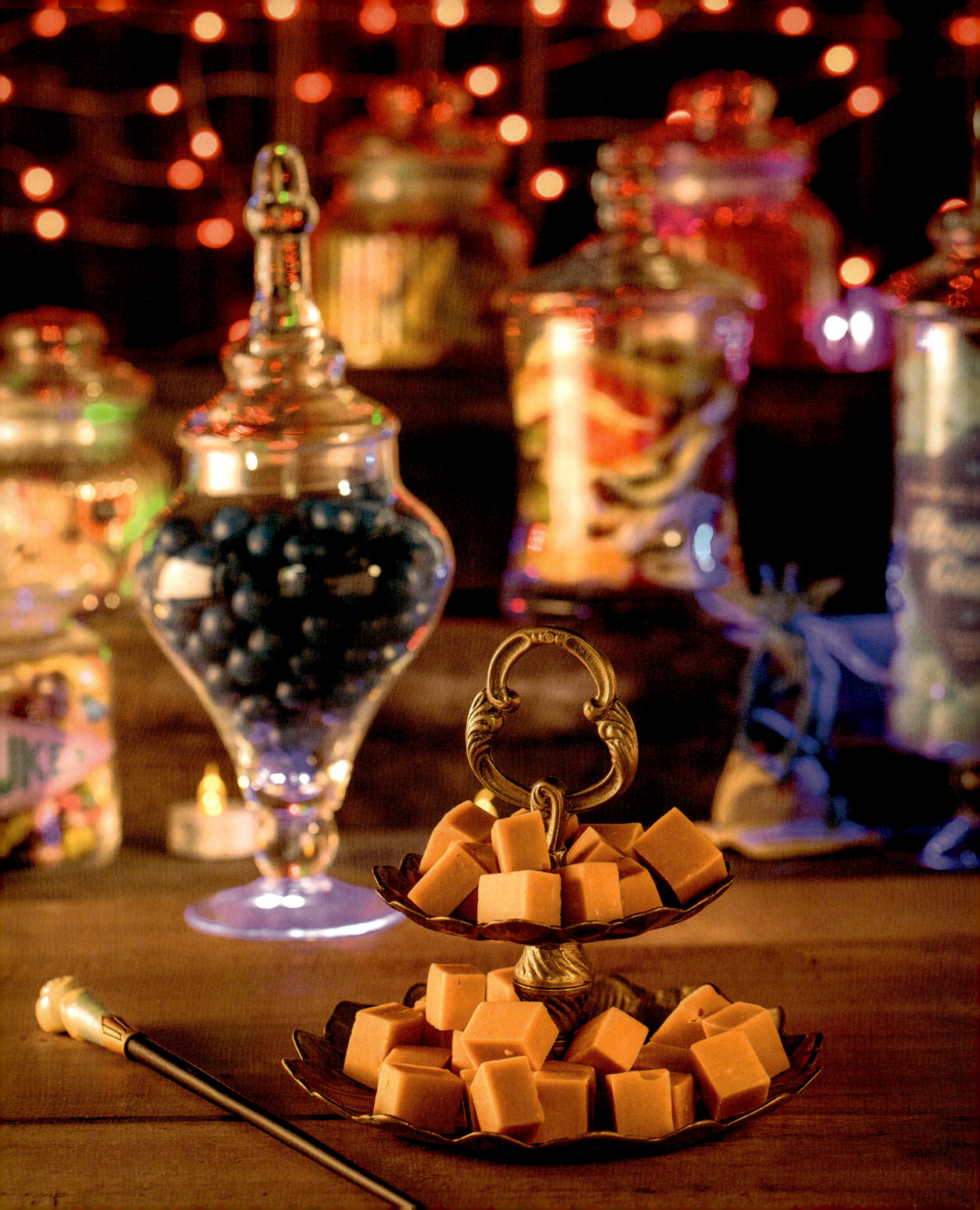

Butterbeer Fudge

INGREDIENTS
FOR ABOUT 12 SERVINGS

1¼ tbsp butter
⅓ cup non-alchoholic beer
¾ cup sugar
2 cups sweetened condensed milk
1 large pinch salt

Also required:
the flattest casserole dish available
(about 9 x 11 cm)

1. Cover a casserole dish with baking parchment so that the paper overlaps the sides. Grease with some of the butter.

2. Put the rest of the butter, the beer, and the sugar in the pan. While stirring constantly, bring to a boil over medium heat. Whisk in the condensed milk and the salt. Simmer gently for at least 20 minutes. Regularly stir, so that nothing burns!

3. Simmer until it becomes visibly thick, with a typical caramel color. Once it has the consistency of creamy, rather firm honey, carefully fill a casserole dish, smooth the top, and allow to cool completely at room temperature (about 3 to 4 hours).

4. Before cutting, place in the freezer for about 20 minutes, so that the fudge isn't sticky to the touch. Then, carefully transfer from the dish to a cutting board, and cut into bite-sized pieces with a large, sharp knife. Keep in a sealable, airtight container.

DOBBY THE HOUSE-ELF'S TIP: If you'd like a little more pep in your butterbeer fudge, just put a shot of rum in the batter!

DROOBLE'S BEST
Blowing Gum
Guaranteed to never lose flavour!

Drooble's Best Blowing Gum

**INGREDIENTS
FOR ABOUT 1 CUP GUM**

½ cup chicle (plain chewing gum)
1 tbsp glucose syrup
1 tsp lemon juice
8–10 drops natural flavor, as desired
2 tbsp glycerin (from the drugstore)
A few drops blue food coloring
1 cup sifted powder sugar, and a little more as a coating

1. Put the chewing gum paste in a plastic bowl with the glucose syrup, the lemon juice, and the natural flavors, and heat for 30 seconds at 1,000 watts; alternatively, use a double boiler. Then thoroughly stir the mixture, and heat it again for 30 seconds, until the plain chewing gum is completely melted.

2. Now, thoroughly stir in the glycerin and work in the food coloring, until the paste has the desired blue color. Then, add the sifted powdered sugar, and knead with the hands until the all of the sugar is carefully worked in. If possible, use disposable gloves, because the paste is very sticky.

3. Roll out the paste on the work surface. Take small pieces, make marble-sized balls, and roll them in powdered sugar so that the gumballs are coated all around. Important: Make the gumballs as quickly as possible, because the more the paste cools, the harder it becomes to shape!

4. Keep in a lightproof container. Keeps for several months.

DOBBY THE HOUSE-ELFS TIP: Chicle is easily available over the Internet!

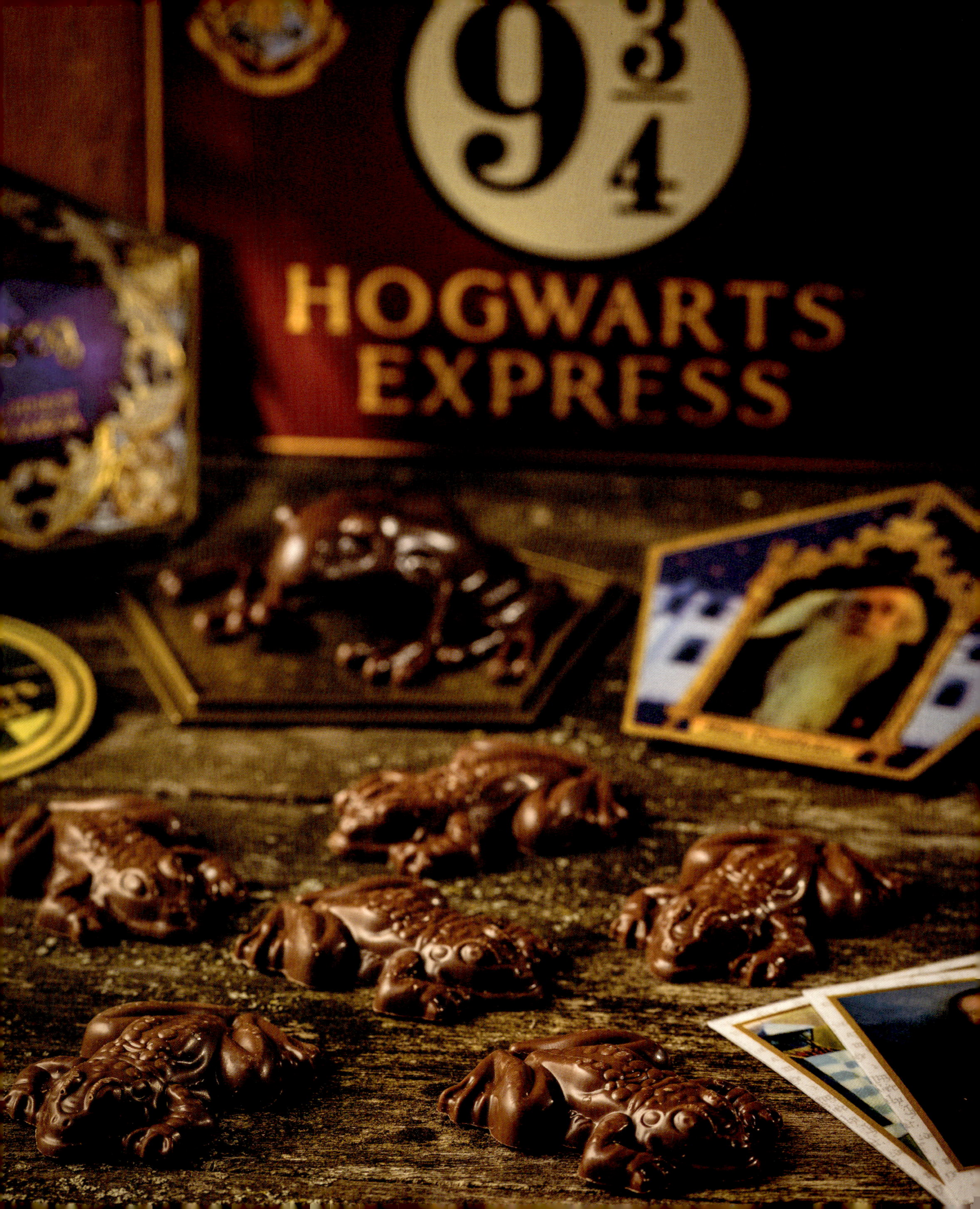
9 3/4
HOGWARTS
EXPRESS

Chocolate Frogs

INGREDIENTS
FOR 6 CHOCOLATE FROGS

1½ cup dark couverture chocolate, finely chopped

2–3 drops peppermint oil

2–3 drops vanilla extract

Also required:
Frog candy mold

1. Put ⅔ of the chocolate in a metal bowl and carefully, stirring regularly, melt in a double boiler. Important: The bowl must not touch the water! When the couverture chocolate is melted, take the bowl from the stove and stir in the remaining third of the chocolate, until it is all dissolved. Add 2-3 drops of peppermint oil and 2-3 drops of vanilla extract and stir thoroughly.

2. Now carefully fill the molds with chocolate, and gently tap the mold with a spoon several times so that any air bubbles can escape. Loosely cover with plastic wrap, place in the refrigerator, and allow to set.

3. Gently remove the chocolate frogs from the mold, and enjoy before Ron beats you and your friends to them! After all, Harry's best friend loves Chocolate Frogs more than anything!

DOBBY THE HOUSE-ELFS TIP: The original Harry Potter Chocolate Frog mold is readily available on the Internet! They even include assorted Chocolate Frog Cards and folding boxes, just like in the movies!

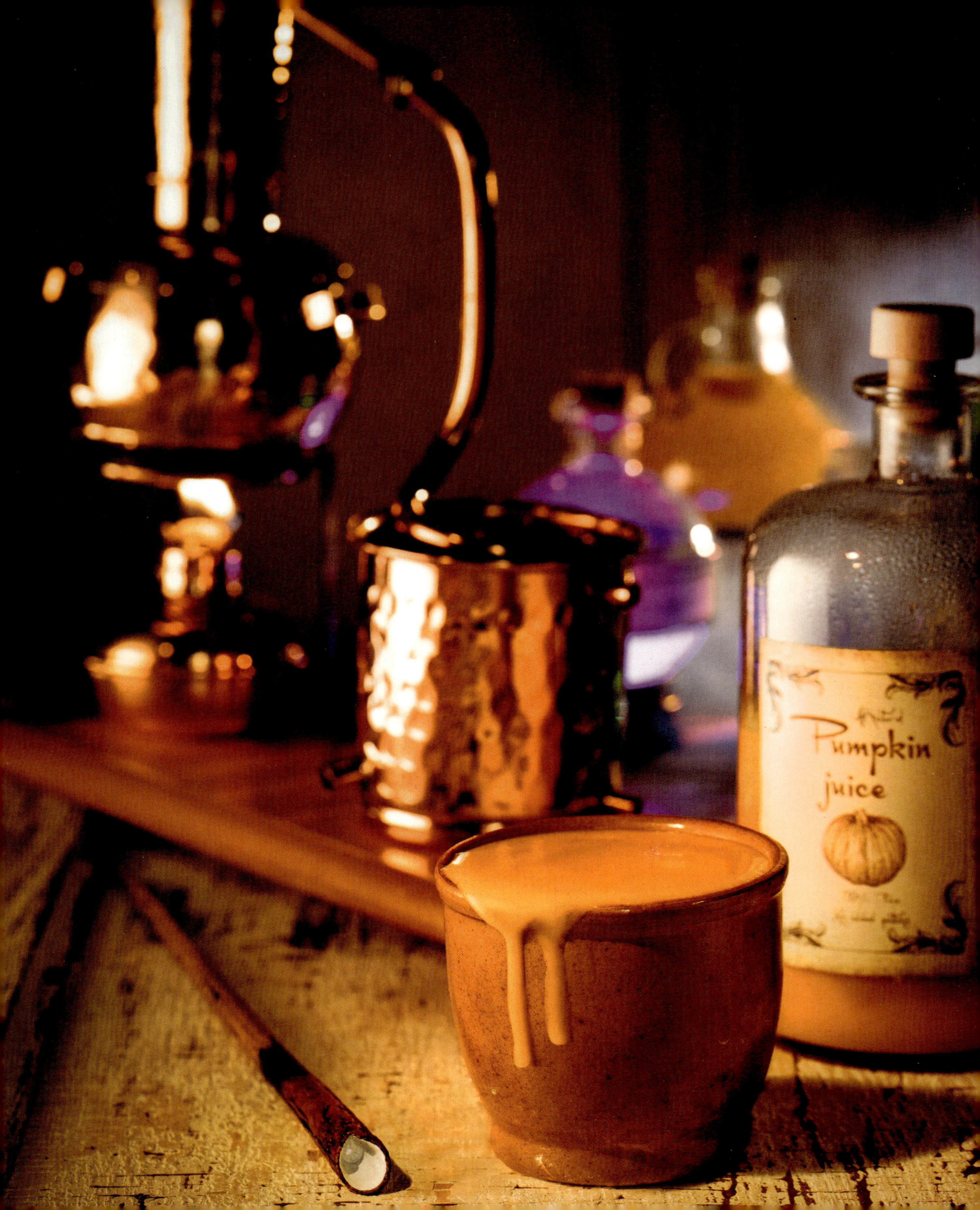
Pumpkin
juice

Pumpkin Juice

INGREDIENTS
FOR ABOUT 2 QT PUMPKIN JUICE

18 oz pumpkin, cut into large cubes
1 cup cane sugar
6½ cups water
2 tsp lemon juice
2 tsp apricot flavoring
1 tbsp vanilla extract
Sparkling water
   (optional)

Also required:
2 empty bottles (34 fl oz each)

1. Preheat the oven to 350°F. Cover a baking tray with baking parchment.

2. Wrap the pumpkin cubes with aluminum foil, put them on the tray, and cook for 20 minutes in the oven, until the pumpkin is soft and the skin easily comes away from the flesh. Put the pumpkin flesh in a bowl and purée finely with an immersion blender.

3. Put the pumpkin purée in a large saucepan with the sugar and water. Bring to a boil, and let simmer while stirring constantly for 20 minutes on low heat. Mix in the lemon juice, the apricot flavor, and the vanilla extract. Mix well, and pour into two 1-L bottles that have been washed with hot water. Close the bottles well and leave them in the refrigerator. If it stays properly cool, the Pumpkin Juice keeps for 3-4 days.

4. If the Pumpkin Juice is too thick, mix it with a little sparkling water right before drinking!

DOBBY THE HOUSE-ELF'S TIP: This Pumpkin Juice recipe is sweet rather than savory, and tastes best chilled!

MR. H. POTTER
The Cupboard under the Stairs
4 Privet Drive
Little Whinging
SURREY

Dumbledore's Favorite Lemon Drops

INGREDIENTS
FOR ABOUT 2 CUPS LEMON DROPS

Neutral tasting oil,
  for the marble slab
1½ cups sugar
7 tbsp glucose
⅓ cup water
2 tsp ascorbic acid
15 drops natural lemon oil
3 drops yellow food coloring
1 good pinch of talcum powder

Also required:
Sugar thermometer; large marble slab (about 14 × 20 in.)

1. Thinly coat the marble slab with water.

2. Put the sugar, the glucose, and the water in a small saucepan, and carefully bring to a boil over high heat. Be very careful at this stage, because the sugar mixture is very hot, and contact with skin can cause serious burns! Regularly check the temperature with a sugar thermometer and heat the mixture until it reaches 310°F (about 10 min.)

3. From this point on, four hands are better than two, so it's best to work with a partner! Now, evenly pour the heated sugar mixture onto the greased marble slab; take care that none goes over the edges! At the same time, quickly loosen the mixture from the slab with a spatula, and knead it. Evenly distribute the ascorbic acid, the lemon oil, and the food coloring on the sugar mixture, and quickly work it in.

4. As soon as the candy mass is cooled enough to safely touch, use your hands to pull it into thin strands, and with household scissors, cut off marble-sized pieces. Put the drops in a freezer bag with the talcum powder, close it, and shake it well so that the drops are covered with the powder and do not stick together.

5. When kept in a lightproof, sealable container, Dumbledore's Favorite Lemon Drops keep for 1-2 months.

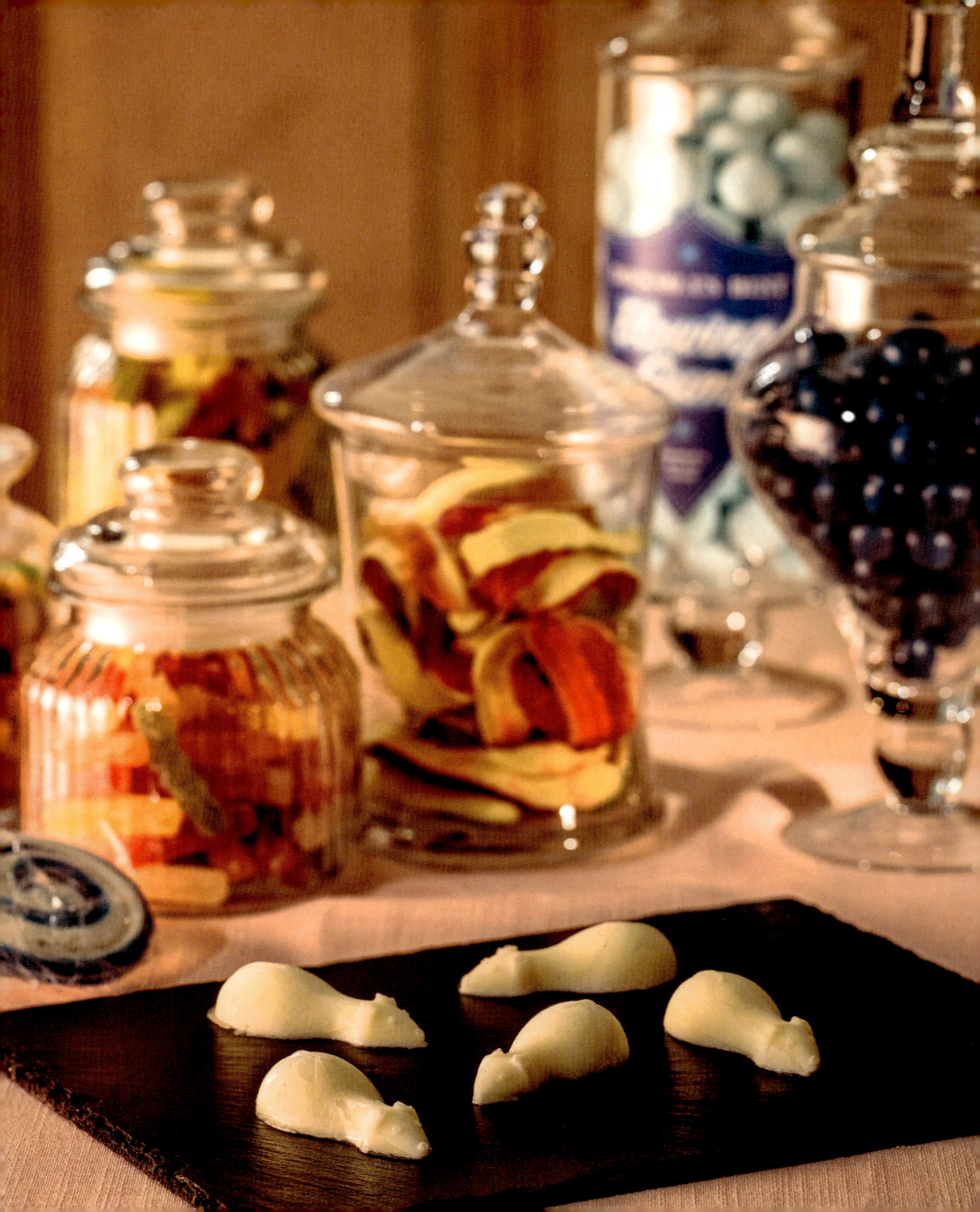

Ice Mice

**INGREDIENTS
FOR 12 ICE MICE**

11 tbsp cream, thoroughly cooled
1½ cups yogurt
¼ cup powdered sugar
1 tbsp lemon juice
1 tbsp vanilla extract

Also required:
Two six-piece silicon mouse molds

1. Whip the cooled cream in a bowl until semi-rigid or creamy.
2. In a separate bowl, thoroughly mix the yogurt with the powdered sugar, lemon juice, and vanilla extract. Fold in the cream.
3. Put it in the spaces in the silicon mouse molds. With the back side of a bread knife, wipe off all excess. Cover the whole molds with plastic wrap, and place in the freezer for 4-5 hours.
4. Remove from the freezer, remove the plastic wrap, and carefully remove the mice from the mold. Use a little warm water on the bottom of the mold, if necessary. Serve immediately.

DOBBY THE HOUSE-ELF'S TIP: The silicon mouse molds are easily found on the Internet!

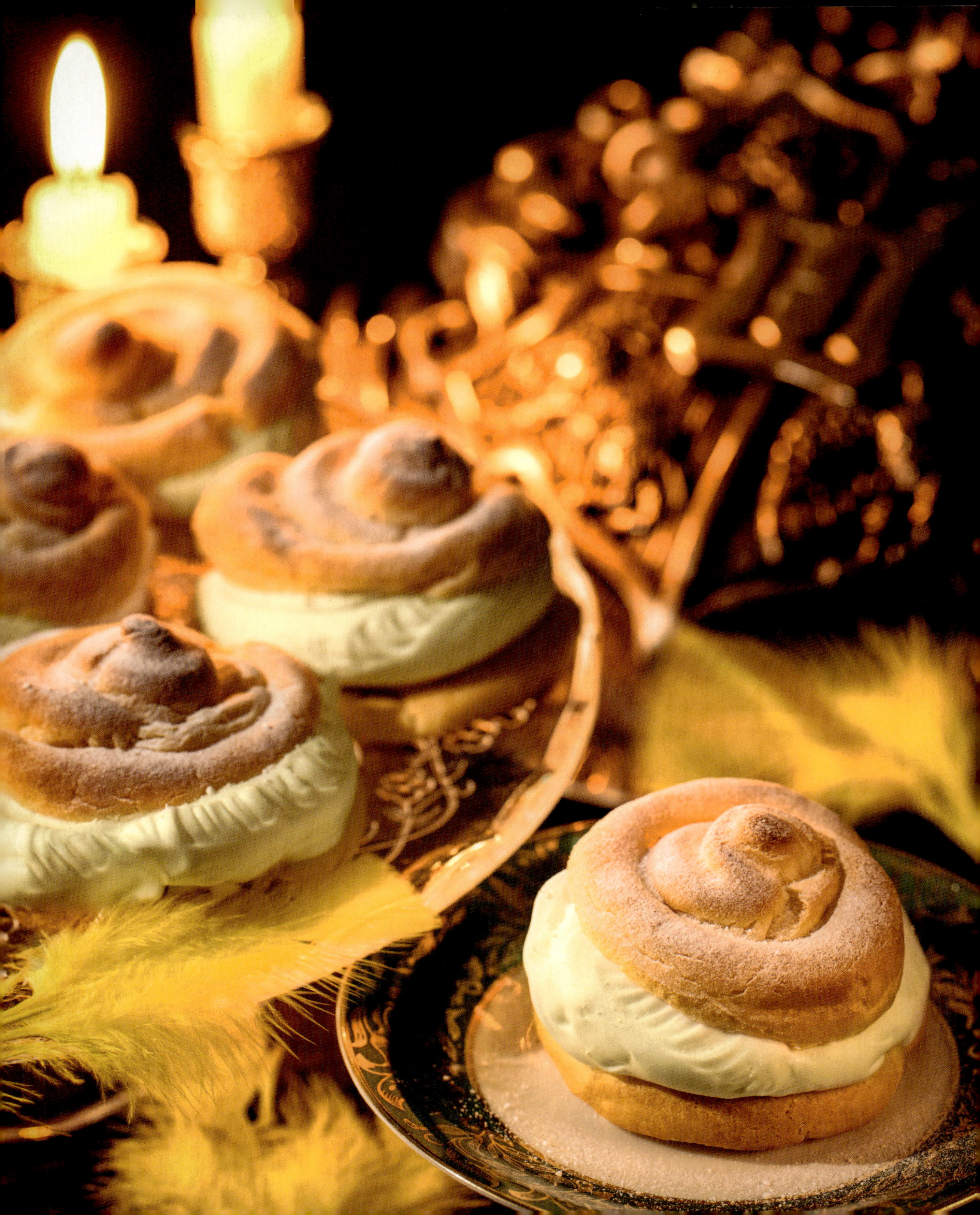

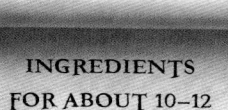

Canary Creams

INGREDIENTS FOR ABOUT 10–12 CANARY CREAMS

For the dough:
½ cup water
1½ tbsp butter
¾ cup flour
1½ tbsp cornstarch
2 eggs
1 pinch baking powder

For the filling:
1¾ cups cream
4 tsp cream stabilizer
2½ tbsp powdered sugar
2 tsp vanilla sugar
Juice of ½ lemon
5 drops yellow food coloring

1. Preheat the oven to 390°F. Cover a baking tray with baking parchment.

2. Bring the water to a boil in a small saucepan with the butter. Remove the saucepan from the stove. Mix the flour and cornstarch in a bowl, and put the mixture in the bowl. Work the mixture into a smooth dough, then heat for 1 minute, stirring constantly.

3. Put the dough in a mixing bowl. Use a mixer on high power with dough hook attachment to mix the eggs into the dough, one at a time. Work in the baking powder.

4. Using a piping bag with large star nozzle, leaving sufficient distance between them, put 10-12 dough puffs onto the baking tray, and bake for about 20 minutes in the preheated oven. Caution: During baking, do not open the oven door, or the pastry will collapse!

5. When the time has finished, remove the puffs from the oven right away, cut away the "lids" with a sharp knife, and allow the pastries to cool completely on a cooling rack.

6. In the meantime, prepare the filling. For this, put the cream in a bowl. Add the cream stabilizer, the powdered sugar, the vanilla sugar, the lemon juice, and the food coloring, and whip until stiff. Once the puffs are cooled, use a piping bag or a freezer bag with a corner cut off to fill the pastries.

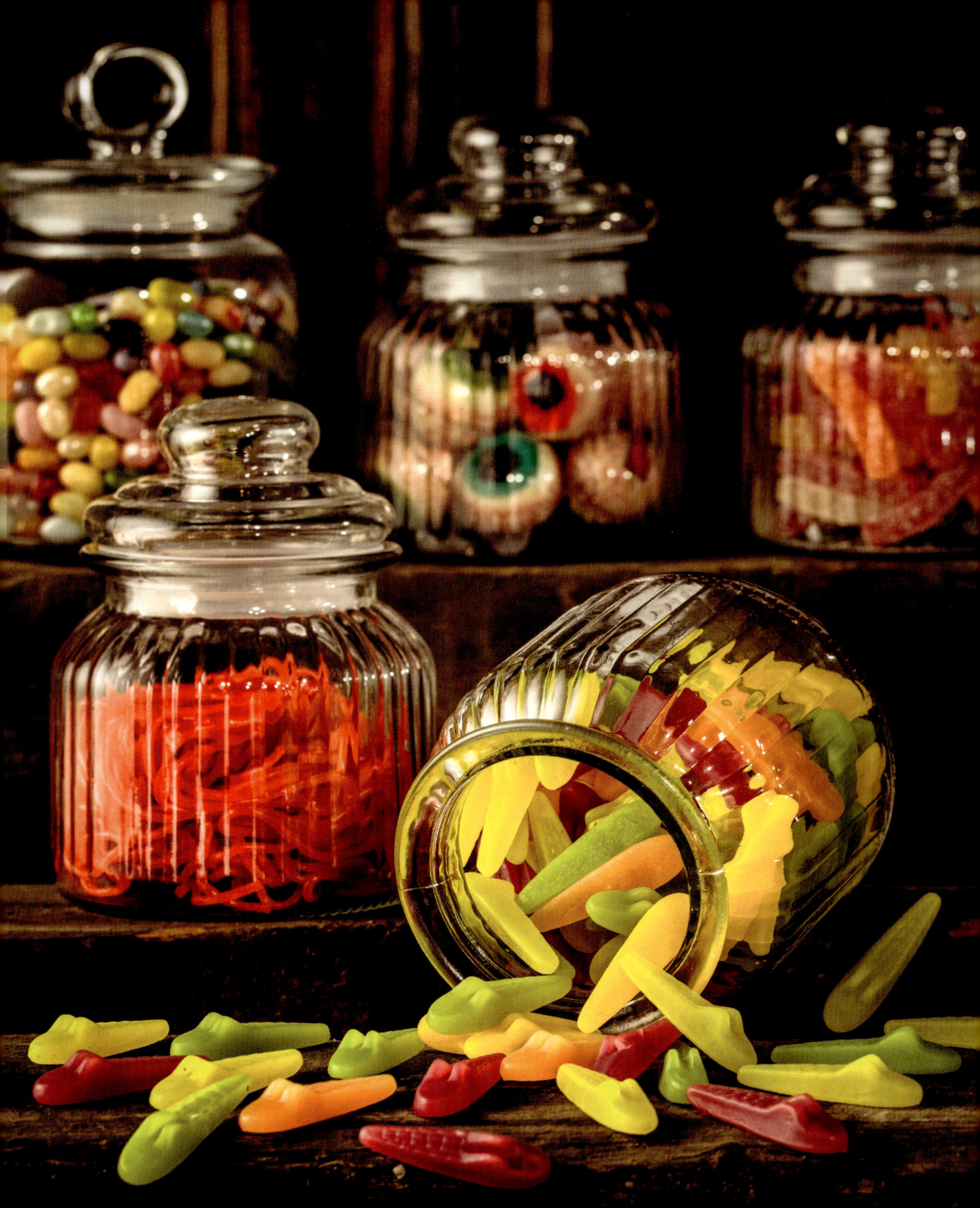

Jelly Slugs

**INGREDIENTS
FOR 12 JELLY SLUGS**

4 tsp powdered gelatin
1 cup fruit juice of your choice
1–2 tbsp lemon juice
1 tbsp sugar
5 drops food coloring of your choice (e.g., red, green, yellow)

Also required:
Two eight-piece slug molds

1. Put the gelatin in a small saucepan. Add the fruit juice, and let the gelatin soak for 5-10 minutes. Then add the lemon juice and sugar.

2. Stirring constantly, completely mix the soaked gelatin and the sugar over low heat. Add and mix in 5 drops of food coloring of your choice. Make sure that the whole thing doesn't boil, but rather simmers gently. Otherwise, the gelatin loses its effect and the Jelly Slugs will not firm up!

3. Carefully put the mixture in the silicon molds, smooth out, wrap as tightly as possible with plastic wrap, and let cool for at least 1 hour in the refrigerator; ideally, let cool overnight.

4. Remove the Jelly Slug from their molds, and enjoy!

DOBBY THE HOUSE-ELF'S TIP: It's easiest to find the silicon molds for the Jelly Slugs on the internet!

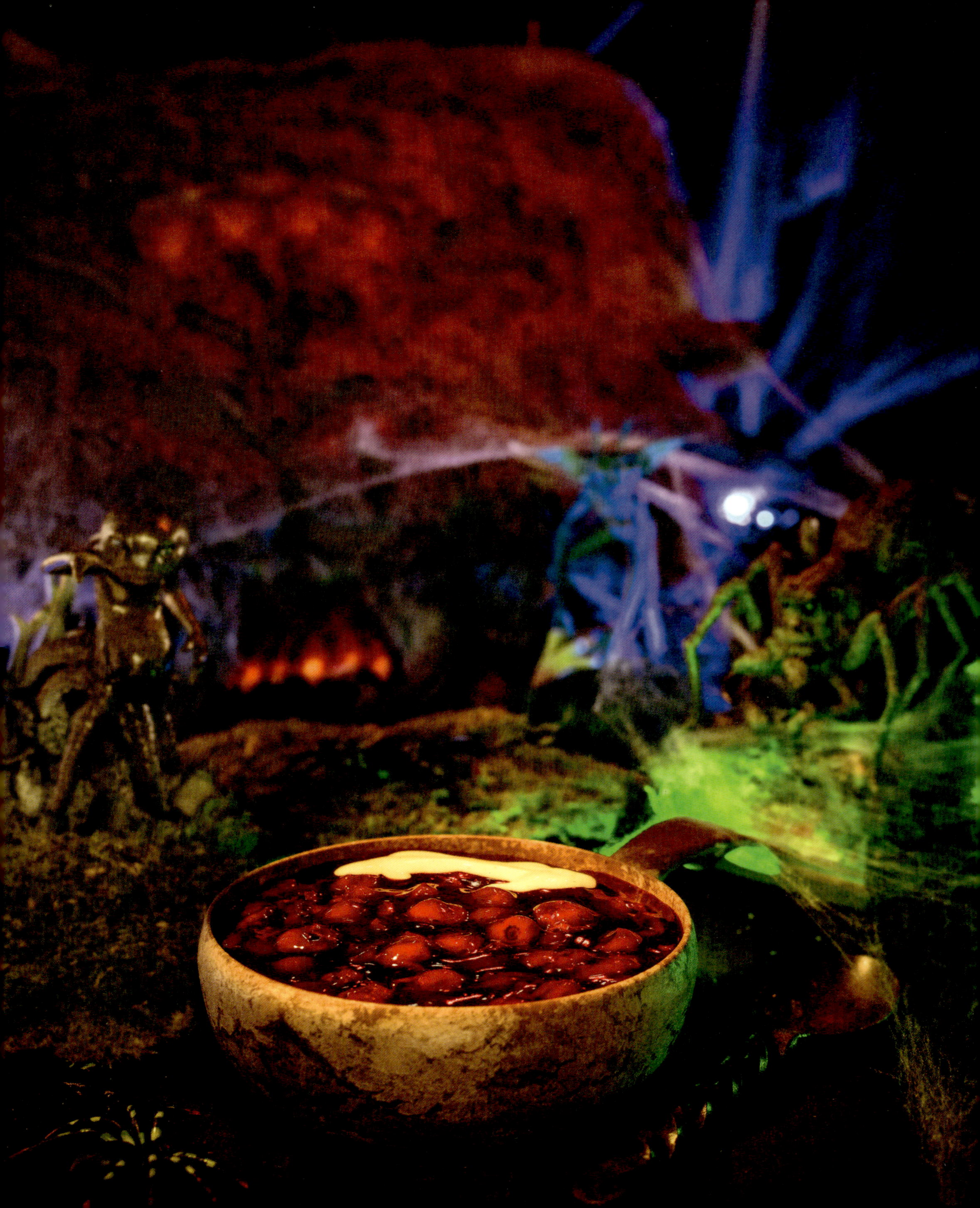

Bat's Blood Soup

INGREDIENTS
SERVES 5–6

4½ cups sour cherries (from a jar)
1 tbsp cornstarch
4 cups frozen mixed berries (e.g., raspberries, blackberries, currants)
3 tbsp sugar
1 cinnamon stick
Vanilla sauce, (optional)

1. Drain the cherries with a sieve; collect the juice.
2. In a small bowl, mix 3 tbsp of the cherry juice with the starch, and set aside. Put the rest of the cherry juice in a saucepan with 2 cups of the frozen berries, the sugar, and the cinnamon stick. Bring to a boil over medium heat, and while stirring constantly, let simmer until the berries slowly fall apart (about 5 minutes).
3. Remove the saucepan from the stove, remove the cinnamon stick, and carefully chop the berries with an immersion blender. When the purée is as fine as possible, sift through a sieve. Then put it back in the saucepan.
4. Thoroughly mix in the stirred starch, then mix with the berry purée. Leave the saucepan on the stove. Bring the purée to a boil, and simmer for about 5 minutes over low heat. Meanwhile, stir repeatedly. Finally, add the sour cherries and the rest of the berries, and bring it all to a boil. Remove from the stove, and let the mixture cool to room temperature. Then leave it in the refrigerator for 4 hours.
5. Divide the Bat's Blood Soup in bowls or dessert dishes, and serve warm or cold. Ideally, serve with vanilla sauce.

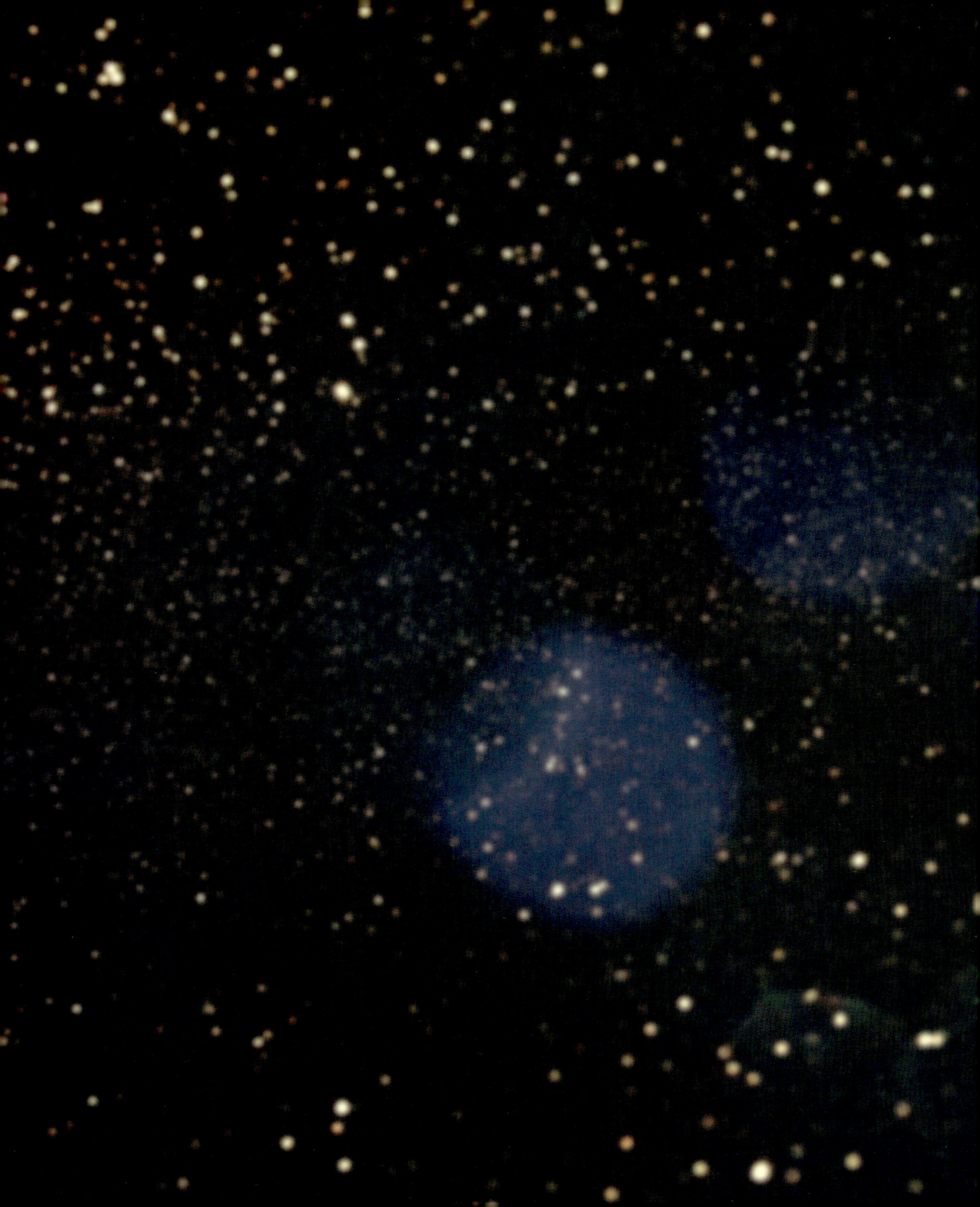

From the Menu of the Leaky Cauldron

Although it might appear that way at first glance, the *Leaky Cauldron* is not just a regular pub. This treasure is the entryway to the legendary Diagon Alley, a labyrinth of wondrous shops and businesses, where you can find anything that your magical heart desires—and in some ways, that also goes for the *Leaky Cauldron*. Because although it isn't a very inviting place, the food and drinks for sale in this rustic atmosphere—Hermione would say "filthy"—have always been very popular.

The butterbeer is excellent, and alongside traditional Scottish dishes such as black pudding and shepherd's pie, the inn is known above all for its soups and stews. But take care: the food can be so delicious that having it can be harmful to your health! No, not because of calories and so on, but because you should ideally eat your pea soup in the *Leaky Cauldron* as quickly as possible—before it turns the tables and
eats *you* instead!

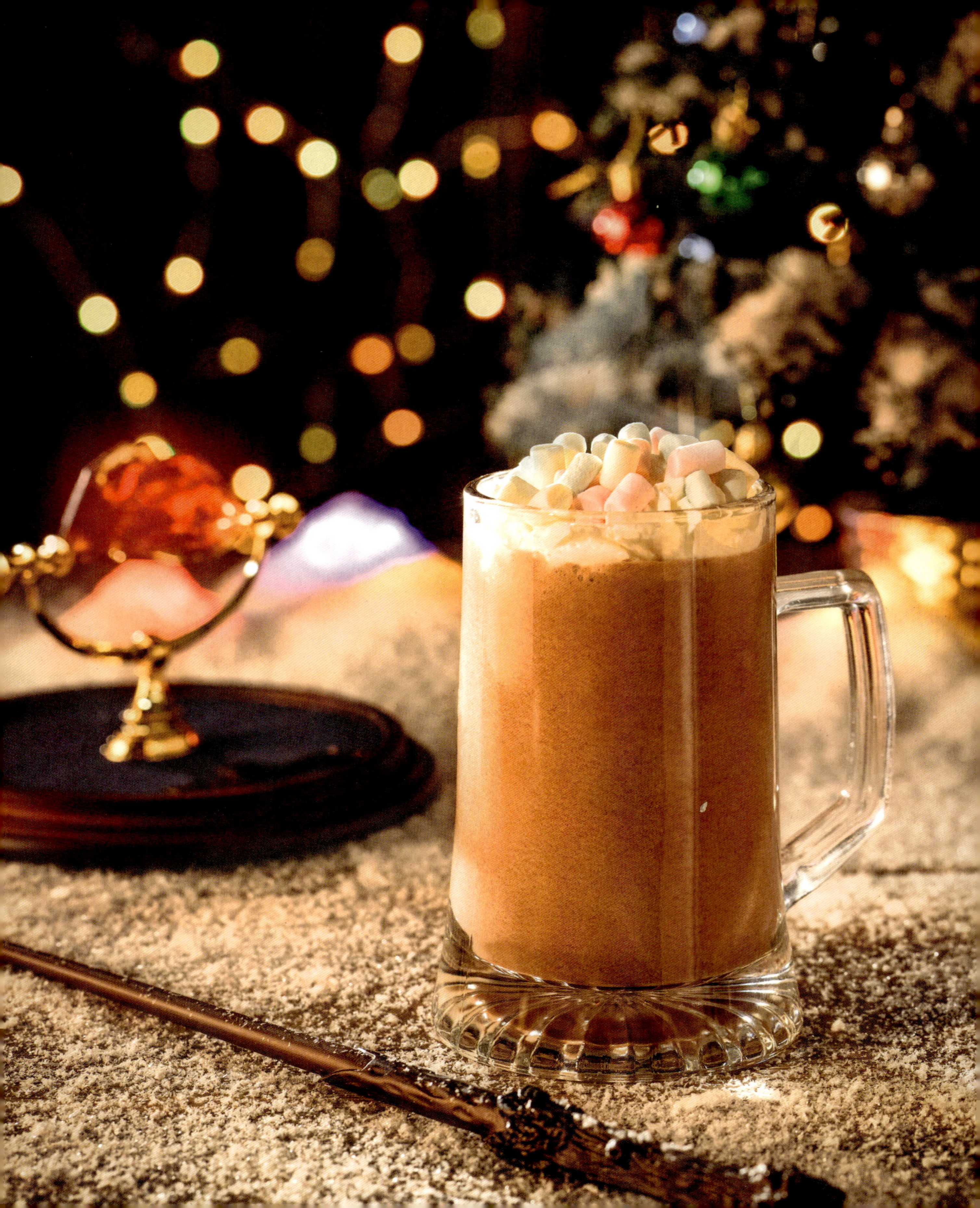

Hot Chocolate

INGREDIENTS
SERVES 2

3½ tbsp cream
2¼ cups milk
2 tbsp unsweetened cocoa
2 tsp vanilla sugar
½ cup dark chocolate, coarsely chopped
1 handful of colorful miniature marshmallows

1. In a mixing bowl, whip the cream stiff.
2. Stirring constantly, heat the milk, the unsweetened cocoa, the vanilla sugar, and the chopped dark chocolate in a saucepan over medium heat until the chocolate is completely melted. Be careful not to let the milk start to boil! If needed, reduce the heat.
3. Remove from the stove, let cool 2-3 minutes, then thoroughly stir and divide between two mugs or heat-resistant glasses. Put as much whipped cream as desired on top of each, and crown with miniature marshmallows. Serve immediately.

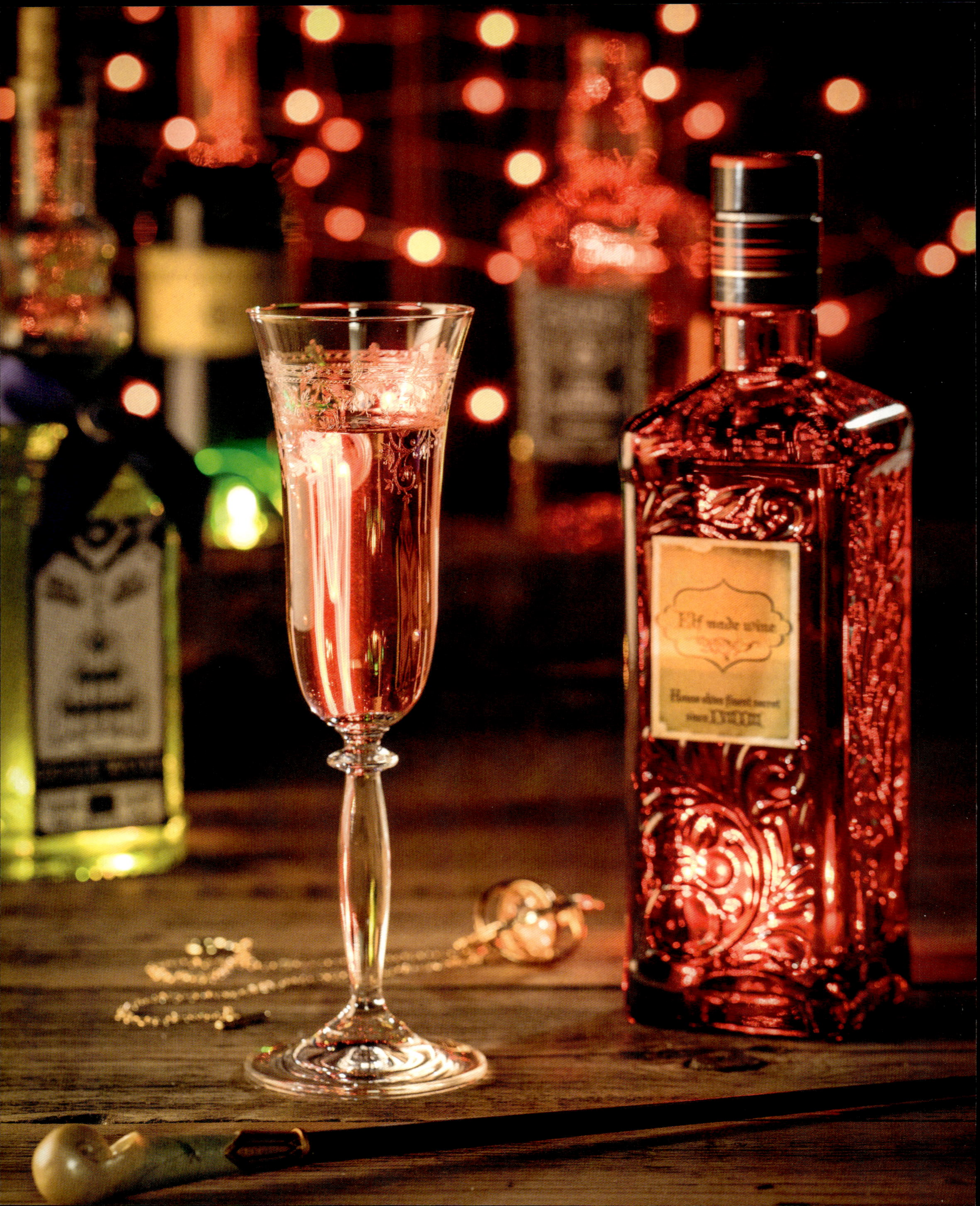
Elf made wine

Elfwine

CONTAINS ALCOHOL

INGREDIENTS FOR 1 DRINK

1.5 fl oz vodka, ice cold
4.5 fl oz Schweppes Russian Wild Berry, ice cold
0.5 fl oz raspberry syrup
Fresh berries (optional)

1. Put the ice-cold vodka in a wine or champagne glass, infuse with Schweppes Russian Wild Berry, and add the raspberry syrup. Gently mix together.
2. Garnish with fresh berries as desired. Serve immediately.

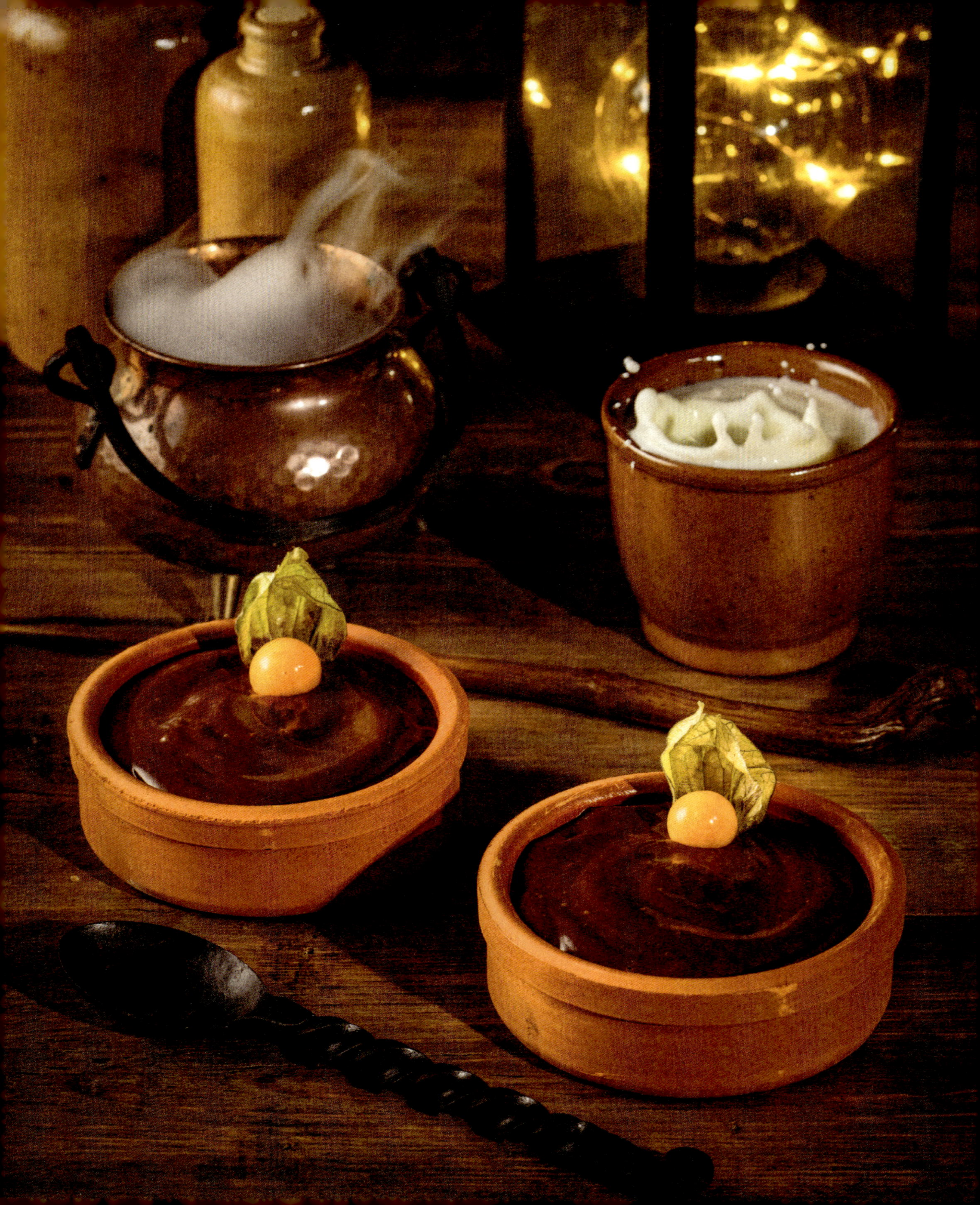

Chocolate pudding

INGREDIENTS
SERVES 2–3

1 cup milk chocolate, coarsely chopped
1¼ cups milk
1 cup cream
1 tbsp cocoa
1 tbsp sugar
4 tbsp cornstarch
1 egg yolk
1 pinch salt
Cape gooseberries (golden berries), as garnish (optional)

1. In a saucepan over low heat, stirring constantly, heat the chopped chocolate with 200 ml milk and ⅓ cup cream. Mix until the chocolate is completely dissolved.

2. In a separate bowl, whisk the rest of the milk and cream together with the cocoa, sugar, cornstarch, egg yolk, and salt. Then mix in the chocolate milk with the whisk. Stirring constantly, let simmer for about 3-4 minutes until the pudding becomes noticeably thicker.

3. The pudding can now be poured into one big bowl or several small ones, garnished with cape gooseberries (or other berries), and served warm or cold.

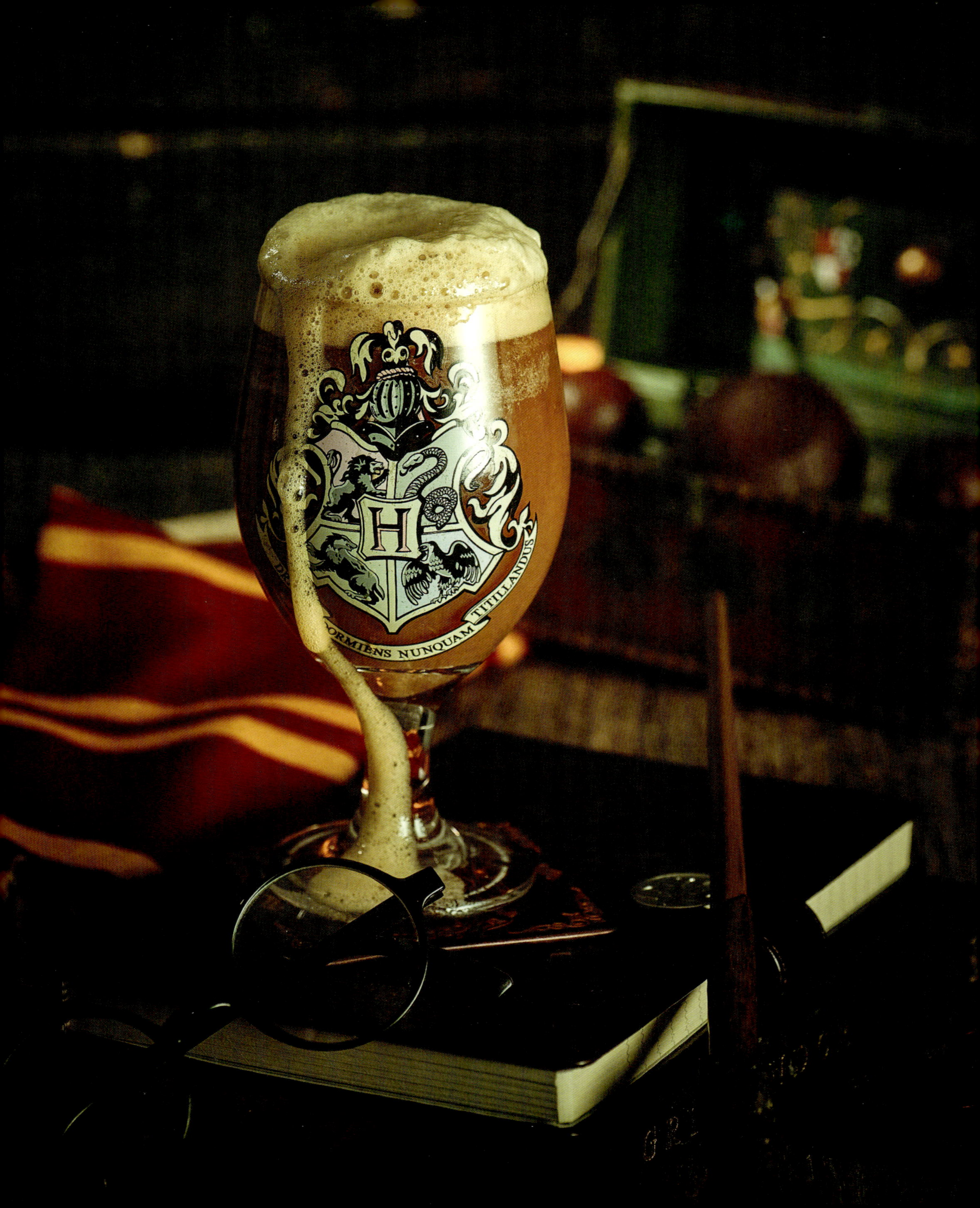
H
DORMIENS NUNQUAM TITILLANDUS

Butterbeer

INGREDIENTS FOR 4 BUTTERBEERS

1 tbsp butter
2 tbsp cane sugar
1 vanilla bean
2¼ cups milk
⅓ cup cream
1 tbsp cinnamon
½ tbsp cocoa powder
1 tsp vanilla sugar
1 cup non-alchoholic beer

1. Melt the butter in a saucepan over low heat. Add the cane sugar and, stirring constantly, let lightly caramelize.

2. Cut the vanilla beans open lengthwise with a sharp knife, and scrape out the seeds. Put the emptied beans and the vanilla seeds in a saucepan with the milk, half of the cream, the cinnamon, the cocoa powder, and the vanilla sugar. Mix thoroughly, and simmer for a short time. Remove the saucepan from the stove and mix in the beer.

3. Warm the butterbeer again briefly, but make sure not to boil it, or flakes will form! Remove from the stove and let cool a little.

4. Meanwhile, whip stiff the rest of the cream. Fill heat-resistant glasses with the warm butterbeer, and top each with a spoonful of whipped cream. Serve immediately.

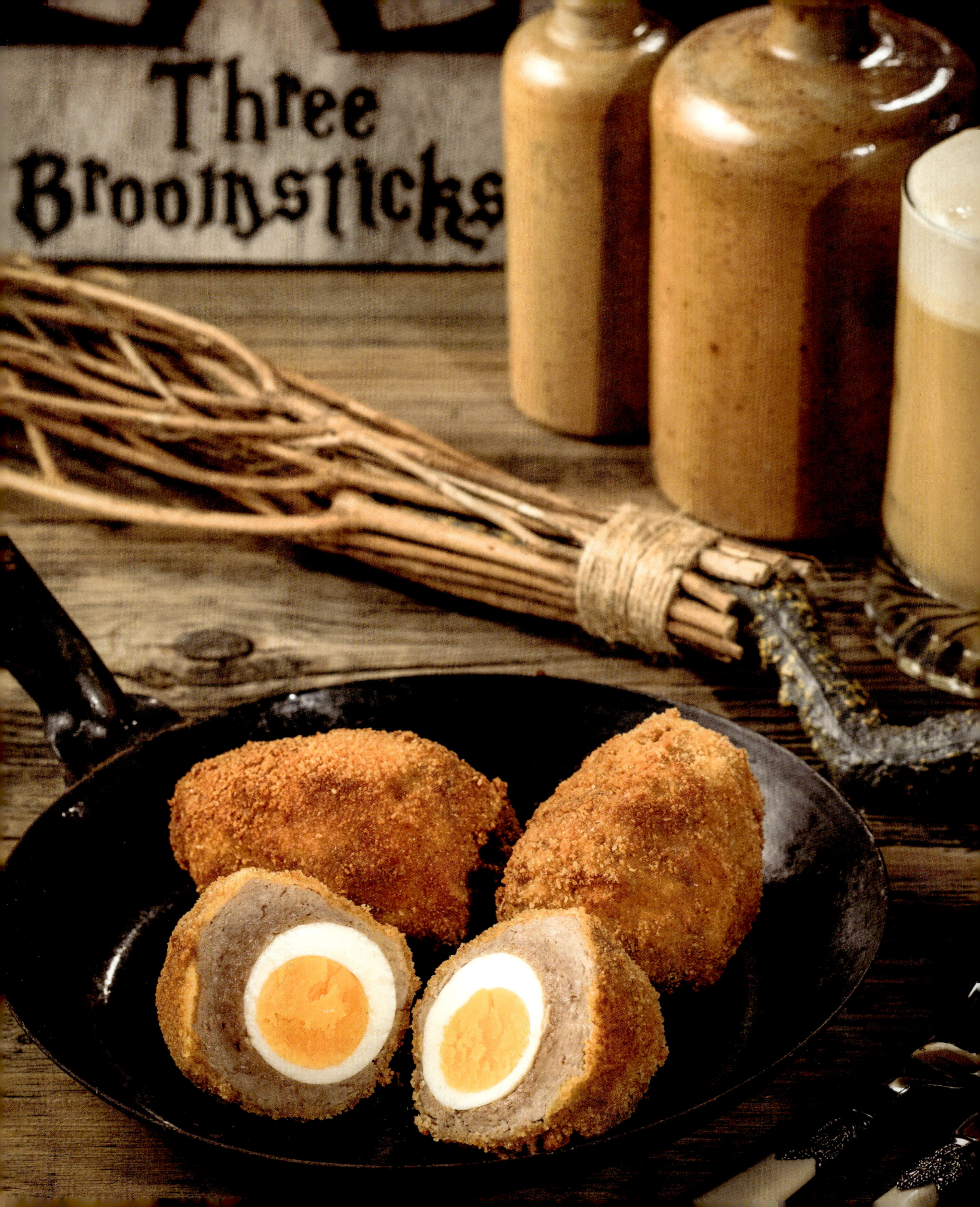
Three
Broomsticks

Scotch Eggs

INGREDIENTS FOR 4 SCOTCH EGGS

6 eggs
9 oz ground pork
1 onion, finely chopped
1 tbsp mustard, medium-spicy
1 tsp nutmeg
Freshly ground black pepper
Some breadcrumbs
Some flour
Vegetable oil for frying (amount depending on saucepan size)

1. Bring water to a boil in a medium-sized saucepan. Place four of the eggs in, and hard-boil them for 8-10 minutes. Drain the water, place the eggs in an ice bath, and peel. Set aside.

2. Put the ground meat in a bowl. Add the diced onion, one of the remaining eggs, the mustard, and the nutmeg, and season to taste with pepper. Mix thoroughly with hands.

3. Thoroughly coat each peeled egg with one-quarter of the meat mixture; press the meat well.

4. Meanwhile, put the breadcrumbs and flour in a separate deep dish. Whisk the last egg on a separate plate. Coat the meat-covered eggs first with flour, then with egg, and finally with breadcrumbs. Make sure that they are evenly breaded.

5. Put the frying oil in a tall saucepan and heat to 320°F over high heat. To test whether the oil is hot enough, try adding one of the breaded eggs; if sizzling bubbles appear, the oil is ready. Then, keeping enough distance between them (in two batches, if necessary), fry until crispy, about 4-5 minutes, stirring the oil occasionally.

6. Removed the fried eggs from the saucepan with a slotted spoon, and place on a plate covered with paper towels, so that the excess oil can drain. Serve hot or cold, perhaps with Fluffy Mashed Potatoes and Gravy (p. 102).

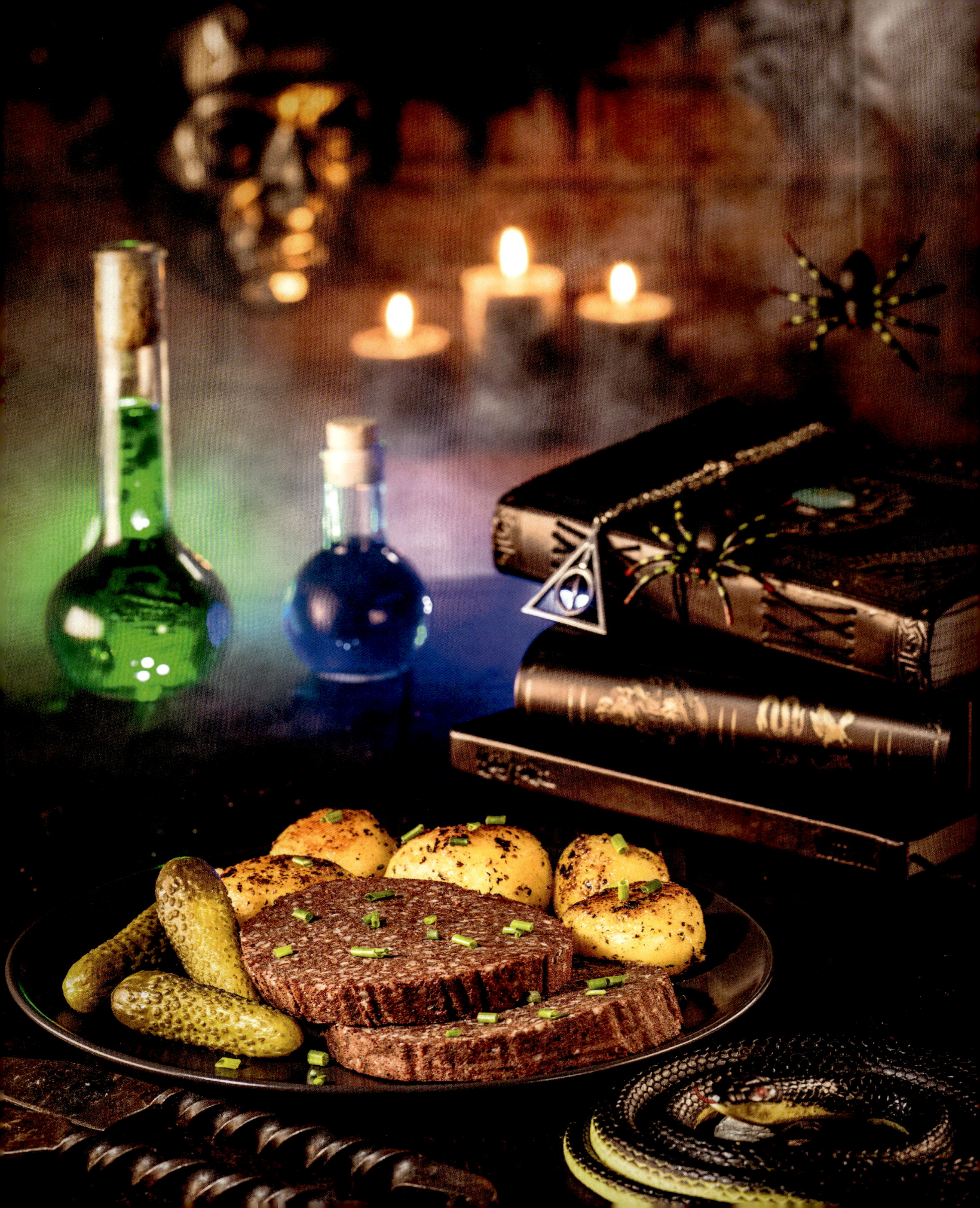

Black Pudding

INGREDIENTS
SERVES 4

1½ lb small early potatoes (waxy)

1 lb fresh blood sausage, from the butcher

1 tbsp clarified butter

2 onions, finely chopped

Salt and freshly ground black pepper

½ tsp powdered clove

2 tbsp butter

2–3 sprigs thyme, stripped, finely chopped

Some fresh chives, finely chopped

Dill pickles, (optional)

1. Wash the potatoes, peel them, and precook them in a large saucepan in heavily salted water for about 15-20 minutes on medium heat. Drain, and set aside the potatoes for now.

2. Preheat the oven to 250°F.

3. Peel the kaszanka/kishka, and cut into pieces ¾-1 ¼ in. thick.

4. Melt the clarified butter in a large pan, and stew the onions until translucent. Add the kaszanka/kishka, and sear on both sides over medium heat (about 2 min. per side). Turn as infrequently as possible, so that the meat does not fall apart. Season liberally with salt, freshly ground black pepper, and a tiny bit of powdered clove. Finally, remove from the pan, place on a plate, loosely cover with aluminum foil, and warm until serving in a preheated oven.

5. Put the butter in the pan, turn the heat to high, and fry the pre-cooked potatoes on all sides with the thyme until golden brown. Liberally season with salt and pepper, sprinkle with fresh chives, and serve with the slices of kaszanka/kishka and the pickles.

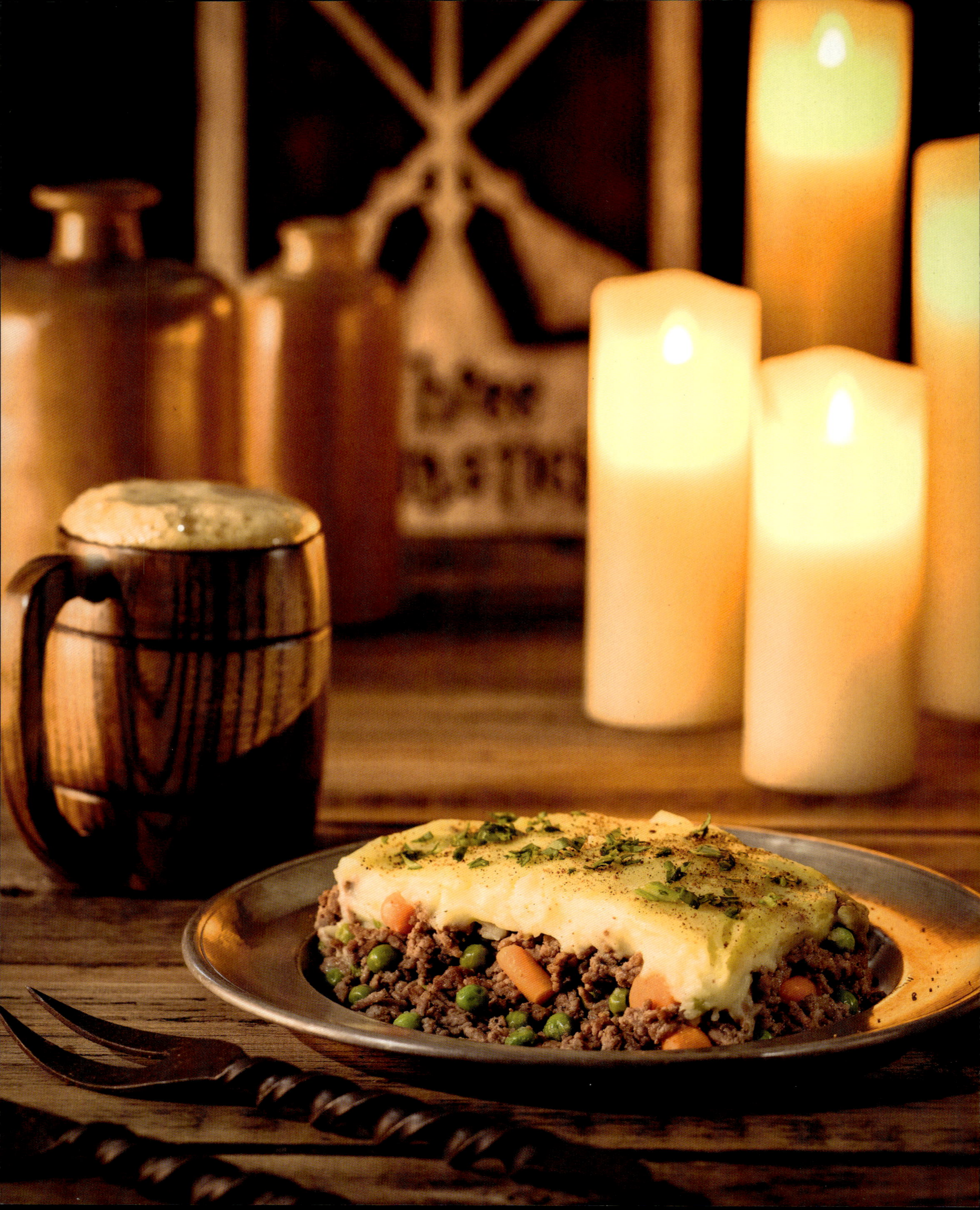

Shepherd's Pie

INGREDIENTS
SERVES 4-5

1½ lb floury potatoes, cut into large cubes
4 tbsp oil
2 onions, finely chopped
1¾ lb ground lamb
2 tbsp tomato paste
1¼ cups beef stock
1⅓ cups frozen peas and carrots
Salt and freshly ground black pepper
1 tbsp powdered paprika (sweet)
3 tbsp butter, in pats, a little more if necessary, to grease the casserole dish
1 cup milk
1 large pinch nutmeg
Freshly chopped parsley

Also required:
Casserole dish (approx. 8 x 10 in.)

1. In a large saucepan, over medium heat, heat heavily salted water. Add the cubed potatoes, and boil for 20 minutes or until they are cooked.

2. In the meantime, heat the oil in a pan on medium heat, and sauté until translucent. Add the ground lamb, and fry until it is golden brown all over and crumbly. Add the tomato paste, infuse with the beef stock, and add the frozen peas and carrots. Mix everything well, and season with salt, pepper and paprika. Let simmer uncovered, stirring constantly, for 10 minutes.

3. Meanwhile, preheat the oven to 390°F.

4. Drain the cooked potatoes, add the pats of butter, and mash the potatoes as finely as possible. Add the milk, liberally season with pepper, salt, and nutmeg, and stir until creamy.

5. Grease a casserole dish with butter. Add the ground meat and vegetable mixture. Evenly spread it in the dish. Spread the mashed potatoes in one layer, smooth, cover loosely with aluminum foil, and place in the preheated oven for 30 minutes. Five minutes before the time is up, remove the aluminum foil so that the top browns and a light crust develops.

6. Remove the dish from the oven, let cool briefly, sprinkle with freshly chopped parsley, and serve in the dish.

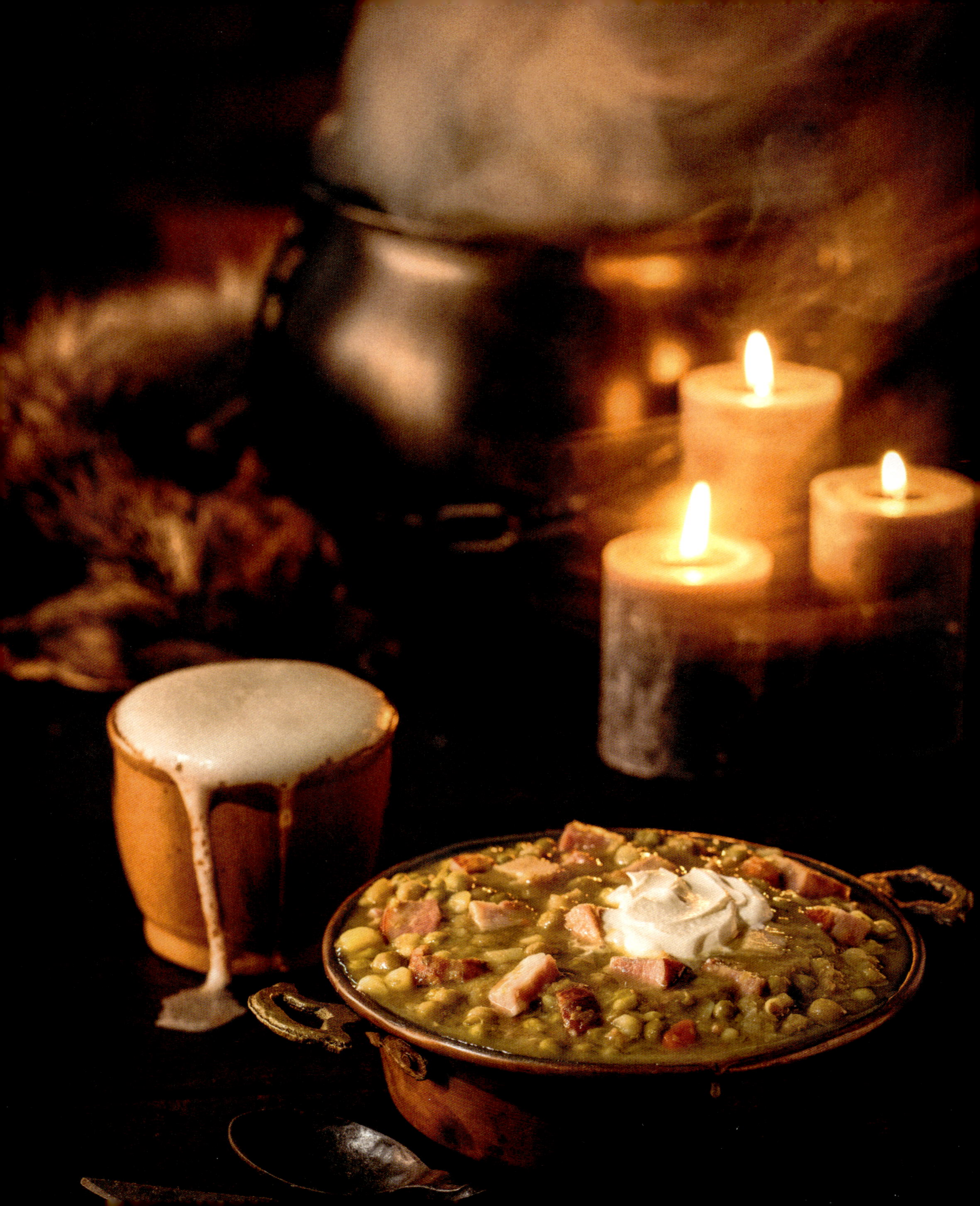

Pea Soup

INGREDIENTS
SERVES 6–8

2 tbsp lard

2 onions, finely chopped

¼ celery root/celeriac, two large carrots, one small leek, all finely chopped

10½ oz pork shoulder, cut into large cubes

8 medium-sized potatoes (floury), peeled and finely diced

4¼ cups vegetable stock

2 cups water

5¼ cups frozen peas

Salt, pepper, celery salt, lovage, and marjoram to taste

1 large splash apple vinegar

Some fresh parsley, finely chopped

1. Melt the lard in a large saucepan over medium heat. Cook the onions in it until translucent. Add the chopped vegetables and sauté. After 2-3 minutes, add the pork shoulder, and 2-3 minutes after that, add the potatoes. Deglaze with the vegetable stock, infuse with water, and add the frozen peas. Let simmer without a lid for 30 minutes.

2. With a potato masher, roughly mash the soup. Season with salt, pepper, celery salt, lovage, and marjoram. Add a healthy splash of apple vinegar and mix in the freshly chopped parsley.

> **DOBBY THE HOUSE-ELF'S TIP:** Like most soups, this one also tastes especially good when you have time to cook it slowly. So, it's ideal to make it the night before, then just warm it up the next day!

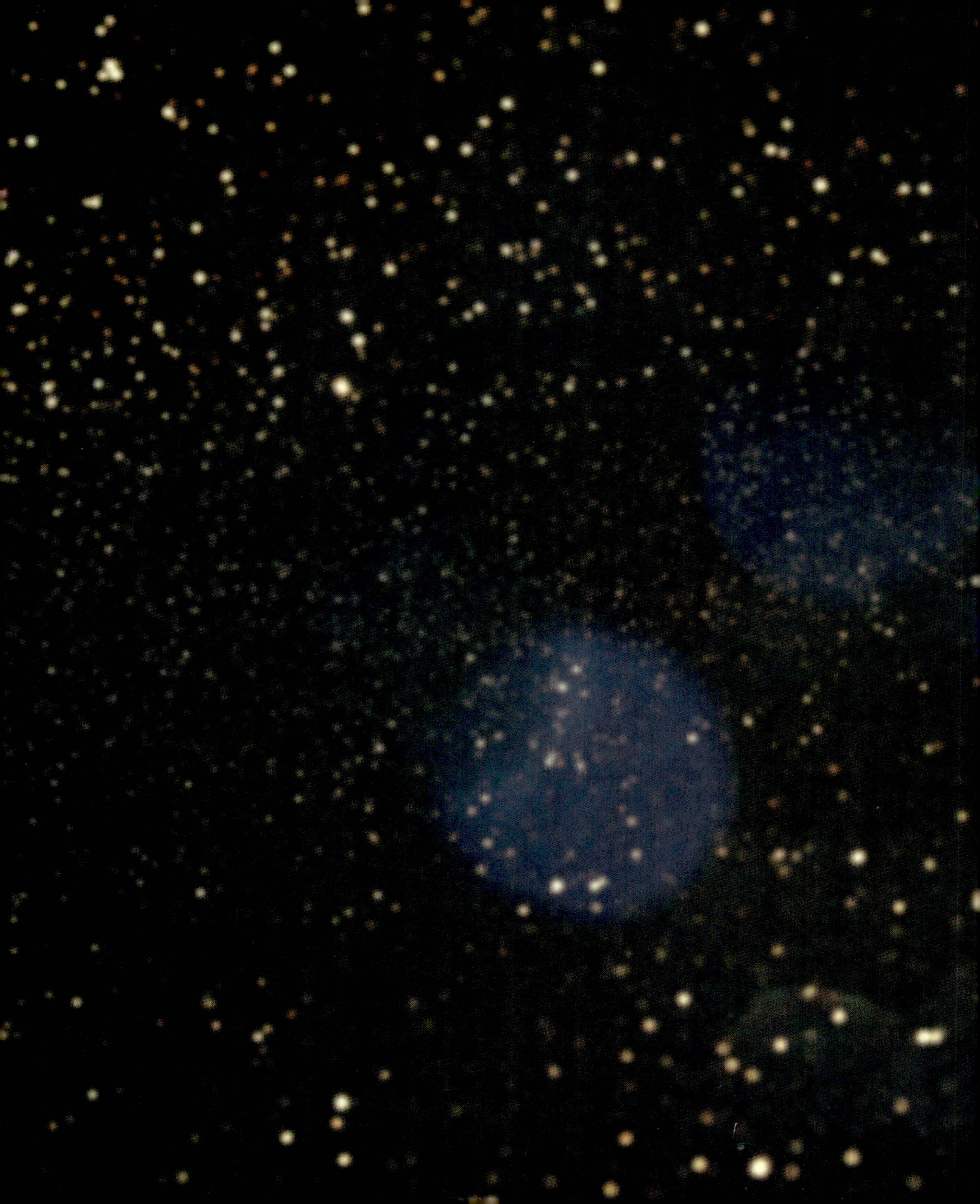

Privet Drive Delicacies

Since the tragic death of his parents, Harry has lived with the Dursleys, at 4 Privet Drive, Little Whinging, Surrey, England; at first, in a tiny, dusty cupboard under the stairs, and later, in a tiny, dusty room on the top floor. Unlike him, his Aunt Petunia, his Uncle Vernon, and his completely spoiled cousin Dudley are completely normal small-town Muggles, and like most completely normal small-town Muggles, they have no truck with magic—on the contrary! Above all, Uncle Vernon will have nothing to do with "that dangerous nonsense." To keep his highly embarrassing link to the magical world from becoming common knowledge and making him the laughingstock of the neighborhood, Uncle Vernon tells everyone that Harry is going to St. Brutus's Secure Center for Incurably Criminal Boys. Otherwise, the Dursleys miss no opportunity to make the boy's life a living hell. Even a world-famous wizard can't choose his family. But no matter what you think about this ghastly family, you have to give Aunt Petunia credit for one thing: She can cook!

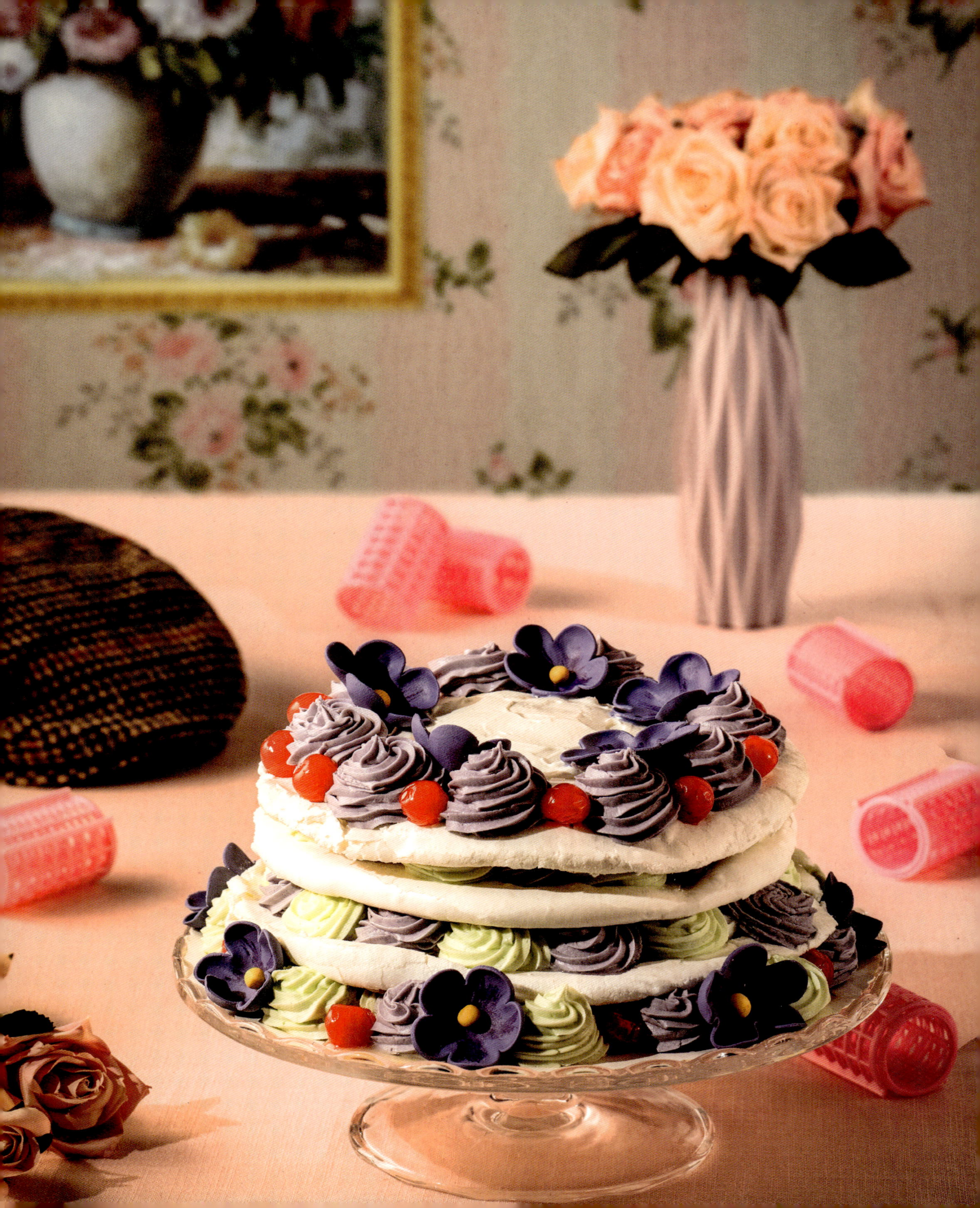

Aunt Petunia's Windtorte Pudding

**INGREDIENTS
FOR 1 WINDTORTE
(ABOUT 10 PORTIONS)**

For the meringue layers:
8 egg whites
2 tbsp lemon juice
1 pinch salt
1¾ cups sugar

For the filling:
1⅓ cups cold whipped cream
1 tbsp vanilla sugar
2 tsp cream stabilizer
3.5 cups mixed fresh berries (such as raspberries, blackberries, currants)

For the cream:
1⅔ cups cold whipped cream
4 tbsp sugar
4 tsp cream stabilizer
A few drops lilac food coloring
A few drops green food coloring

Candied cherries, as garnish

Also required:
14 violet decorative flowers made of fondant or marzipan

1. Preheat the oven to 210°F.
2. Spread a piece of baking parchment on the counter and, with a pencil, draw one circle 8 in. in diameter and three circles 6 in. in diameter. With the markings on top, place it on two baking trays and set aside.
3. In a bowl, beat the egg whites with a hand mixer on medium speed. Then, add the lemon juice and salt, and slowly add the sugar little by litter. Beat the mixture until stiff peaks appear. Now put the meringue mixture in a piping bag with large nozzle, and evenly cover the circles that you have drawn on the baking parchment.
4. Place in the oven, and bake for at least 1 hour, until the meringue becomes stiff and is easily removed from the parchment.
5. In a bowl, whip the cream using the hand mixer. When the cream is foamy, sprinkle in the vanilla sugar and the cream stabilizer, then whip until stiff peaks form. Mix in the berries, cover with plastic wrap, and leave in the refrigerator until ready to use. In another bowl, whip the whipped cream at medium speed. When the cream is foamy, sprinkle in the sugar and the cream stabilizer, then whip until stiff peaks form. Remove ¾ of the whipped cream, and in a separate bowl, color it lilac with a few drops of food coloring. Color the rest of the whipped cream mint green. Put the colored creams in a piping bag with a medium-sized star nozzle.
6. Place the larger meringue on a serving plate or a round dish. Place some of the fruit filling in the middle, and evenly spread; leave about 2 in. of space to the edge. Place one of the smaller meringues on top and spread some more of the filling on top, smooth, and once more leave 2 in. of space to the edge. Repeat the process with the last meringue.
7. With the piping bags containing the green and lilac cream, create evenly spaced, alternating, large rosettes on the edge of the torte. Do this for each layer of the torte. Line the top layer's edge with continuously piped lilac cream. Attach the candied cherries on the bottom and top layers, and decorate the torte all around with the violet decorative flowers (see picture).

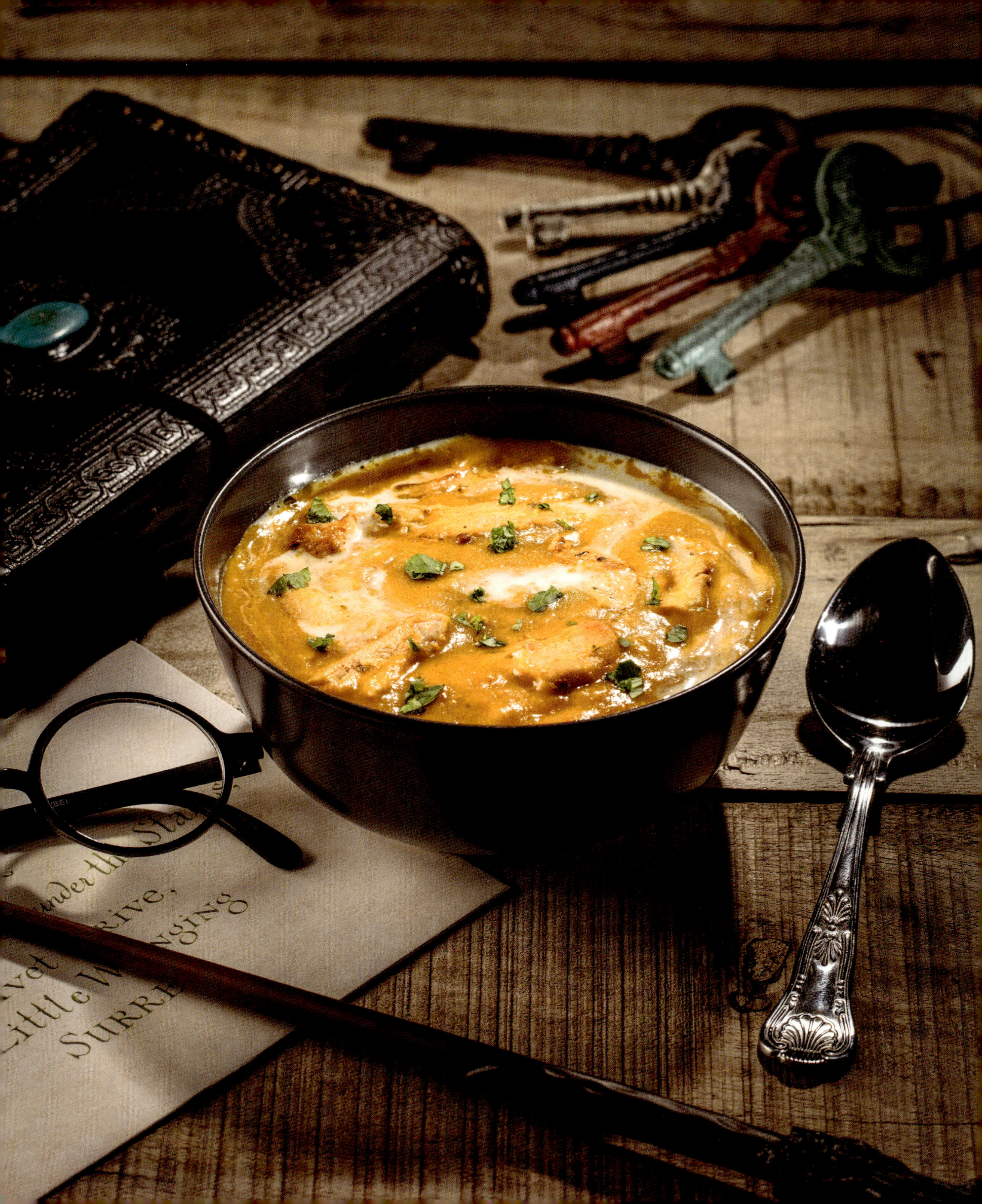

Hearty Mulligatawny Curry Soup

INGREDIENTS FOR 4 PEOPLE

¼ celery root/celeriac, two large carrots, one small leek, all finely diced

2 tbsp olive oil

1½ tbsp Madras curry powder

1 tbsp mild curry paste

3½ cups chicken stock

1 cup coconut milk,
   or abit more, reserve a little for dressing

Some lemongrass

½ tsbp. sambal oelek

3 tbsp mango chutney

Some corn starch (optional)

Pepper, salt

5½ oz chicken breast

½ cup wood ear mushrooms, soaked

1. In a large cooking pot on medium heat, gently sauté the diced vegetables with a little olive oil until colorless. Add the madras curry and the curry paste, add the chicken stock and the coconut milk, and let gently simmer 15 minutes.

2. Flatten the lemongrass at the lower, thicker end, and put it in the soup. Let simmer 2-3 minutes. Then flavor it with the sambal oelek, mango chutney and some salt. Then, pass it through a sieve into a clean saucepan, briefly bring to a boil once more, and bind with some stirred-in cornstarch if needed to give the soup the desired consistency.

3. Finely dice the chicken breasts, season with salt and pepper, and sauté in a pan with some oil for 2-3 minutes, until the meat has color all around. Along with the soaked and drained wood ear mushrooms, fill a soup bowl or deep dish with hot soup, add a blob of coconut milk, and serve immediately.

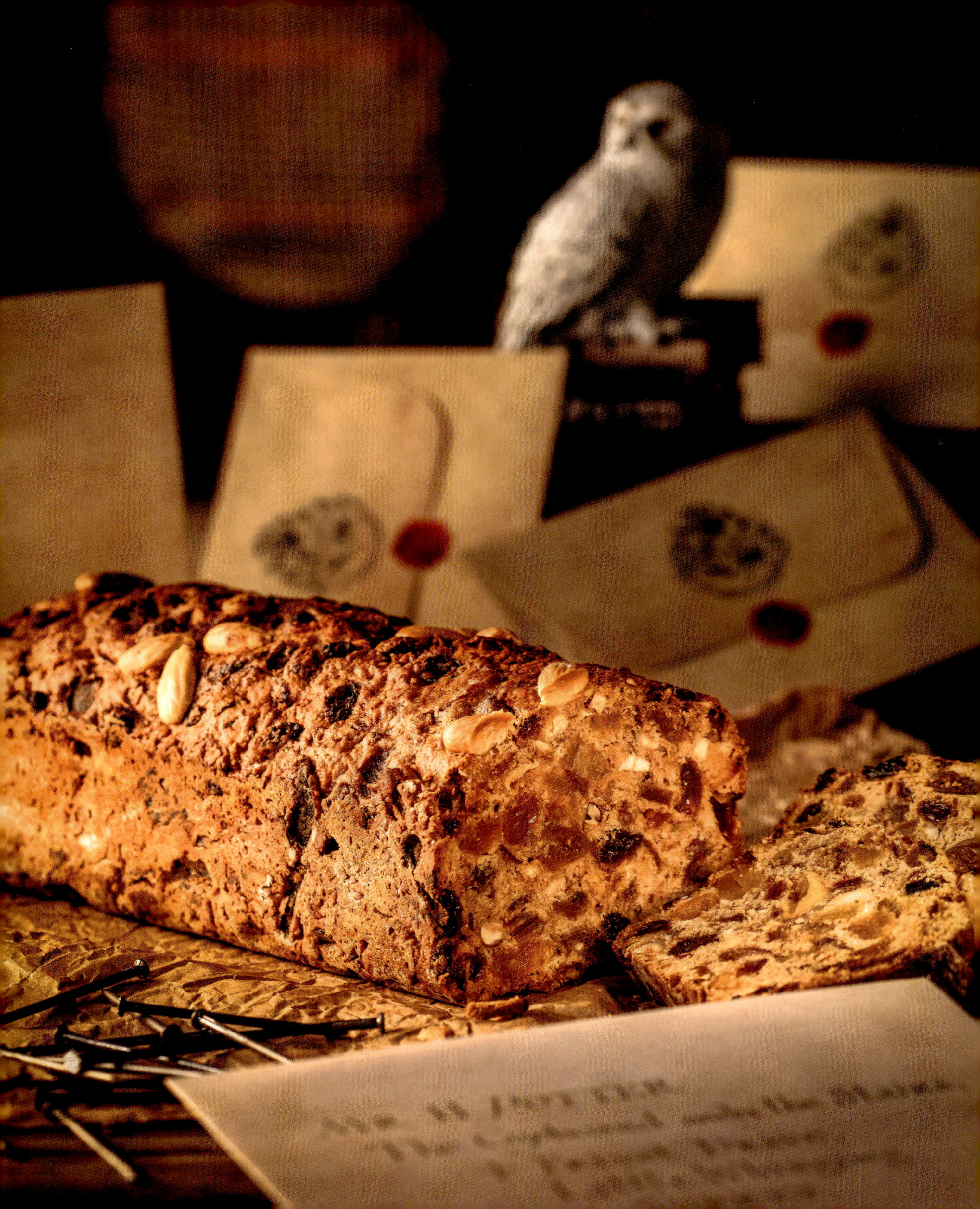

Fruitcake

CONTAINS ALCOHOL

INGREDIENTS FOR 1 FRUITCAKE

4 cups apples, peeled and sliced
4 cups dried fruit of your choice (e.g., figs, raisins, dates, apricots), coarsely chopped
1¼ cups brown sugar
1¼ cups nuts, roasted and finely chopped
2 tsp gingerbread spice
1 pinch salt
½ tbsp cocoa powder
2 fl oz rum
Some butter
4 cups flour, and some more for the loaf tin
2 tsp baking powder

Also required:
Loaf tin (approx. 5 x 12 in.)

1. Put apples, dried fruit, sugar, nuts, gingerbread spices, salt, and cocoa powder in a large bowl, and thoroughly mix. Add the rum, mix well, cover the bowl tightly with plastic wrap, and leave overnight.

2. Preheat the oven to 360°F. Grease a loaf pan with some butter, and dust it with flour.

3. In a bowl, mix 3 ¼ cups flour with the baking powder. Mix in the dried fruit and rum mixture, and work it all into a smooth dough., mi Fill the loaf pan with it, smooth the top, and bake 70-80 minutes in the preheated oven.

4. Remove it from the oven, let cool in the tin for 15 minutes, and then place it on a cutting board. Cut into finger-thick slices. Enjoy sweet or savory.

DOBBY THE HOUSE-ELFS TIP: Fruitcake tastes best when you wrap it in plastic wrap as soon as it is cool, and leave the flavors to infuse for at least a day!

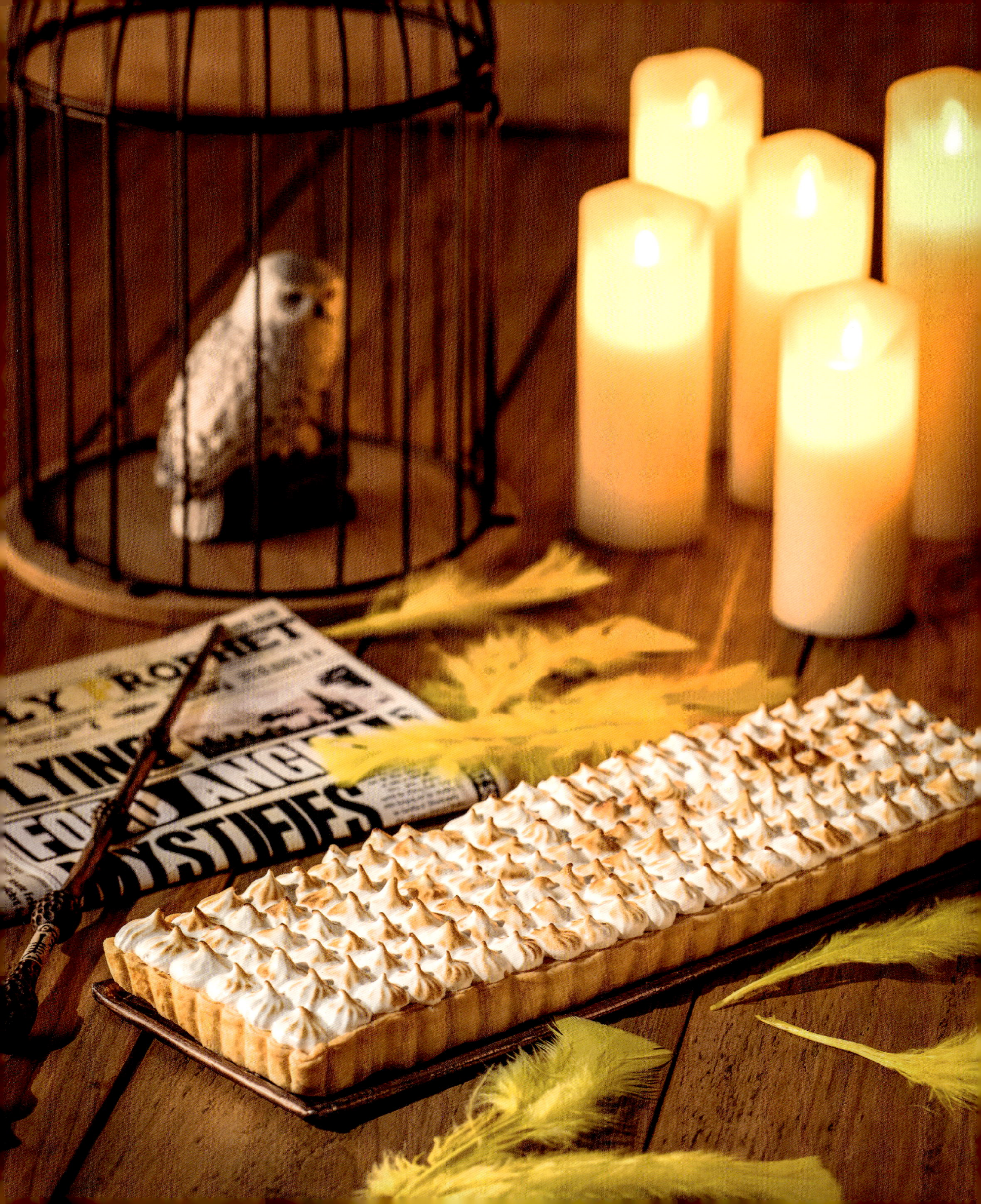

Lemon Meringue Pie

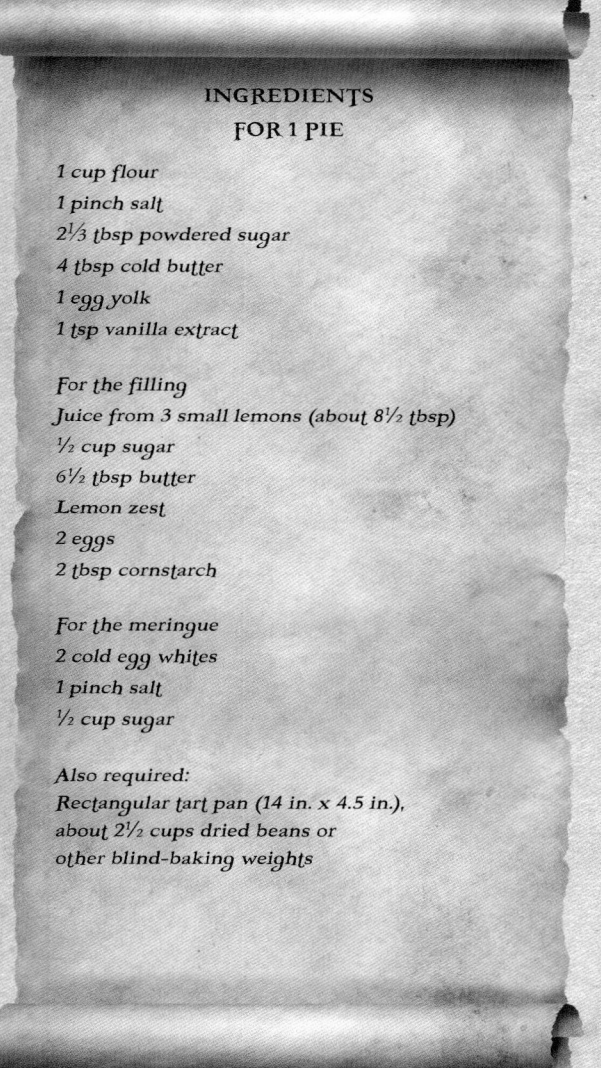

INGREDIENTS FOR 1 PIE

1 cup flour
1 pinch salt
2 1/3 tbsp powdered sugar
4 tbsp cold butter
1 egg yolk
1 tsp vanilla extract

For the filling
Juice from 3 small lemons (about 8 1/2 tbsp)
1/2 cup sugar
6 1/2 tbsp butter
Lemon zest
2 eggs
2 tbsp cornstarch

For the meringue
2 cold egg whites
1 pinch salt
1/2 cup sugar

Also required:
Rectangular tart pan (14 in. x 4.5 in.), about 2 1/2 cups dried beans or other blind-baking weights

1. Preheat the oven to 360°F.
2. Mix the flour, salt, and powdered sugar in a bowl. Add the butter, egg yolk, and vanilla extract, and work into a smooth dough using the dough hook attachments of a mixer. Press the dough slightly flat, wrap tightly in plastic wrap, and cool for at least 1 hour in the refrigerator.
3. Grease the pie pan with butter, and lightly dust with flour. Cut a piece of baking parchment that is a little bit bigger than the pie pan.
4. Unroll the dough into a rectangle on a counter lightly sprinkled with flour. Then carefully roll it out with the rolling pin, and unroll it once more over the pie pan. Press the dough into the pan, press against the sides, and use a fork to puncture it a few times. Cut away the excess dough.
5. Blind bake the dough: Place dried beans or baking weights on the baking parchment in the form, and bake it about 20 minutes on the bottom rack of the oven. Remove from the oven. Remove the weights and baking parchment, and leave the tart base to cool completely in the pan on a cooling rack. In the meantime, make the lemon filling.
6. Heat the lemon juice, sugar, butter, and lemon zest over low heat in a small saucepan. Leave aside and let cool for 30 minutes. Meanwhile, whisk the eggs in a bowl. Heat the cooled lemon juice mixture again while stirring constantly.
7. Thoroughly mix 3 tbsp of warm lemon juice with the cornstarch in a small bowl, and add to the remaining lemon juice. Mix well. Finally, stirring constantly, add to the whipped eggs, fill the pot once again, and (still stirring continuously) simmer until a thick cream develops. Spread it evenly over the crust.
8. In a dry bowl, whip the cold egg white with a pinch of salt using the whisk on a hand mixer. Whipping continuously, trickle the sugar into the mixture little by little, and thoroughly work in. Continue whipping the meringue mixture until the suer is completely dissolved and a firm, shiny cream has formed, with stiff peaks.
9. Fill a piping bag with the meringue mixture and apply to the lemon tart. Place the tart in the upper third of the oven for a few minutes, and broil it until the meringue is caramelized and turns golden brown. Remove from the oven, let cool, and serve.

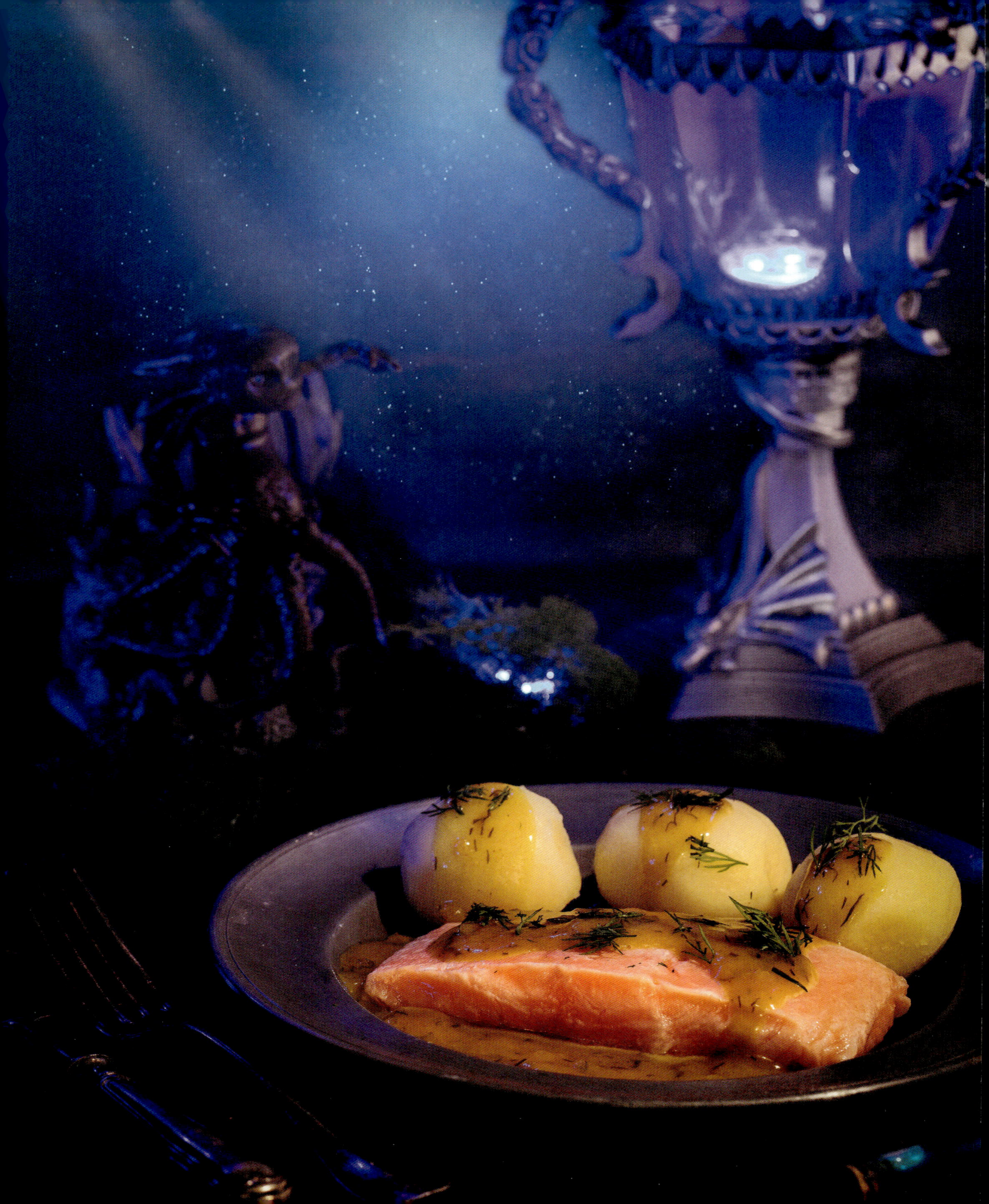

Poached Salmon with Honey Mustard Dill Sauce

INGREDIENTS
SERVES 4

For the salmon:
2 cups white wine
2 cups fish stock
1 shallot, peeled and halved
Juice of 1 lemon
1 tbsp peppercorns
4 salmon steaks (each about 5½ oz)
2 tbsp olive oil
Some sea salt

For the honey mustard dill sauce:
4 tbsp honey
6 tbsp mustard (medium-spicy)
2 tsp lemon juice, freshly pressed
2 tsp neutral oil
3 tbsp fresh dill, finely chopped

For the salmon:
1. In a large enough saucepan (the salmon steaks should have space side by side), warm the white wine and the fish stock over medium heat. Add the halved shallots, the lemon juice, and the peppercorns, and simmer 5 minutes.

2. Reduce heat to low. Rinse the salmon steaks in cold water, and pat dry with paper towels. Place in the broth and let simmer 6 minutes, covered. Remove the fish with a ladle, drizzle with some olive oil, sprinkle with a little sea salt, and serve with the Honey Mustard Dill Sauce (see below). Salted potatoes go wonderfully with it.

For the Honey Mustard Dill Sauce:
3. In a small bowl, mix the honey, mustard, and lemon juice. Stir in the neutral oil, add the finely chopped dill, mix well, and let stand for at least 15 minutes, longer if possible. Before serving, mix well once more.

CONTAINS ALCOHOL

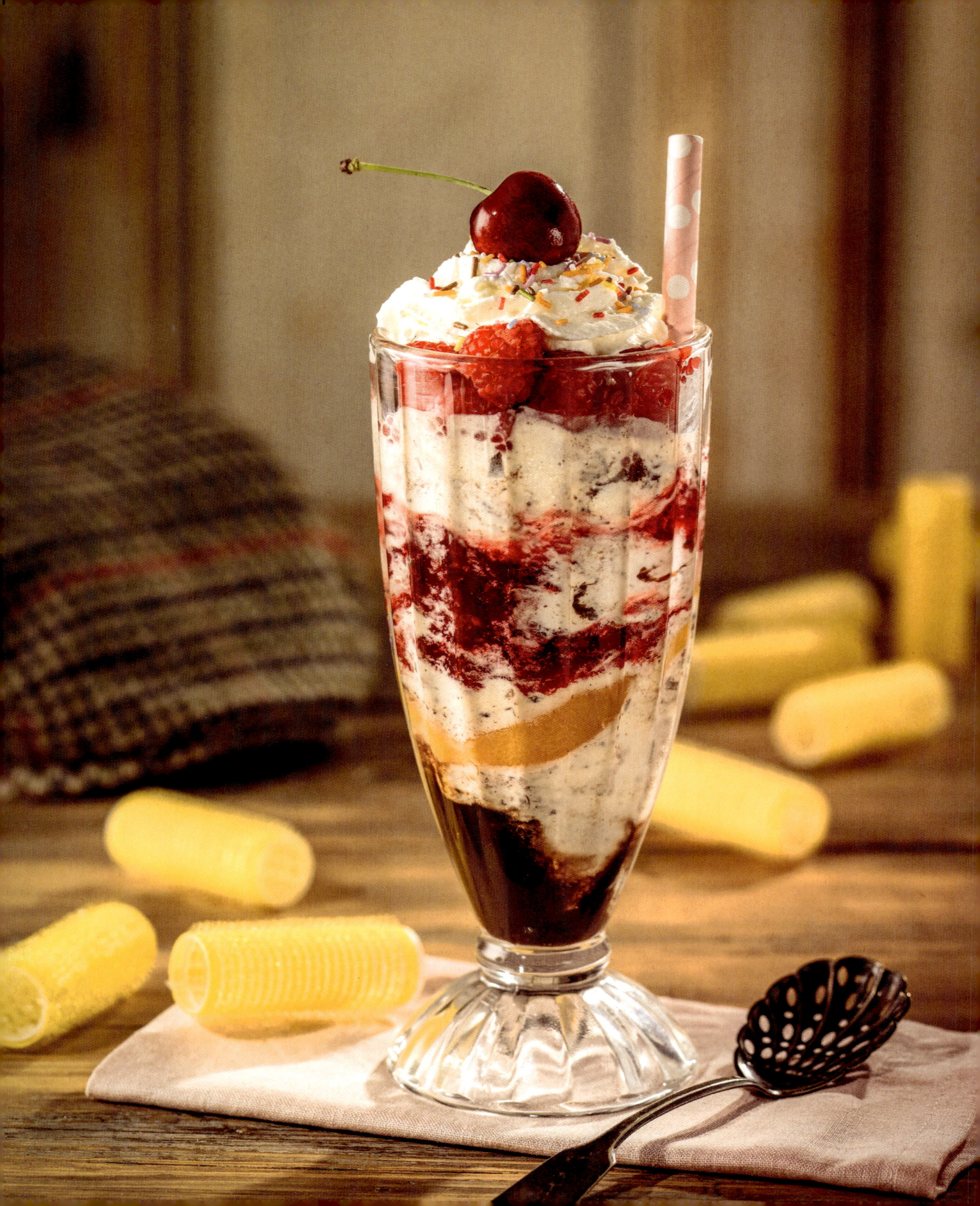

Knickerbocker Glory

INGREDIENTS FOR 1 PORTION

¼ cup cream
Chocolate syrup, (optional)
3 scoops vanilla ice cream
2 halves of a peach (canned), drained
2 tbsp raspberry purée
Fresh seasonal fruit, e.g., raspberries
1 fresh cherry or maraschino cherry
Colorful sprinkles, (optional)

Also required:
tall sundae glass, long ice cream spoon

1. Whip the cream stiff in a mixing bowl.
2. Pour some chocolate syrup into the bottom of a tall sundae glass. Add a scoop of vanilla ice cream, then ½ peach, 1 tbsp raspberry purée, and some more chocolate syrup, followed by the second ice cream scoop and the second peach half. Pour the rest of the raspberry purée over the top, add the last ice cream scoop, and top with fresh seasonal fruit.
3. Heap the whipped cream on top, crown with a single (ideally fresh) cherry, and add colorful sprinkles if desired. Serve with a long ice-cream spoon.

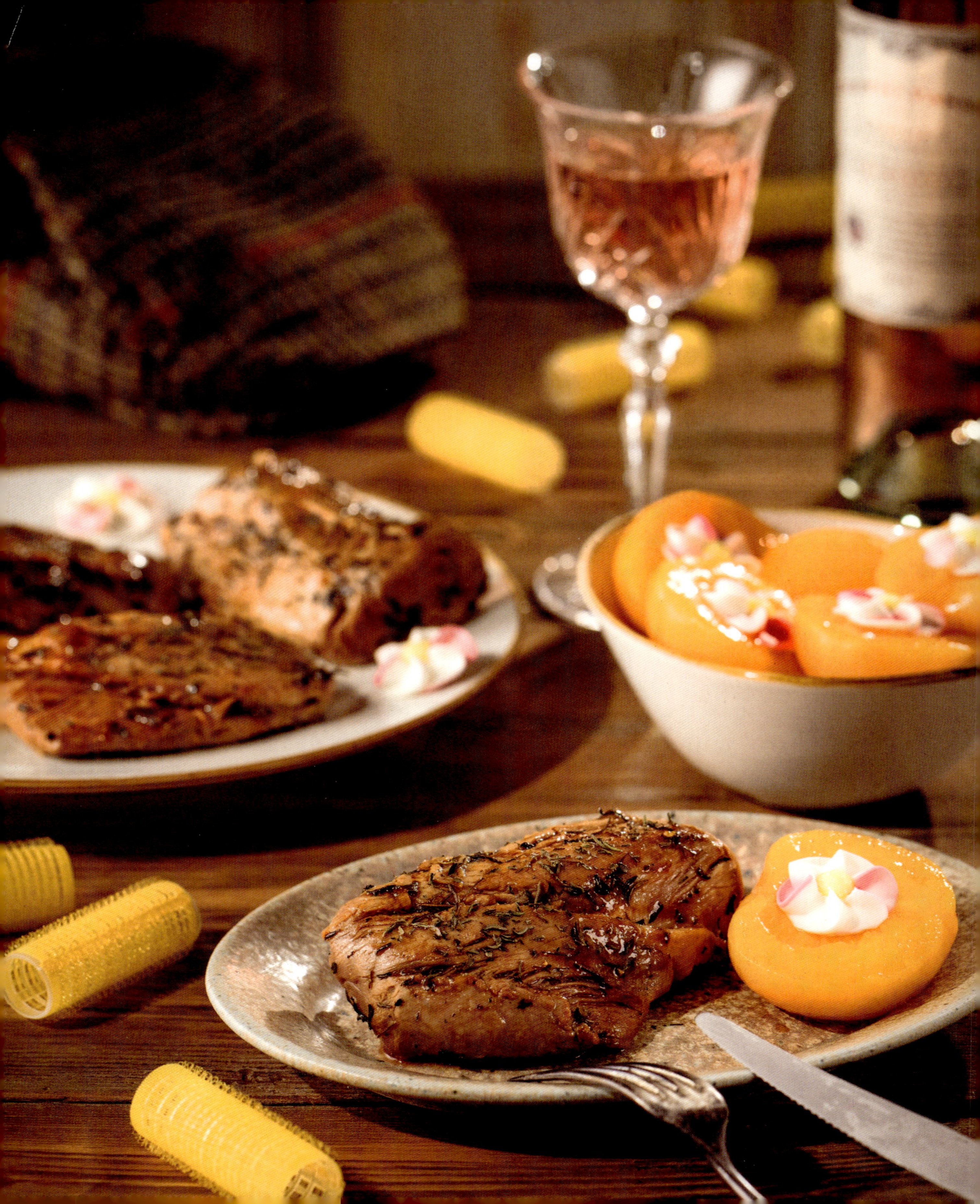

Pork Loin with Apple Glaze and Peach

INGREDIENTS FOR 4 PEOPLE

4 filet tips from a pork tenderloin (about 7 oz each)
2 tbsp dried thyme
1 garlic clove, finely chopped
2 tbsp salt flakes
Freshly ground black pepper
¼ cup peach juice
⅓ cup olive oil
8 peach halves (canned)

For the apple glaze:
5¼ tbsp apple butter (from a jar)
1 tbsp salt
1 tbsp mustard (medium-spicy)
2 tbsp butter
5 tbsp apple cider vinegar

1. Carefully remove silver skin and excess fat from the filet tips. Remove the dried thyme leaves from the sprigs, and chop finely with a knife. In a small bowl, mix the thyme with the garlic, salt flakes, freshly ground black pepper, and some juice from the canned peaches. Add the olive oil, carefully stir with all the rest, and put in a lightproof, sealable container with the filet tips. Massage the meat with the marinade so that it is covered all over. Put in the refrigerator, and let stand for at least 2 hours, ideally overnight.

2. Put the apple butter in a saucepan over low heat, stirring constantly, until liquid. Add the salt, mustard, butter, and vinegar, and mix well. Let softly simmer 8-10 minutes. Remove from heat.

3. About 20 minutes before sautéing, remove the pork filet from the refrigerator. Preheat the oven to 300°F. Prepare a baking tray.

4. Over medium heat, warm a large pan, and along with the marinade, add the pork tenderloin. Briefly sear, then turn. Generously cover the top with the apple glaze. After 1 minute, turn again and cover the other side with the glaze. Repeat these steps twice more. Wrap the pork filets tightly in aluminum foil, and cook for 10 minutes in the preheated oven. Then, check the temperature in the middle of the meat with a grill thermometer, if available. At 160°F, the meat is medium.

5. Remove from the oven, and let stand in the aluminum foil for 5 minutes. Then carefully unwrap, once more cover both sides with a little bit of glaze, and dress with the halved peaches. Serve immediately.

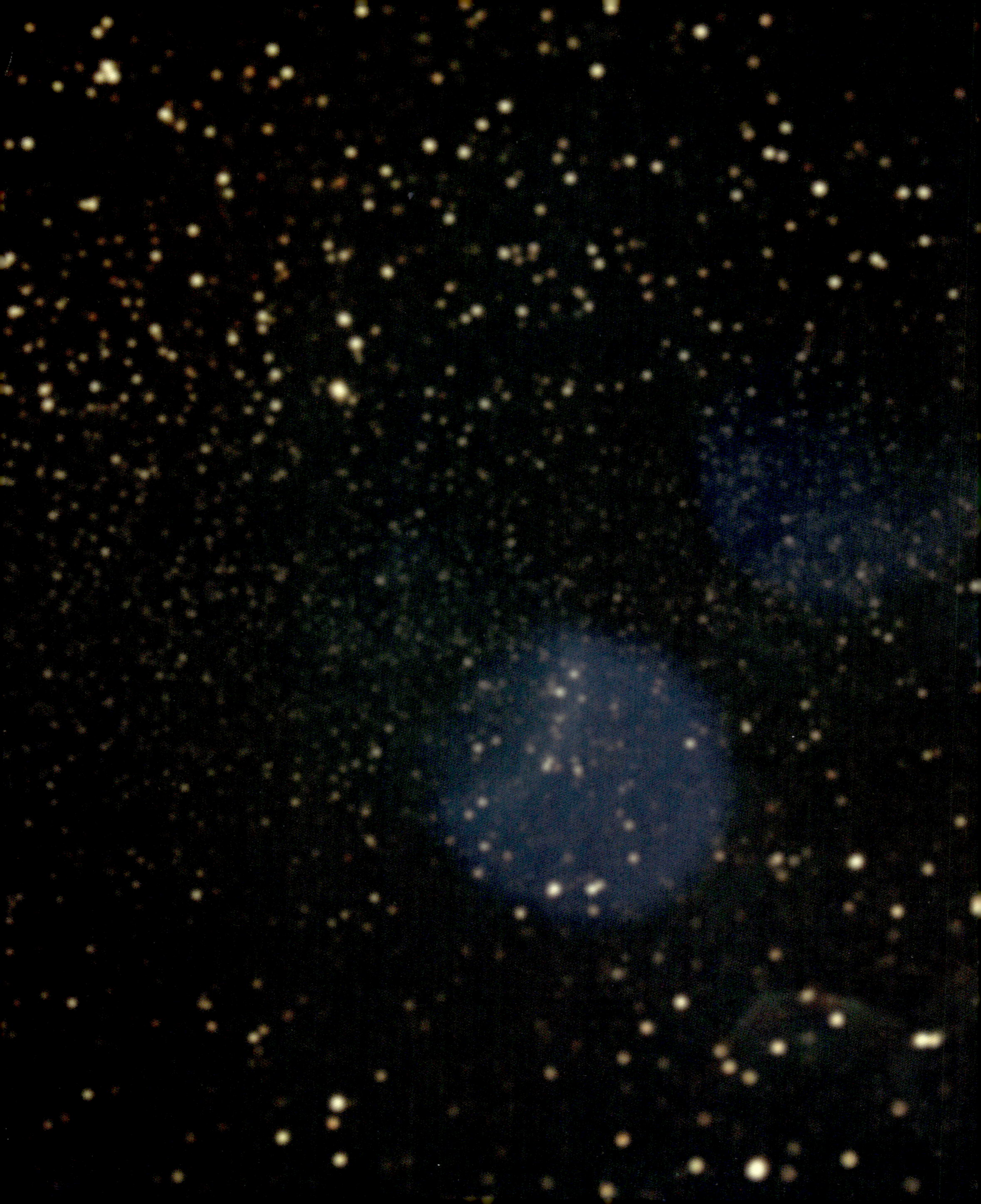

From the "World's Best Cook"

Harry considers Molly Weasley, the mother of his best friend Ron, "the world's best cook." And for good reason! During his first visit to the Burrow, the cozy home of his best friend Ron's family, "[b]ooks were stacked three deep on the mantelpiece"—and it's no coincidence that these were all cookbooks, with promising titles like *Charm Your Own Cheese*, *Enchantment in Baking*, and *One Minute Feasts—It's Magic!* Harry loves everything that Mrs. Weasley makes. She has all kinds of hearty dishes ready day and night, to warm both body and soul. Her traditional Christmas packages, too, are hugely popular with the boys, because next to unbelievably ugly sweaters sit piles of unbelievably tasty treats, like ginger snaps, pumpkin pasties, mince pies, and Mrs. Weasley's legendary—and legendarily delicious! —Christmas cake. It makes the "feast of love" twice as joyful!

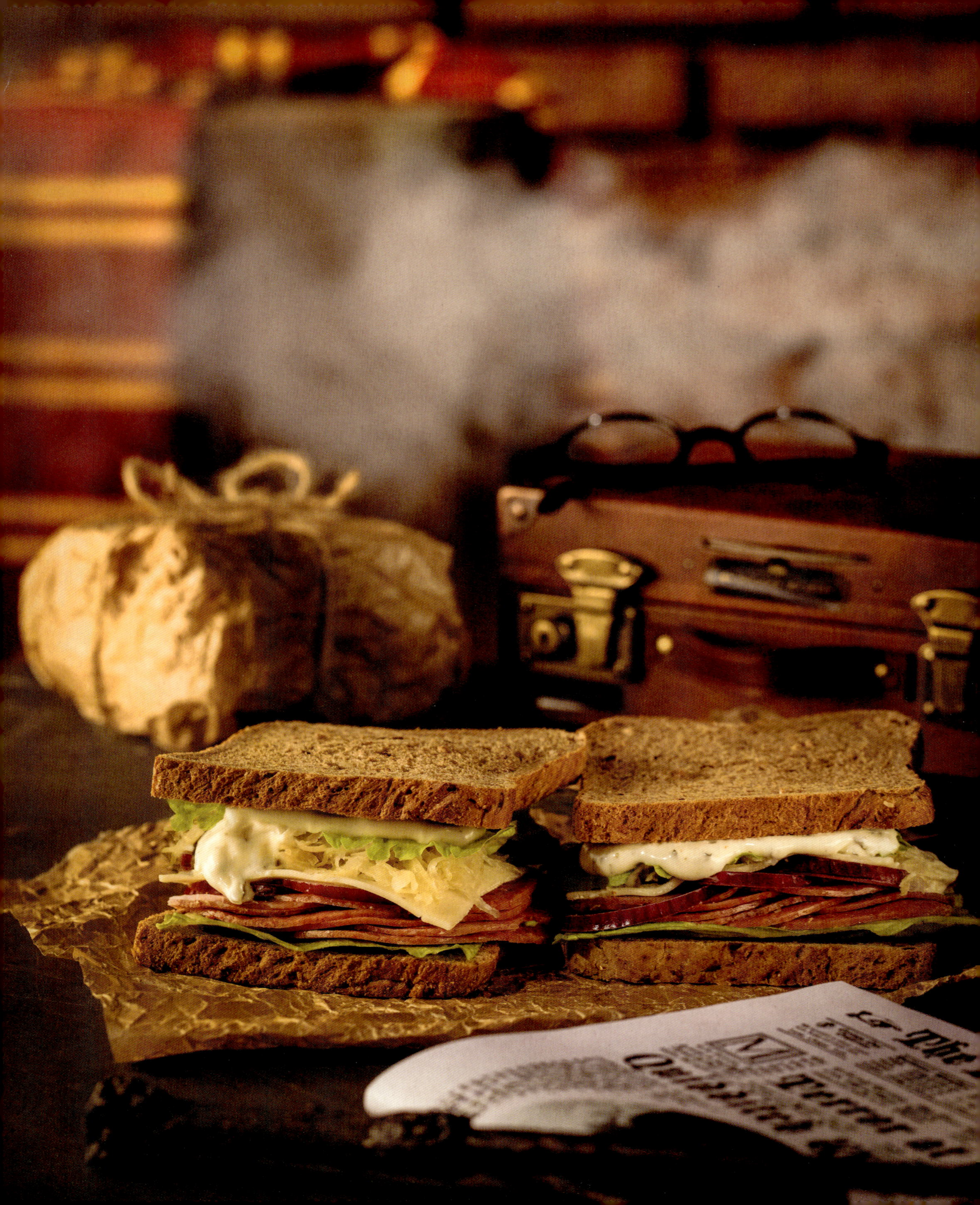

Corned Beef Sandwich

INGREDIENTS FOR 4 PEOPLE

½ red onion, finely chopped
4 tbsp remoulade
1 tsp horseradish
1 tsp Worcestershire sauce
3 tbsp tomato ketchup
8 slices or 1 small can corned beef (about 9 oz)
1 cup sauerkraut, drained
8 slices rye bread
Butter
Leaf lettuce, washed
4 slices cheese
Salt, pepper, Tabasco sauce

1. In a small bowl, mix the chopped onion with the remoulade, horseradish, Worcestershire sauce, and ketchup.
2. Cut the corned beef into thin slices, and rip up the sauerkraut a little.
3. Preheat the oven to 390°F.
4. Spread some butter on each slice of bread. Place a large lettuce leaf, some sauerkraut, two slices of corned beef, and cheese on half of the bread slices. Season with salt and pepper, and sprinkle some Tabasco sauce (optional). Finally, place another buttered slice of bread on top of each one.
5. Wrap the sandwiches in aluminum foil, and bake 10-15 minutes in the preheated oven. The cheese should melt, and the bread should become crispy at the edges. Let cool before serving!

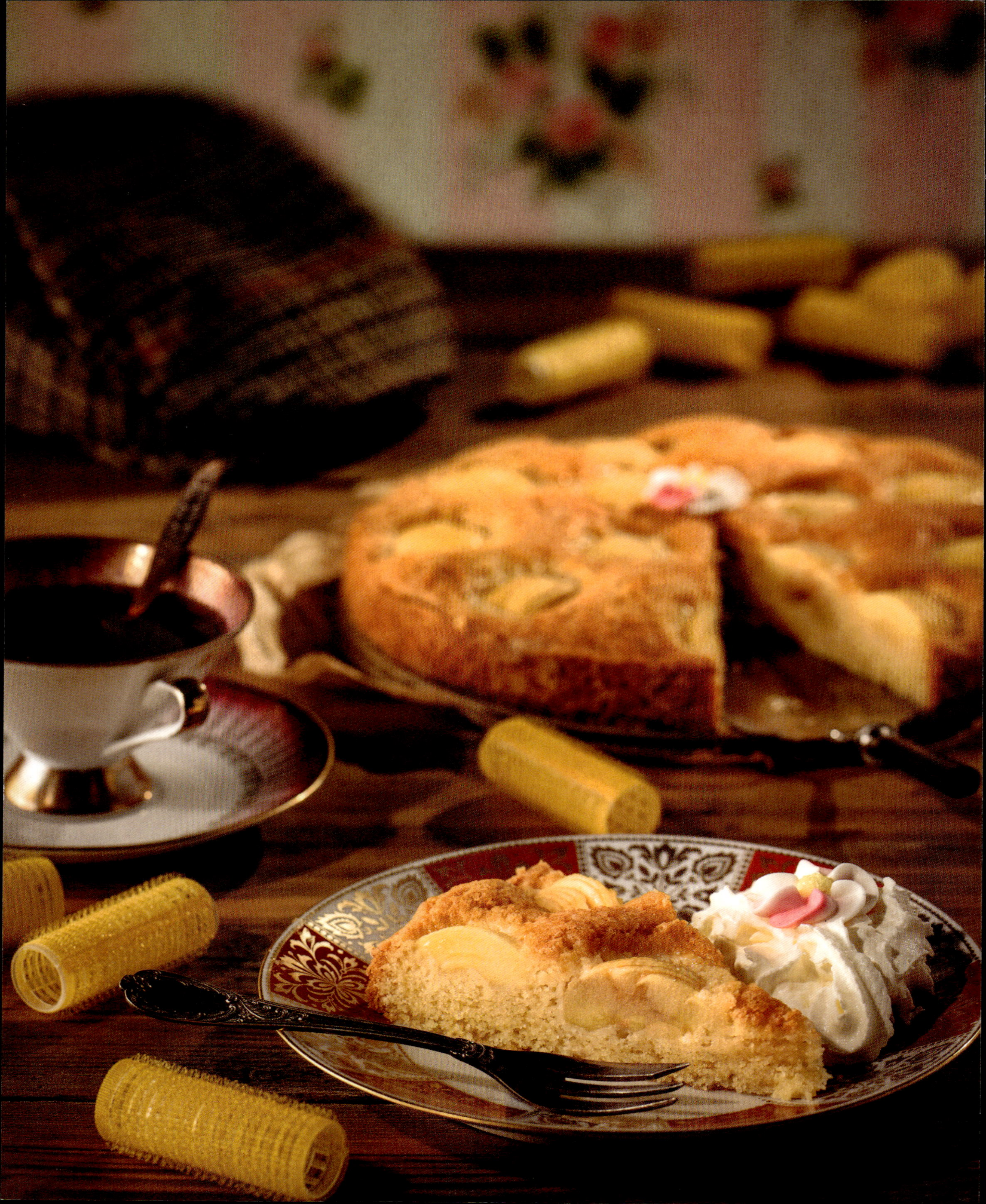

Apple Cake

**INGREDIENTS
FOR 1 CAKE**

½ cup butter, plus a little more to grease the pan
1 cup sugar
2 eggs
Zest of ½ lemon
1 pinch salt
2 cups flour
2 tsp baking powder
2 tbsp milk
6 apples, peeled and quartered
Powdered sugar, (optional)

Also required:
Cake pan (about 10 in. diameter)

1. In a bowl, with a hand mixer, stir the butter and the sugar until frothy. Little by little, add the eggs, the lemon zest, and the salt. Mix well.

2. In a separate bowl, mix the flour and the baking powder, and sift into the butter-egg mixture. Mix into a dough, and work in the milk.

3. Preheat the oven to 340°F. Grease the cake pan with some butter.

4. Make several small slits on the tops of the apple quarters.

5. Fill the prepared cake tin with the dough, smooth the top, and press the apple quarters lightly into the dough, leaving some space between them. On the middle rack of the preheated oven, bake for 40-50 minutes, or until the cake is golden brown and when you stick a toothpick into the middle and remove it, no residue sticks. Finally, remove from the oven, cool on a cooling tray, and last but not least, dust with powdered sugar, as desired.

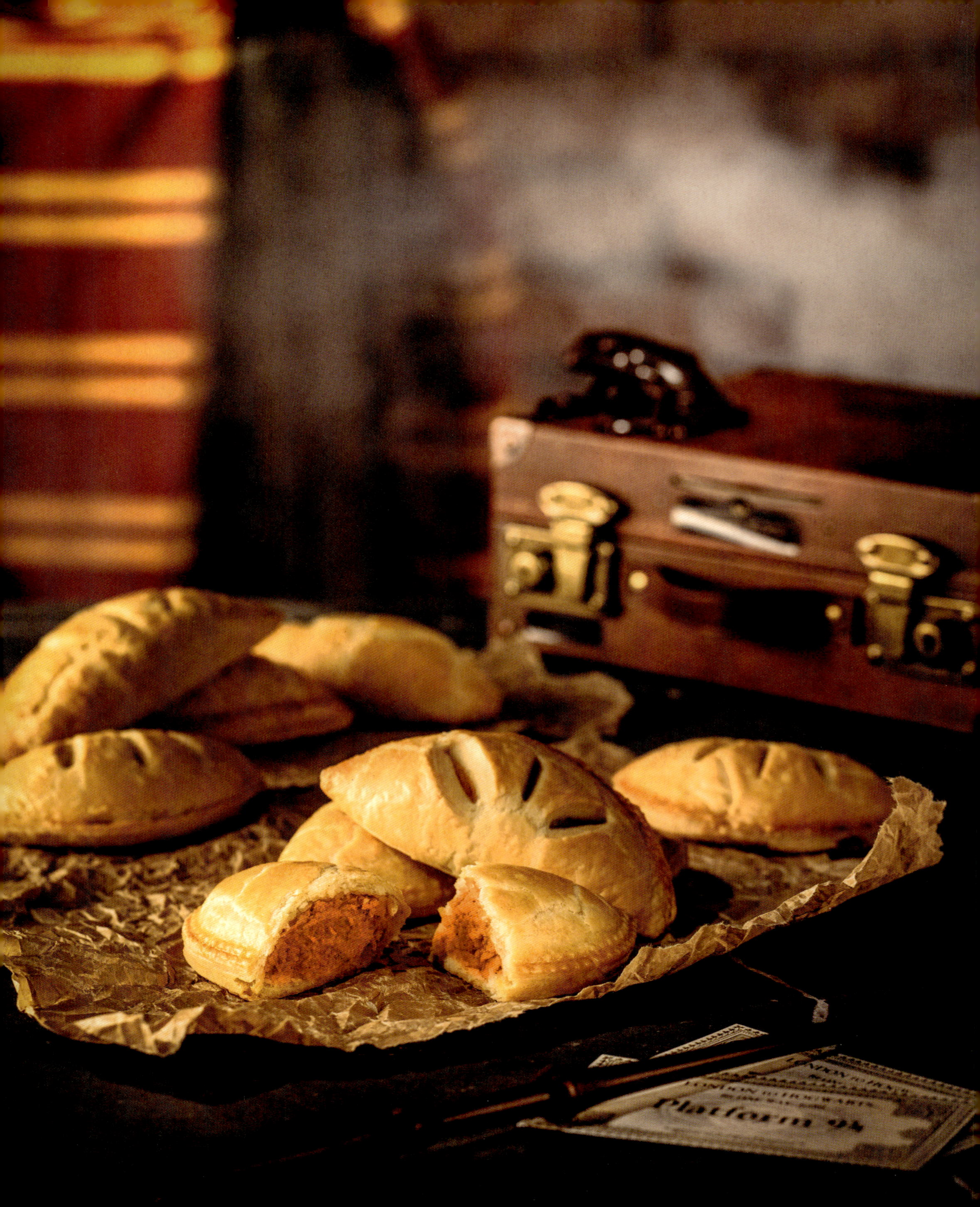
Platform

Pumpkin Pasties

INGREDIENTS
FOR ABOUT 8 PASTIES

For the dough:
3½ cups flour, plus a little more to dust the countertop
1 cup butter
1¼ cups sour cream

For the filling:
1 small Hokkaido pumpkin, de-seeded, puréed
Some pumpkin seed oil
1 pinch salt
7 tbsp sour cream
1 pinch pepper
1 large pinch nutmeg
1 egg

For the glaze:
1 egg
1 tbsp milk

Also required:
round cookie cutters (about 4 in. diameter)

1. In a bowl, knead the flour, butter, and sour cream into a smooth, pliable dough. Cover tightly with plastic wrap, and place in the refrigerator for 1-2 hours.

2. Preheat the oven to 350°F. Cover a baking tray with baking parchment.

3. Roll out the dough onto a countertop lightly dusted with flour, and with a cookie cutter, cut out eight circles about 4 in. in diameter. Place them on the prepared baking tray with some space between them.

4. Cook pumpkin flesh until soft with the pumpkin seed oil and some salt in a big enough saucepan over medium heat, regularly stirring. Then, purée as smooth as possible in the saucepan with an immersion blender. Add the sour cream, and season with pepper and nutmeg. Add the egg, and mix everything thoroughly. Remove from the stove and let cool a little.

5. Put 1 tbsp of pumpkin filling on each dough circle on the baking tray. Fold each circle over once, and with fingers or a fork, press the edges together. With a knife, cut three slits in each dough pouch, so that air can escape during baking.

6. Mix 1 egg and 1 tbsp milk in a small bowl. With this mixture, glaze each pasty all over, and place in the oven for about 20 minutes, until they are golden brown; at the halfway point, turn once. Remove them, and let cool on the tray for 5-10 minutes. Best served warm.

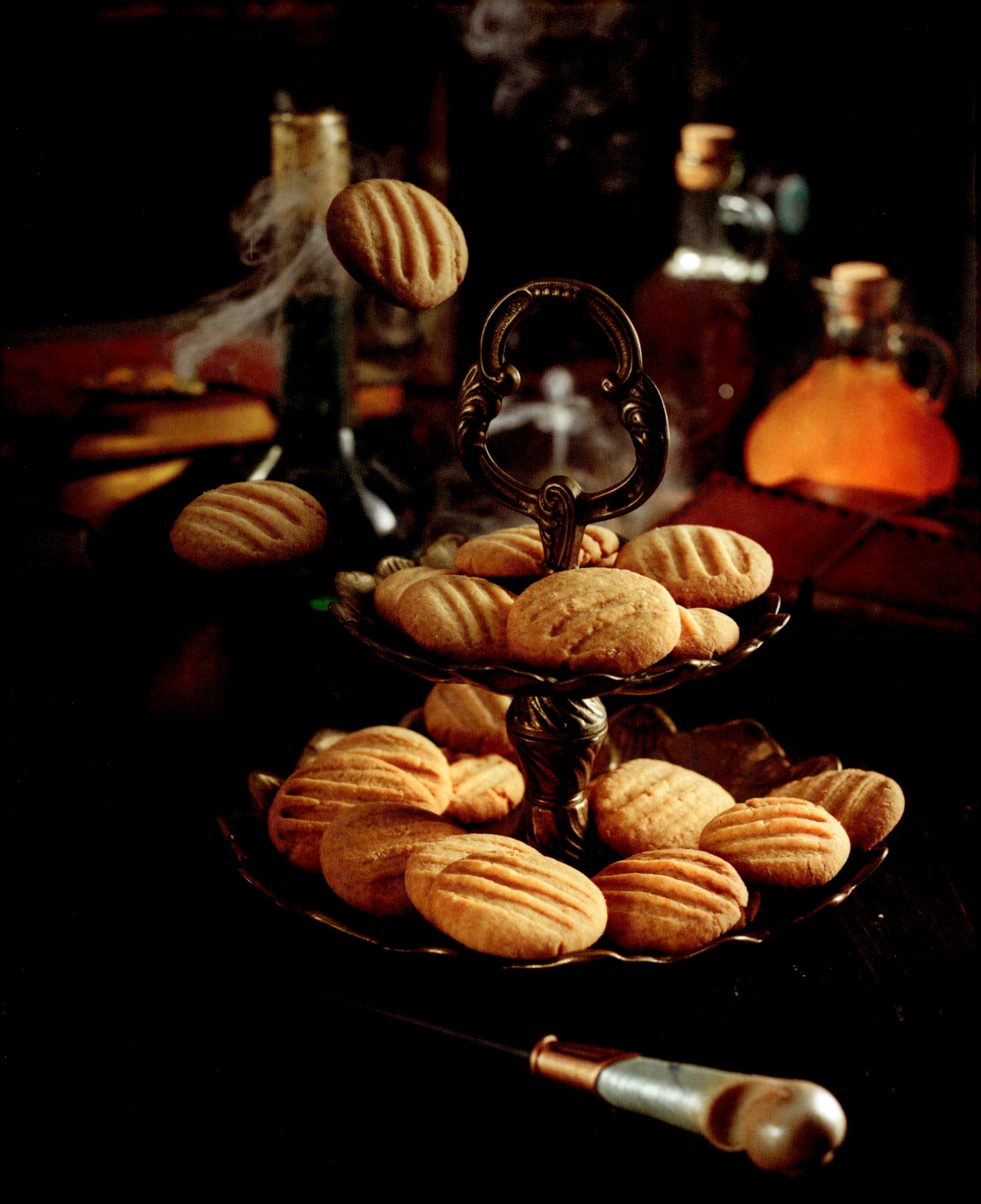

Ginger Snaps

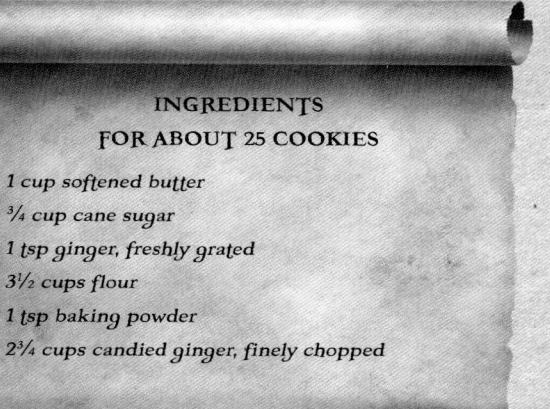

**INGREDIENTS
FOR ABOUT 25 COOKIES**

1 cup softened butter
¾ cup cane sugar
1 tsp ginger, freshly grated
3½ cups flour
1 tsp baking powder
2¾ cups candied ginger, finely chopped

1. Preheat the oven to 390°F. Cover a baking tray with baking parchment.
2. Whip the softened butter in a mixing bowl with the cane sugar. Mix in the ginger.
3. In a separate bowl, mix the flour and the baking powder, and sift into the butter-sugar mixture. Mix everything together thoroughly. Add the ginger and, with hands, work into a supple dough., a
4. Make about 25 walnut-sized balls from the dough, place them on the prepared baking tray, and with a moistened fork or your hands, flatten them to a ½-inch thickness. Bake the ginger snaps for 12-15 minutes, until golden brown. Remove them from the oven and let them fully cool on a cooling rack.

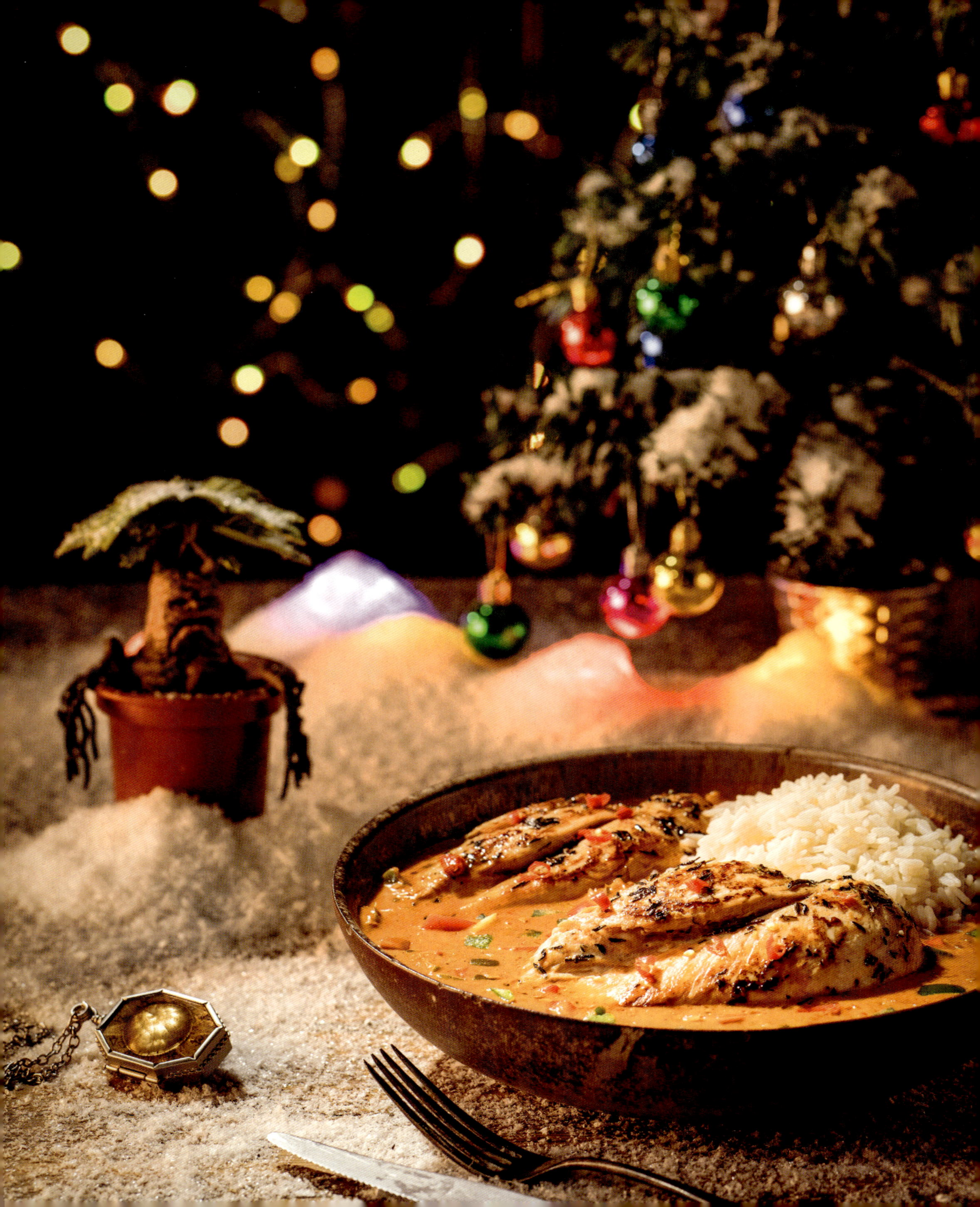

Ginny Weasley's Pepperup Paprikash

INGREDIENTS
SERVES 4

2 tbsp olive oil

4 chicken breast filets

1 onion, finely chopped

2 garlic cloves, finely chopped

1 tbsp tomato paste

3 tbsp powdered paprika (sweet)

1 red pepper, seeds removed, cut into thin strips

1 green pepper, seeds removed, cut into thin strips

1¾ cups water

1 bouillon cube

1½ cups sour cream

2 tbsp flour

Salt and freshly ground black pepper

1. In a large pan, over medium heat, heat the olive oil. Heavily season the chicken breast filets all over with salt and pepper, and sear on all sides (about 3-4 minutes). Remove the meat from the pan, put on a plate, cover with aluminum foil, and briefly set aside.

2. In the juice, sauté the onion and garlic. Mix in the tomato paste and paprika powder, and add the pepper strips. Add the water and the bouillon cubes. Boil briefly; put the meat in the pan and cook, covered, for about 15 minutes.

3. Remove the meat. In a bowl, mix the sour cream and flour with some water until smooth, and sift it into the sauce, which should not be boiling. Mix in well, briefly bring everything to a boil once more, and finally season with salt and pepper. Put the meat back in, and let the Pepperup Paprikash stand in the sauce for 5 minutes. Serve with rice.

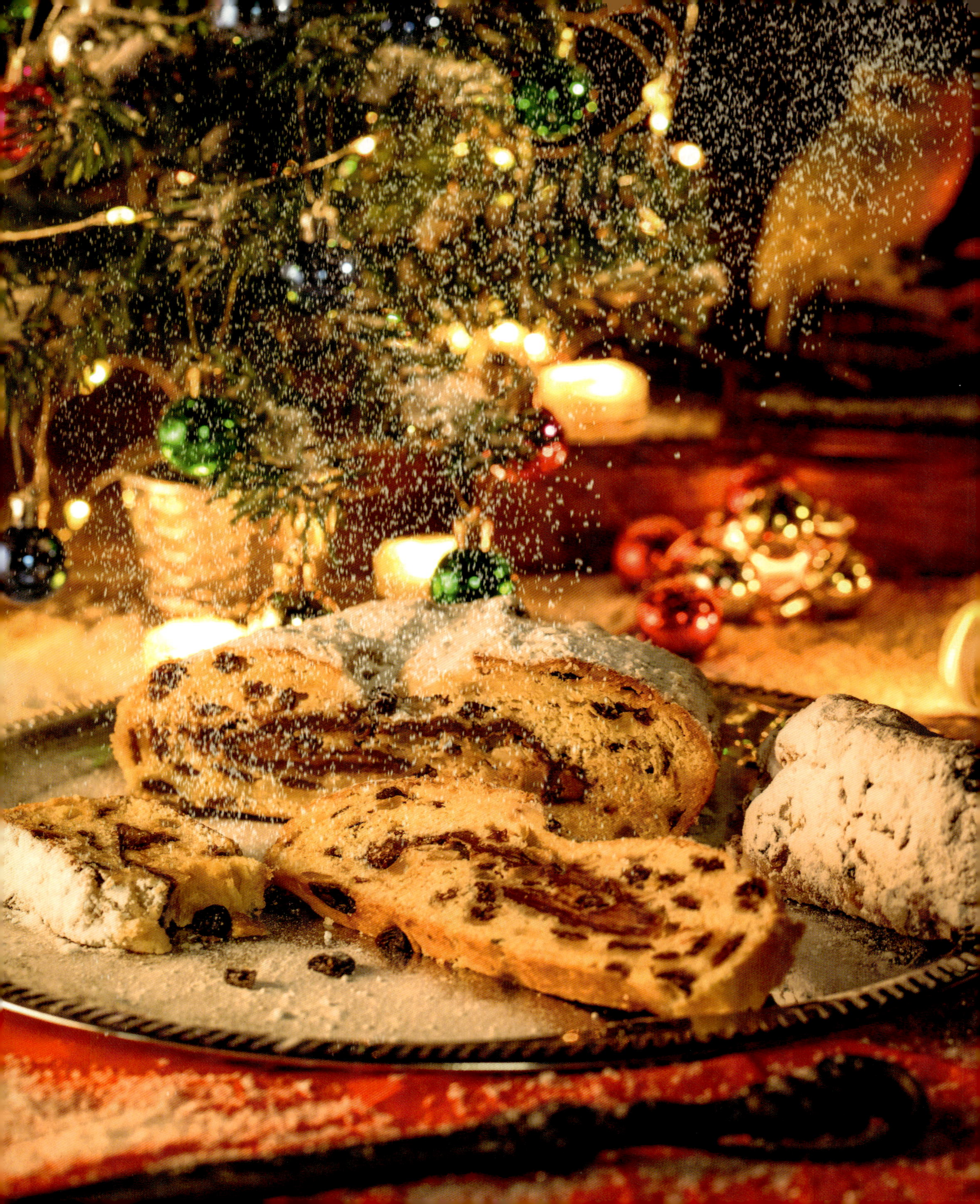

Christmas Cake

CONTAINS ALCOHOL

INGREDIENTS FOR 1 CHRISTMAS CAKE

For the dough:
1 cup raisins
½ tsp lemon zest
¼ cup candied orange peel
¼ cup candied lemon peel
2 fl oz rum
½ cup ground almonds
4¼ cups flour
1 tbsp fresh yeast
⅓ cup lukewarm milk
¼ cup sugar
7 tbsp butter
1 egg
2 tsp vanilla sugar
½ pinch salt
½ tsp cinnamon
¼ tsp cardamom
¼ tsp nutmeg

For the glaze:
3 tbsp butter
½ cup powdered sugar

1. In a large bowl, mix the raisins, lemon zest, candied orange peel, and candied lemon peel with the rum and the ground almonds. Let infuse at least 1 hour, preferably overnight.

2. Put the flour in a large bowl, and add yeast. Add 2 tbsp lukewarm milk and a pinch of sugar, and mix briefly. Leave covered in a warm place for about 30 min.

3. Put the butter in the flour, in small pieces. A little at a time, add the egg, remaining sugar, vanilla sugar, salt, cinnamon, cardamom, and nutmeg, and briefly mix each time. Then, using a hand mixer on high power with dough hooks attached, knead well for at least 10 minutes. Meanwhile, little by little, add the remaining milk and knead it in. Finally, work in the fruit-nut-rum mixture, and leave covered for 30 minutes.

4. Cover a baking tray with baking parchment.

5. Knead the dough briefly, and form an elongated loaf. With a rolling pin, flatten slightly over the long side until halfway. Fold the thicker side over, and make the loaf into the desired shape with your hands. Place on the baking tray and leave covered 30 minutes. Meanwhile, preheat the oven to 390°F on a convection setting.

6. Bake the cake for about 40-45 minutes in the preheated oven. After 30 minutes, reduce the temperature to 355°F. If the cake is too dark, cover with aluminum foil until it is completely baked.

7. In the meantime, melt 2¾ tbsp butter in a saucepan over low heat. Remove the cake from the oven, and coat with the butter. Let cool a little, then coat again with melted butter, and generously sprinkle with powdered sugar.

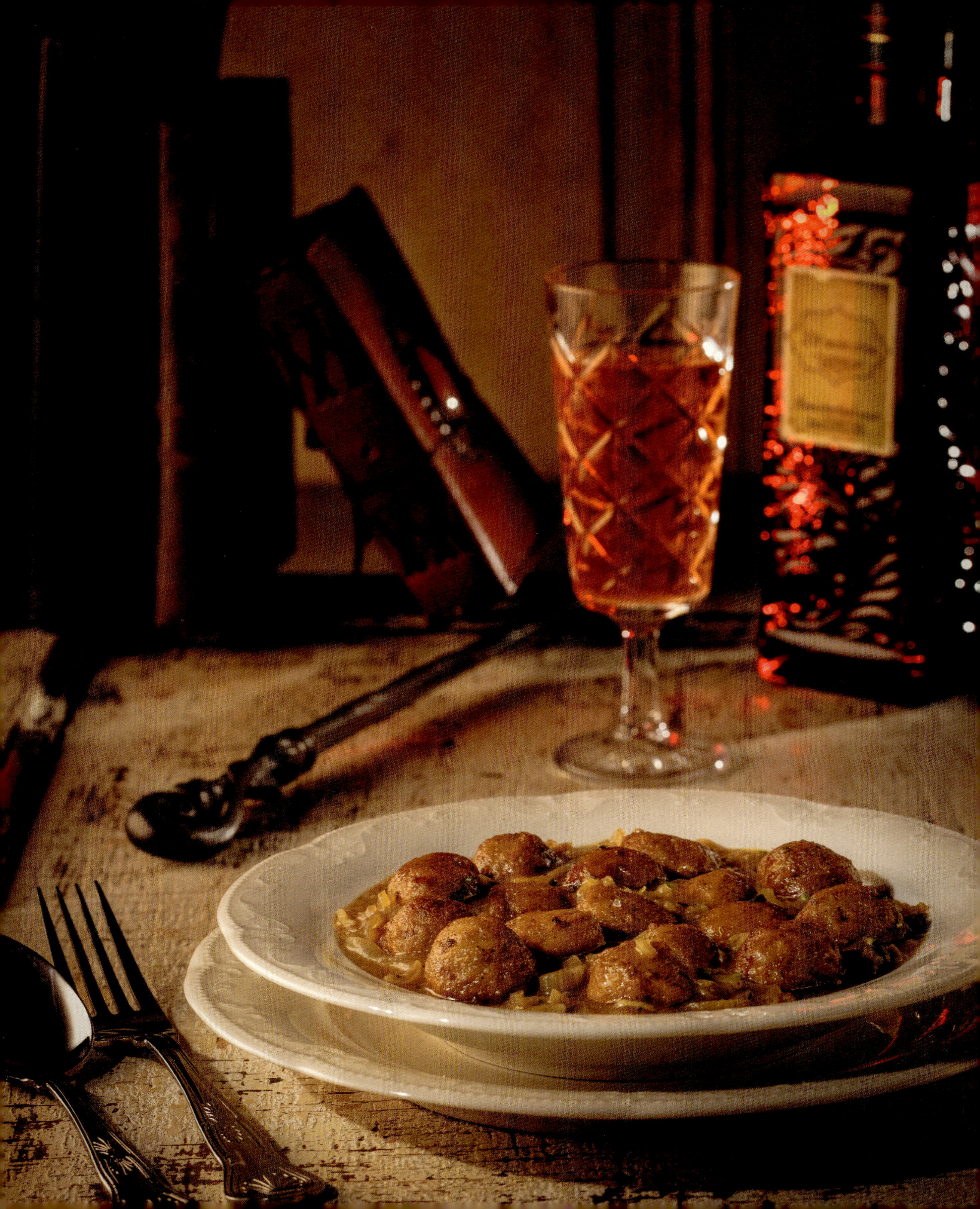

Meatballs in Onion Sauce

CONTAINS ALCOHOL

INGREDIENTS
SERVES 4

For the meatballs:
1⅓ lb ground meat, mixed
3 tbsp breadcrumbs
1 egg
1 shallot, finely diced
2 tbsp mustard (medium-spicy)
Salt, pepper
1 pinch nutmeg
2 tbsp butter

For the onion stock:
3 cups onions, cut into rings
1 garlic clove, finely diced
1¼ cup beef stock
¾ cup white wine
1 tbsp lemon juice
2 tbsp sour cream
Salt and freshly ground black pepper

1. Put the ground meat, breadcrumbs, egg, shallot, and mustard in a large bowl. Season with salt, pepper, and nutmeg, and knead thoroughly. Make golf-ball-sized balls from the meat mixture with lightly moistened hands.

2. In a large pan over medium heat, melt the butter, and fry the meatballs on all sides until they are golden brown all over (about 5 minutes). Remove from the pan and set aside.

3. Put the onion rings in the fat in the pan, and sauté until they have taken on some color all over. Now add the garlic and sauté together. Deglaze with the beef stock and white wine. Add the lemon juice and briefly boil. Mix in the sour cream, season with salt and pepper, and warm the meatballs in the hot onion sauce for a few minutes.

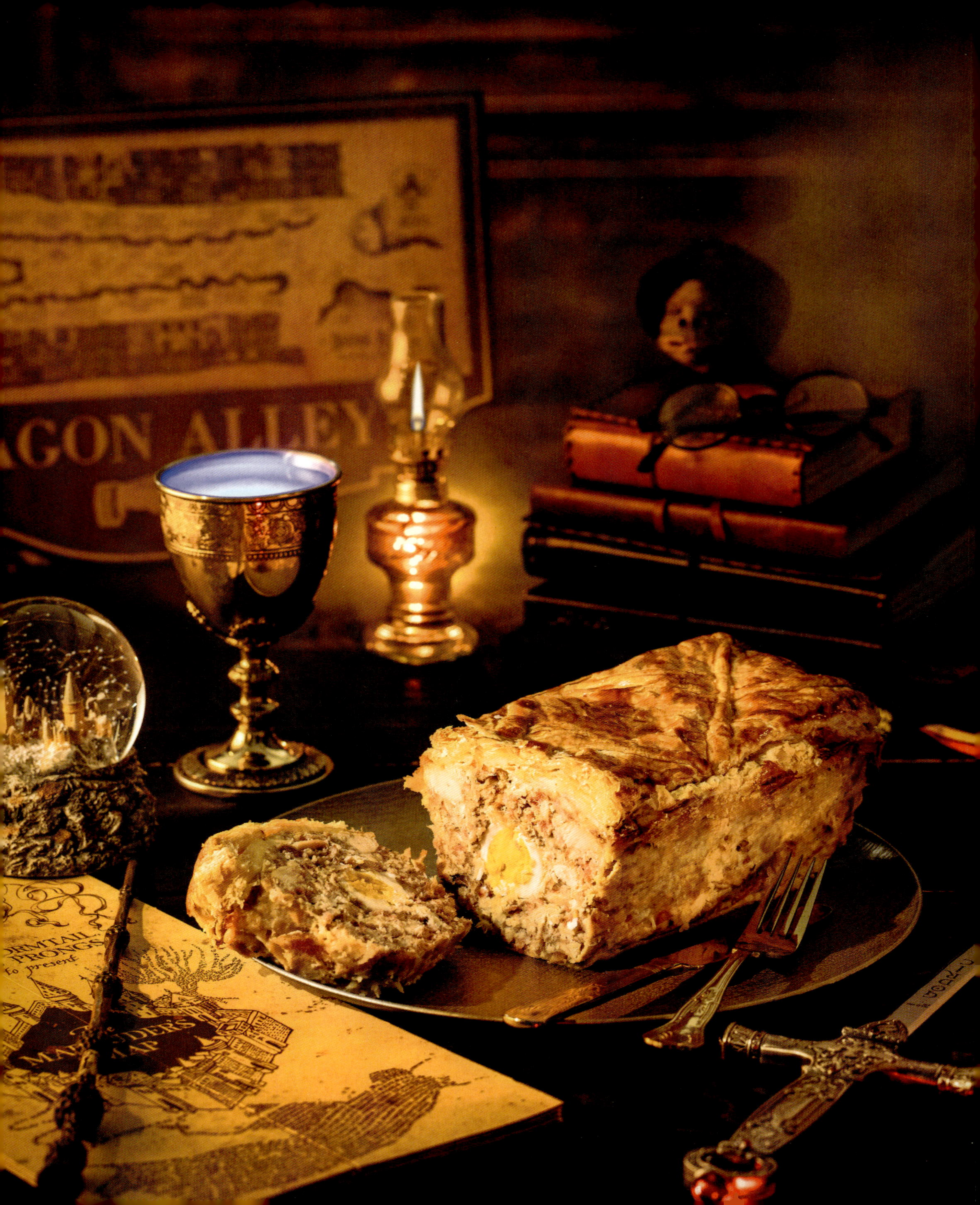
AGON ALLEY
PRONGS
to present

Chicken and Ham Pasty

INGREDIENTS
SERVES 6-8

2¼ lb cooked frozen chicken, in bite-sized pieces
7 oz diced ham
1 lb ground pork
1 small shallot, finely diced
Salt and freshly ground black pepper
Butter, to grease the pan
1 pack frozen puff pastry
3 hard-boiled eggs, peeled
1 egg yolk

Also required:
Tall loaf mold (approx. 4 x 10 in.)

1. Defrost the frozen chicken to room temperature, and drain excess liquid.

2. Put the defrosted chicken, the ham, the ground pork, and the shallot in a large bowl, season with salt and pepper, and mix well.

3. Preheat the oven to 320°F on a convection setting. Cover a loaf pan with baking parchment so that the paper overlaps the edges. Grease thinly with butter.

4. Roll out the pastry on a countertop, not too thick. Place in the pan and press the sides; make sure that enough puff pastry is left over the sides so that they can be pressed together to "close" the pasty. Evenly place half of the chicken/ground-meat filling inside. Flatten the top, and place the hard-boiled eggs in a row in the middle of the loaf. Add the remaining filling, smooth the top, and fold over the overhanging puff pastry so that the filling is completely covered. Loosely cover with aluminum foil, and bake for 1 hour in the preheated oven. Every 20 minutes, drain the excess liquid from the pan!

5. The last time you drain the fat, coat the top of the pasty with the egg yolk and remove the aluminum foil. This gives the crust color and makes it nice and crisp. After the cooking time, remove from the oven. Let cool briefly, then carefully remove from the pan using the leftover baking parchment.

6. Raise the temperature to 390°F and set the oven to broil. Cover a baking tray with baking parchment. Carefully place the pasty on the tray, and put in the oven again for 5 minutes, until the crust is golden brown and crispy all over. Finally, remove from the oven, let cool briefly, and with a large, sharp knife, cut into approximately 1-inch slices. Best served with cranberry jam and Fluffy Mashed Potatoes with Gravy (p. 102).

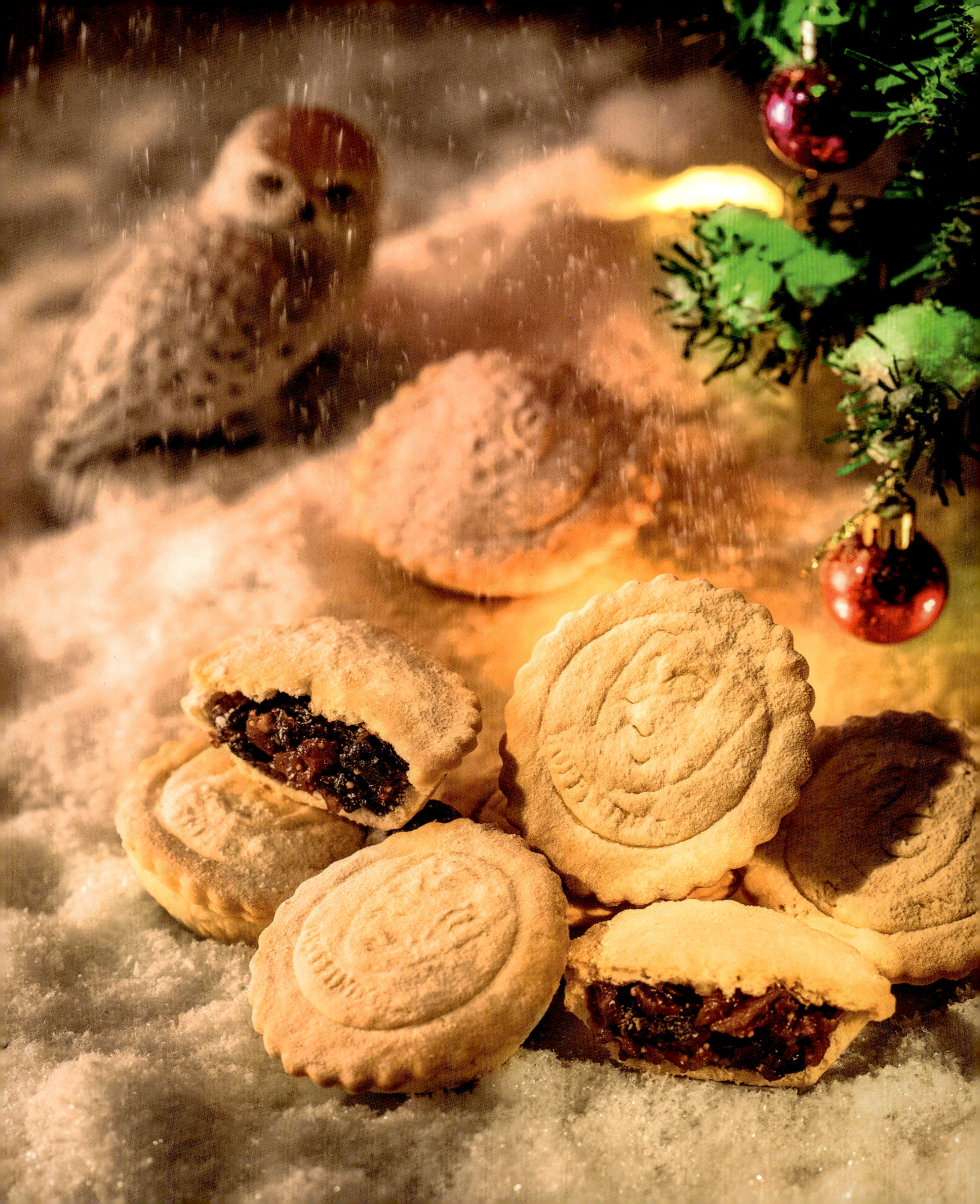

Mince Pies

CONTAINS ALCOHOL

INGREDIENTS
FOR 8 MINCE PIES

For the filling:
1 cup mixed dried fruit, finely diced
1 cup raisins
Zest of 1 orange
½ cup cane sugar
1 tsp cinnamon
1 tsp ginger
½ tsp ground nutmeg
⅓ cup rum
A few drops of almond extract
½ tsp vanilla extract
2 tbsp honey

For the shortcrust pastry:
1 cup softened butter
3¾ cups flour
10½ tbsp sugar
1 pinch salt
2 eggs
Powdered sugar

Also required:
round cookie cutter (about 4 inches),
round cookie cutter (about 3 inches), silicone
Hogwarts stamp, 8-muffin pan

1. In a bowl, mix the finely diced dried fruit, raisins, orange peel, cane sugar, cinnamon, ginger, and ground nutmeg, and thoroughly blend in the rum, almond and vanilla extracts, and honey. Cover with plastic wrap, and leave in the refrigerator for at least 12 hours.

2. Put the butter and flour in a bowl. Add the sugar, the salt, and an egg. With a hand mixer with dough hooks, work the mixture into a supple dough. Pat with a clean paper towel, and let cool 10 minutes in the refrigerator.

3. Grease a loaf pan with some butter, and dust it with flour. Preheat the oven to 430°F.

4. Roll out the dough as thinly as possible (about 1/8 inch), on a well-floured countertop. With a round cookie cutter, cut 8 circles that are large enough to cover the bottom and sides of one of the molds in a muffin pan. Carefully put the circles in the molds, and gently press. Reknead the rest of the dough, roll it out again, and make 8 smaller circles. Carefully press the Hogwarts silicone stamp into these.

5. Put the dried fruit filling in the muffins, cover each with a stamped dough circle, and press all around the edge.

6. In a small bowl, whisk the second egg, and glaze the top of the mince pies with it. Bake in the preheated oven for 20 minutes, then let cool a little and sprinkle with powdered sugar. Enjoy warm or cold.

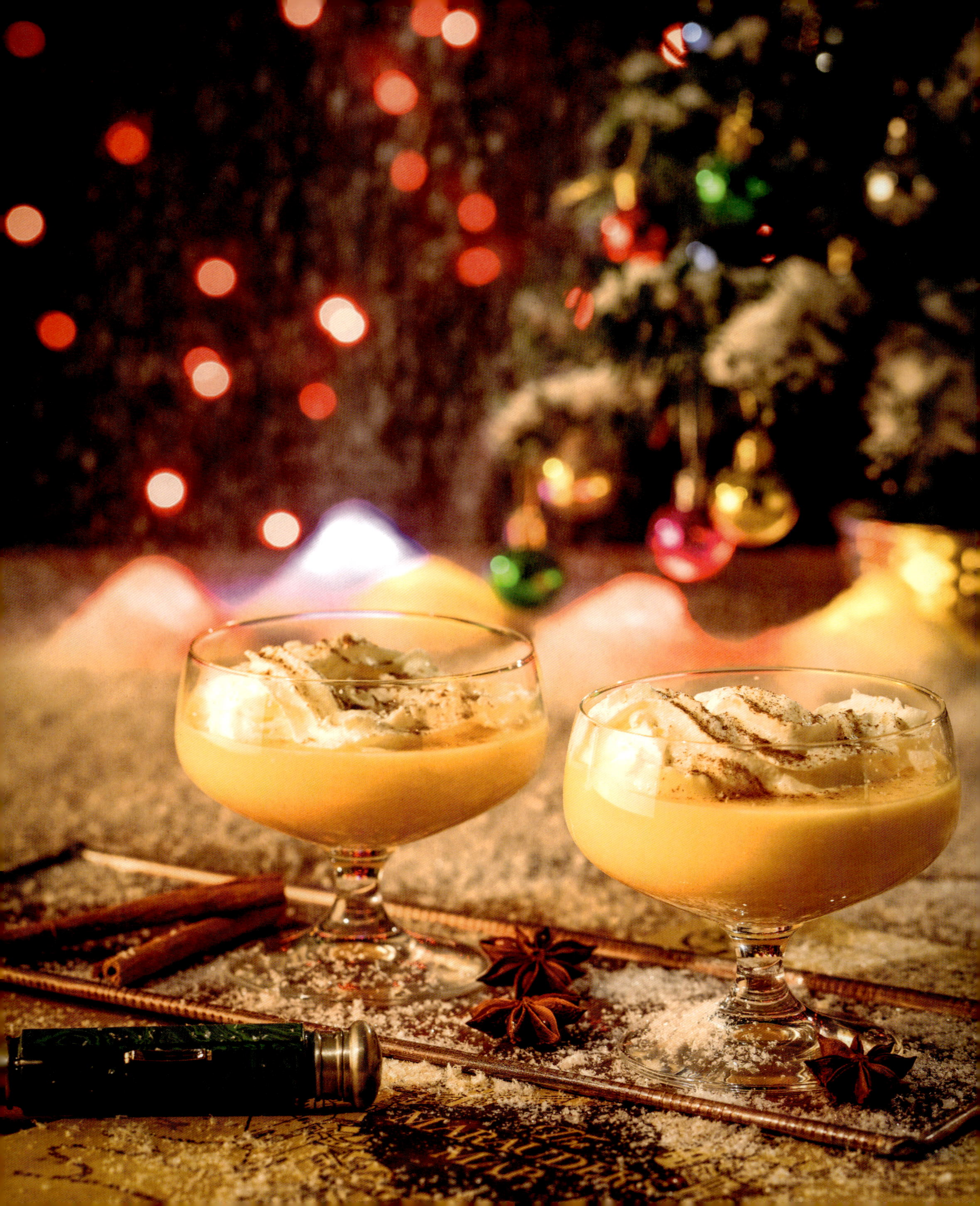

Eggnog

CONTAINS ALCOHOL

INGREDIENTS FOR 8 GLASSES

8 egg yolks
¾ cup sugar
½ tbsp cinnamon, plus some more as garnish
2–3 tbsp lemon juice
½ cup cream
3⅓ cups dry white wine
4 tbsp rum
Whipped cream
Cinnamon

1. Put the egg yolk in a mixing bowl, Using a hand mixer with whisk attachment, whip along with the sugar, cinnamon and lemon juice until foamy, about 10 minutes.
2. In a separate bowl, whip the cream.
3. Put the egg cream in a tall cooking pot. Mix in the white wine and rum. Stirring constantly, warm over low heat, making sure nothing burns or sets. Finally, whip again briefly. Pour into glasses, or into a hot-washed, sufficiently large bottle if the eggnog is going to be drunk later. In this case, keep it in the refrigerator!
4. Serve the eggnog warm or cold, with a heap of whipped cream on top, sprinkled with some cinnamon!

DOBBY THE HOUSE-ELFS TIP: This recipe can also be made without alcohol with no problems. Instead of white wine, add the same amount of whole milk, and substitute some black tea for the rum!

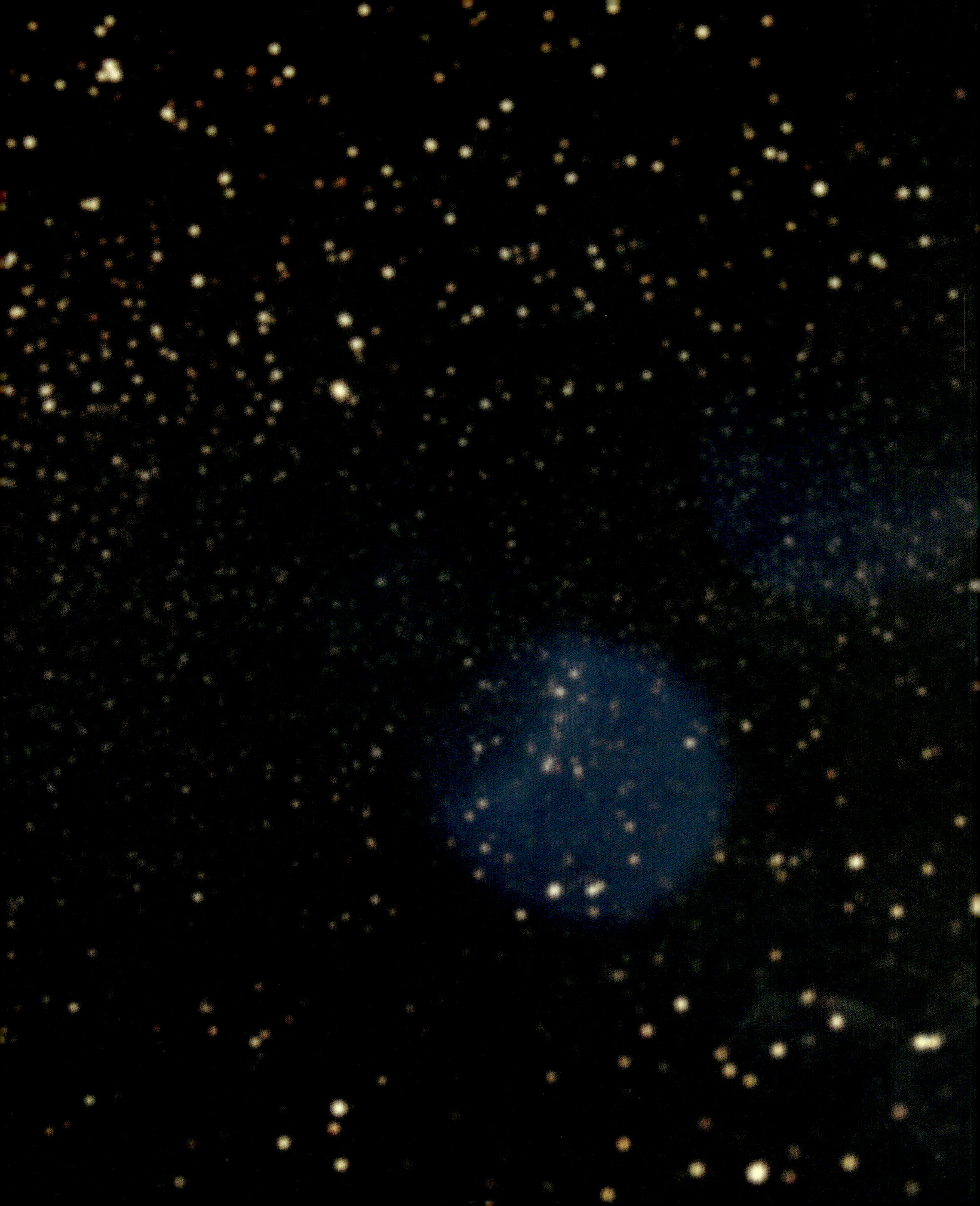

Hogwarts Culinary Delights

The Hogwarts School of Witchcraft and Wizardry is a boarding school for children with magical abilities. It is one of the most famous magical schools in the world. Since its founding in the year 993 by the four greatest magicians of their time—
Godric Gryffindor, Helga Hufflepuff, Rowena Ravenclaw, and Salazar Slytherin—pupils here are trained in the ways of magic. At Hogwarts, Harry learned for the first time in his life what it means to have a real home—and in a real home, good food and drink always have a place! Happily, there is lots in Hogwarts! In the Great Hall, fine dishes are served at every mealtime, prepared by the school's hardworking house elves in such abundance that you can only hope Ron (a well-known lover of food) knows a good weight-loss spell...

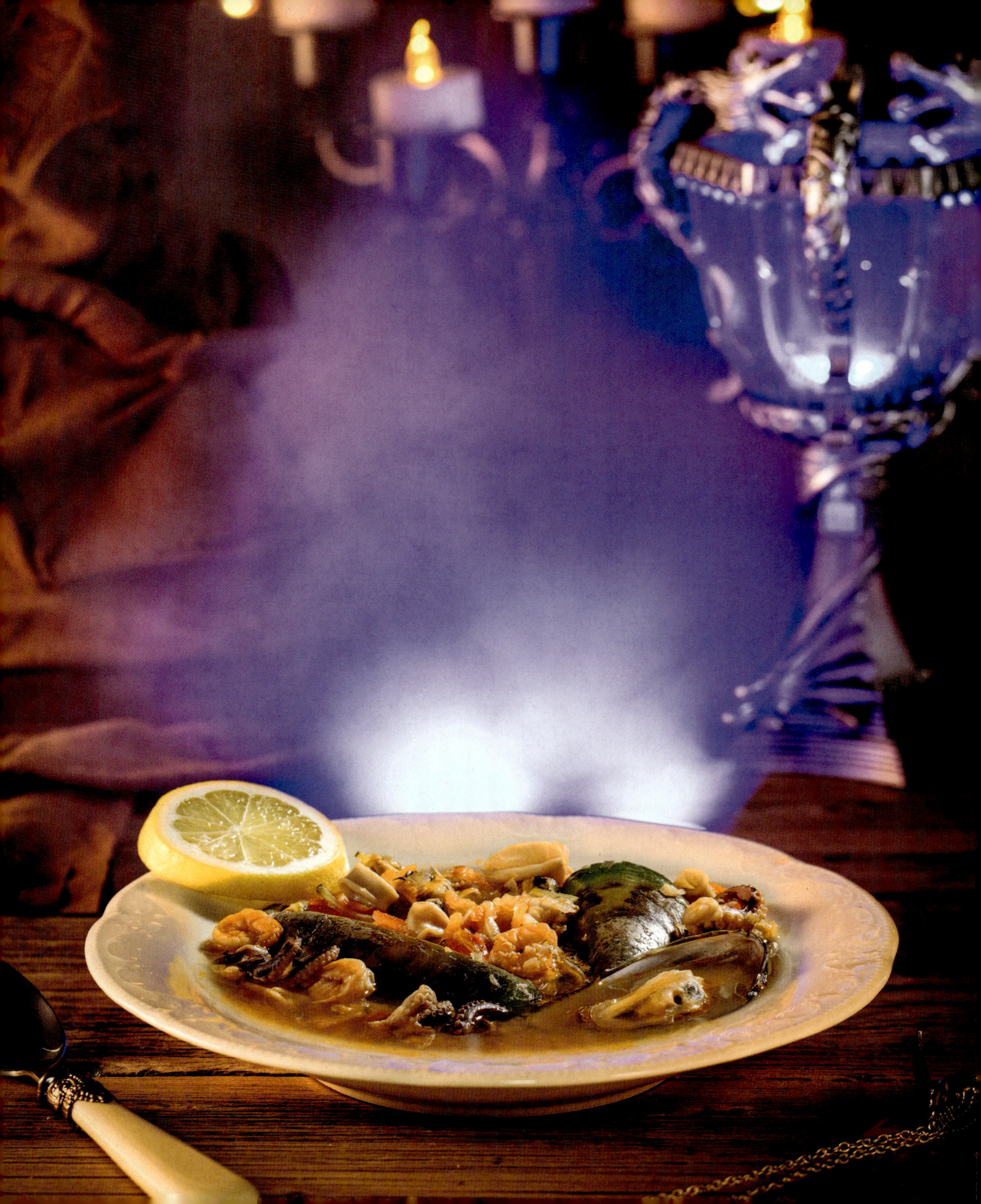

Beauxbatons Bouillabaisse

CONTAINS ALCOHOL

INGREDIENTS
SERVES 6

5 tbsp olive oil

2 onions, finely chopped

4 garlic cloves, finely chopped

½ small zucchini, julienned

¼ celery root/celeriac, two large carrots, one small leek, all coarsely chopped

1 small fennel bulb, coarsely chopped

1 tbsp tomato paste

3 cups white wine

1¼ cups pureed tomatoes

2 cups fish stock

¼ cup apple juice

1 pinch saffron

5–6 sprigs fresh thyme, leaves removed

5–6 sprigs fresh savory, leaves removed

3 bay leaves

3–4 juniper leaves

1 small dried chili pepper, finely chopped

1 lb mixed frozen fish filets (e.g., monkfish, bream, mullet)

10½ oz fresh mussels

7 oz frozen seafood (e.g., shrimp, baby squid)

Salt and freshly ground black pepper

½ bunch fresh parsley, finely chopped

1. In a large pot, sauté the onions and garlic with a big splash of olive oil. Add the zucchini, the coarsely chopped vegetables, and the fennel, and while stirring regularly, sear for 5–10 minutes. In the meantime, add the tomato paste, and mix in well.

2. Deglaze with some white wine, boil down, and add the rest of the wine. Add the pizza tomatoes, fish stock, apple juice, saffron thyme, savory, bay leaves, juniper berries, and chopped chili, and a large pinch of freshly ground black pepper. Fill with enough water to cover the mixture with liquid. Over medium heat, simmer about 15–20 minutes without a lid.

3. Wash the fish filets, pat dry with paper towels, check for bones, and cut into bite-sized pieces. Clean the mussels and seafood; be sure to discard opened shells! Put everything in the pot, and if needed, add enough water to cover with liquid. Over medium heat, gently simmer about 15 minutes. Important: The soup must not boil from now on!

4. Taste the soup, and season to taste with salt and pepper. Remove the bay leaves and juniper berries.

5. Serve the bouillabaisse in deep dishes. Add the fish pieces, seafood, mussels and vegetables, and serve sprinkled with freshly chopped parsley. Goes very well with a fresh baguette.

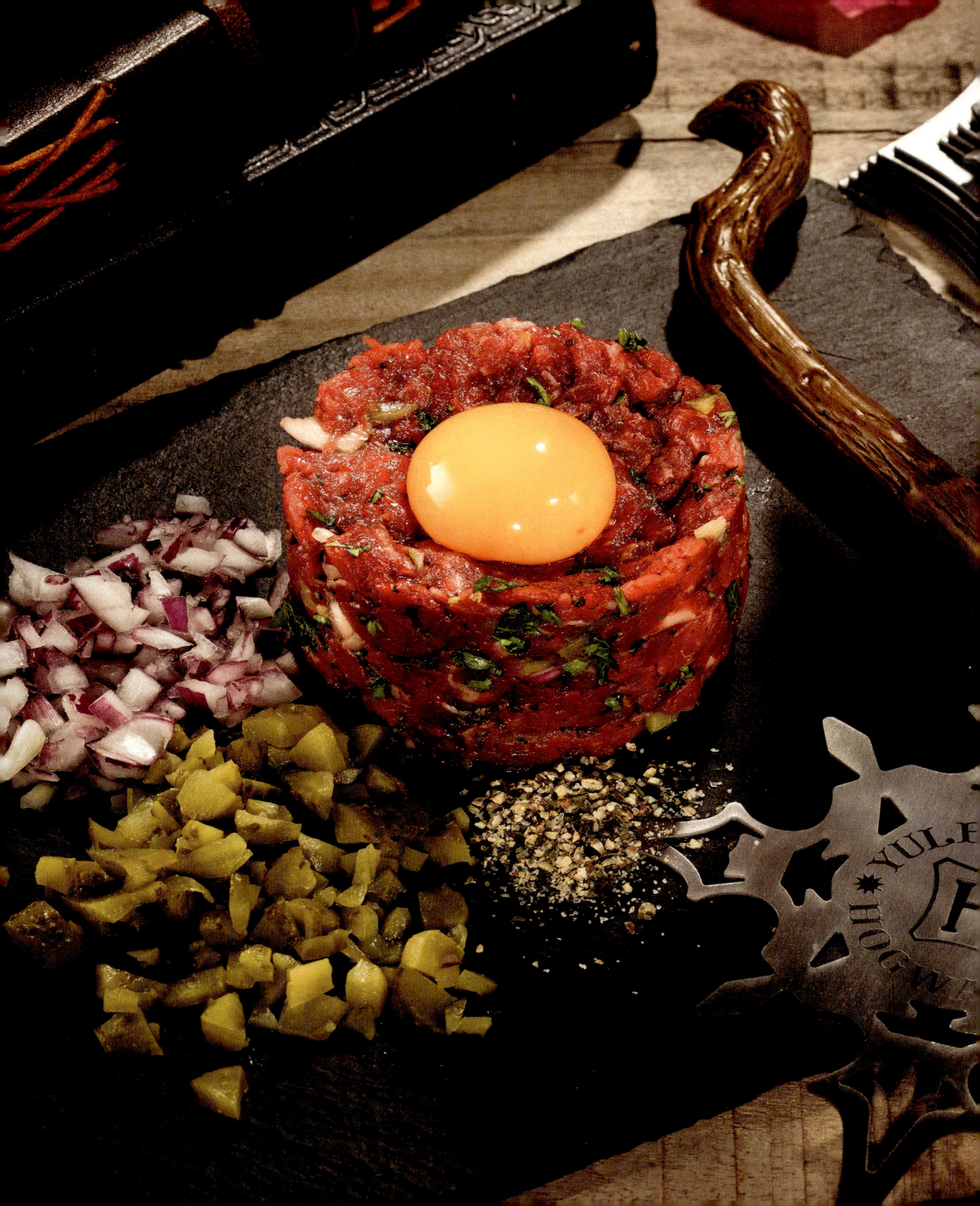

Dragon Meat Tartare

CONTAINS ALCOHOL

INGREDIENTS
SERVES 4

1 lb beef filet, finely diced
Salt and freshly ground black pepper
1 tbsp canola oil
2 shallots, finely chopped
1 tsp horseradish
2 tsp Cognac
Some freshly chopped parsley
4 raw egg yolks
2 pickles, finely diced
1 small jar of capers (non-pareil), drained

Also required:
Round ring (about 4–5 in. diameter)

1. With a large, sharp knife, cut the filet into small cubes (or buy already minced meat) and put in a bowl. Season liberally with salt and pepper. Add the oil, horseradish, Cognac, and chopped parsley, and half of the shallots. Mix thoroughly. Loosely cover with plastic wrap, and place in the refrigerator until serving.

2. Blanche the rest of the shallots in a saucepan with salted water, drain through a sieve, and rinse under cold flowing water.

3. With a round ring, put portions of tartare one by one on a large, flat plate or a serving platter. On top, with the fingers, gently make a shallow indent on the tartare, and carefully put an intact egg yolk on. Surround with the finely chopped pickles, the drained capers, and the blanched shallots. Serve with bread and fresh salad.

DOBBY THE HOUSE-ELF'S TIP: After cutting, tartare should be eaten as soon as possible, because otherwise the meat loses its nice red color and becomes more unsightly than You-Know-Who's face!

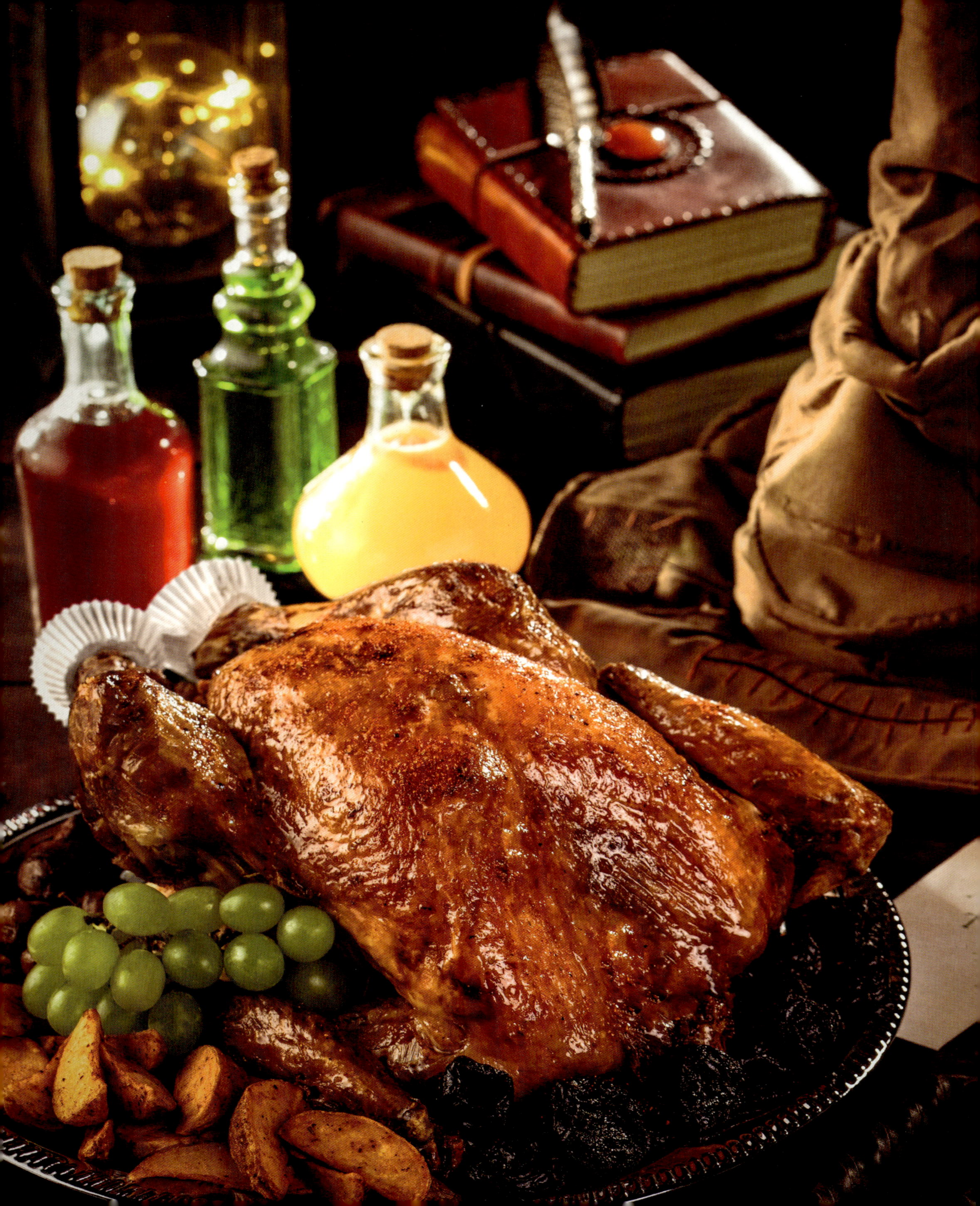

Stuffed Feast Day Turkey

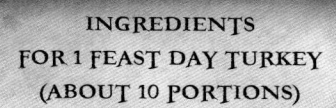

INGREDIENTS
FOR 1 FEAST DAY TURKEY
(ABOUT 10 PORTIONS)

2 large onions, finely chopped

1 apple (sour), seeded, peeled, and finely diced

3½ oz poultry liver, finely diced

½ lb ground pork

¼ bunch celery, very finely diced

2 garlic cloves, finely chopped

½ bunch fresh parsley, finely chopped

⅔ cup chicken stock

Salt and freshly ground black pepper

3 tbsp olive oil

2 garlic cloves, pressed

3 tbsp paprika powder

1 turkey (about 9-11 lbs.), ready to cook

2 tbsp orange juice

¼ cup white wine (or water)

2 tbsp cranberry jam

Sauce thickening agent (optional)

Also required:
Toothpicks

1. Mix the onions, apple, liver, ground pork, celery, garlic, and parsley in a large bowl with the chicken stock. Season with some freshly ground pepper, and set aside.

2. Preheat the oven to 360°F. Place a large pan filled with a finger of water on the bottom of the oven, to collect the fat later.

3. Mix the olive oil, pressed garlic cloves, paprika powder, some salt, and a generous pinch of pepper in a small bowl.

4. Rinse the turkey, pat dry, and stuff with the meat-apple filling. Close the "opening" with toothpicks. Place the bird on a cooling tray, and massage in the marinade all over. Put the turkey on the lowest rack in the preheated oven, and cook for about 5 hours, depending on weight. The rule is: 2.2 lbs turkey = 1 hour of cooking time. During this time, regularly (every 15-20 minutes) brush generously with the remaining marinade and the liquid from the collection pan.

5. Finally, pass the juice from the pan through a sieve into a pot. Flavor with orange juice, white wine, and 2 tbsp cranberry jam. (optional), season with salt and pepper. Bring to a boil over low heat, and thicken with sauce thickener if it is necessary because the sauce is too runny. Serve with the turkey. Fluffy Mashed Potatoes (p. 102), green beans (p. 108) or roast corn on the cob (p. 133) are good alongside.

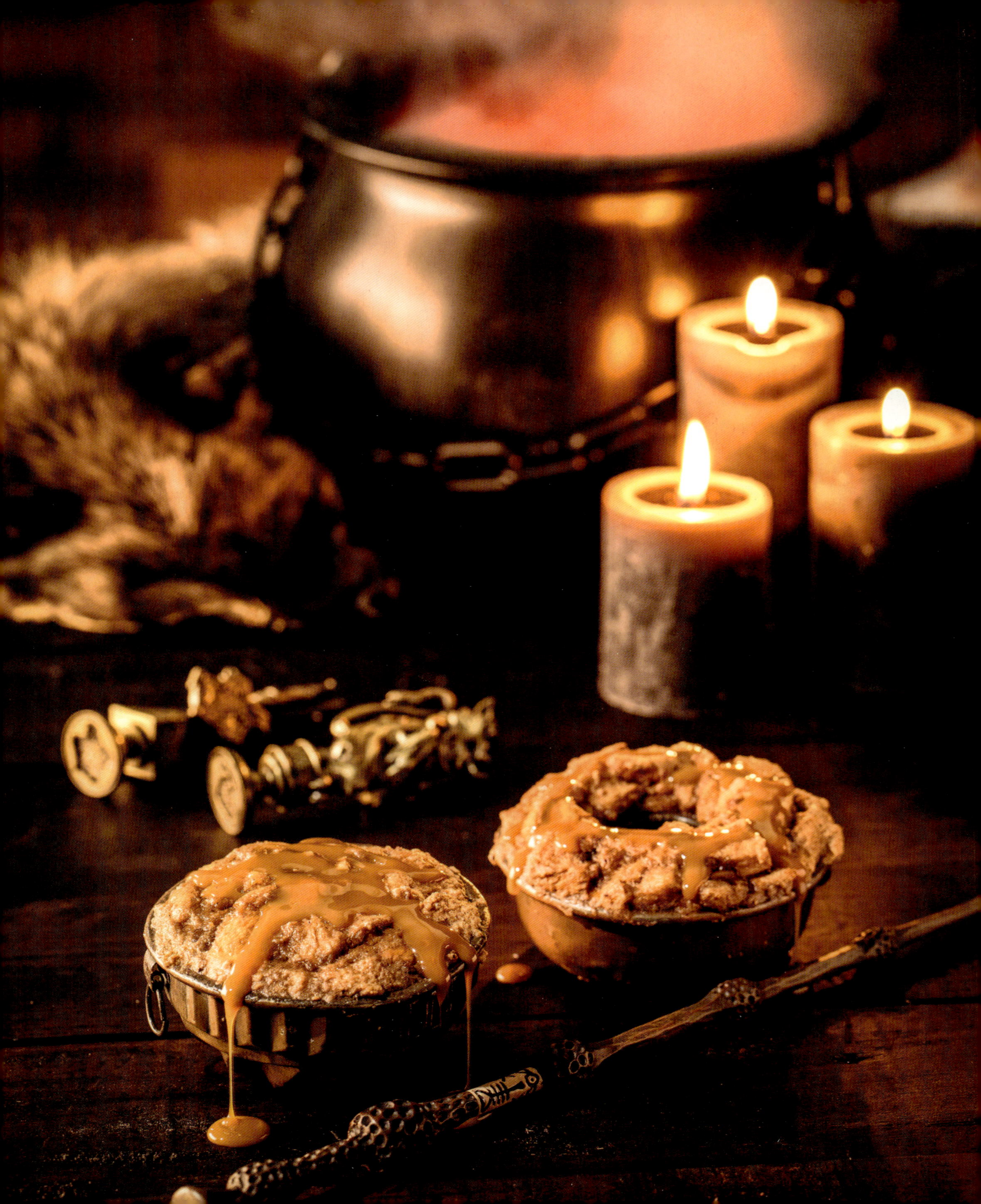

Bread Pudding

INGREDIENTS
SERVES 4

3 cups vanilla ice cream
2 eggs
6½ cups brioche, in bite-sized pieces
1 small pinch salt
Caramel sauce

Also required:
4 small casserole dishes

1. Take the vanilla ice cream from the freezer, put it in a large bowl, let melt, then stir vigorously.
2. Preheat the oven to 360°F.
3. In a small bowl, whisk the eggs and add to the ice cream. Add a small pinch of salt, and mix everything well.
4. Add the brioche into the bowl, mix well, and let soak 10-15 minutes. Fill the casserole dishes with the mixture, smooth the top, and bake 25 minutes in the oven.
5. Generously drizzle with caramel sauce, and enjoy right away!

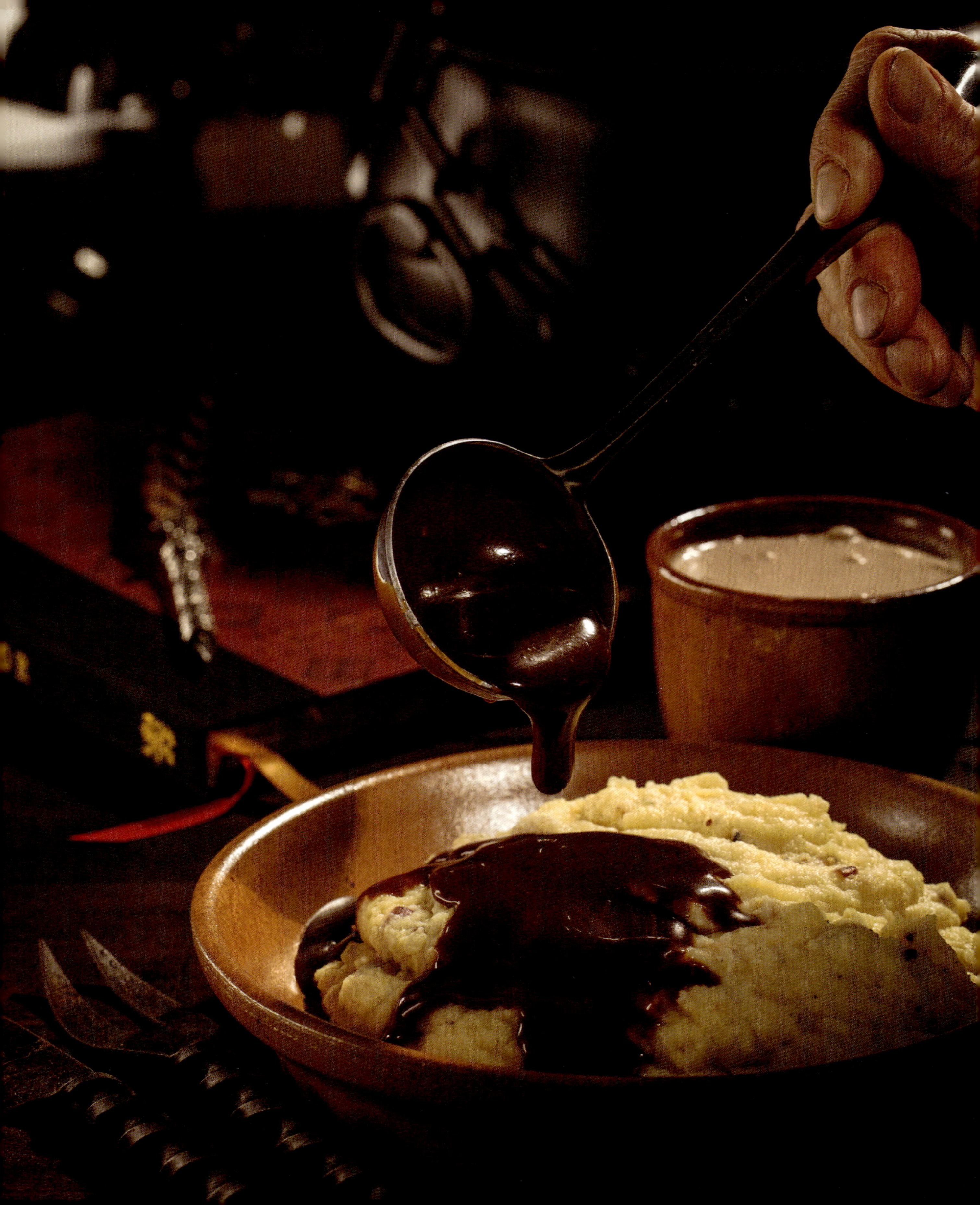

Fluffy Mashed Potatoes with Gravy

INGREDIENTS
SERVES 4

For the mashed potatoes:
8 medium potatoes (floury)
⅔ cup milk
⅓ cup cream
5 tbsp butter, in flakes
Salt and freshly ground black pepper
1 large pinch nutmeg, freshly grated

For the gravy:
2 tbsp neutral oil
1 large onion, finely chopped
¼ celery root/celeriac, two large carrots, one small leek, all finely chopped
1 tbsp tomato paste
Salt, pepper
1 pinch sugar
2 cups water
A sauce thickening agent, if needed

For the mashed potatoes:
1. Peel and quarter the potatoes.
2. In a sufficiently large saucepan, over medium heat, bring salted water to a boil. Add potatoes and let simmer for about 30 minutes, until they can be effortlessly pierced with a knife.
3. Drain the water. Put the potatoes in a large bowl, let the steam evaporate, and evenly mash with a potato masher. Don't be too thorough, because the mashed potatoes should be lumpy!
4. Add the milk, cream, and flaked butter to the bowl, and mix until the mashed potatoes are still relatively lumpy, but also creamy and fluffy. Season with salt, pepper, and a healthy pinch of freshly grated nutmeg.

For the gravy:
5. In a large pan, heat the oil over high heat and sauté the onions until it is translucent and aromatic. Add the vegetables and sauté with a little stirring, until they have taken on a strong color all around. Toast the tomato paste with it. Gently season with salt, pepper, and a pinch of sugar.
6. Deglaze with 2 cups water. Carefully dissolve the juice from the bottom of the pan, bring to a boil, and boil down for a few minutes without a lid, until the vegetables are nice and soft. Pour the mixture through a sieve into another saucepan, and carefully push the vegetables through.
7. Once more, season the gravy and bring to a boil. If needed, thicken with a thickening agent.

DOBBY THE HOUSE-ELF'S TIP: The sauce is made without meat or bones, so it is also suitable for vegetarians. If you want, you can refine it with a little brandy.

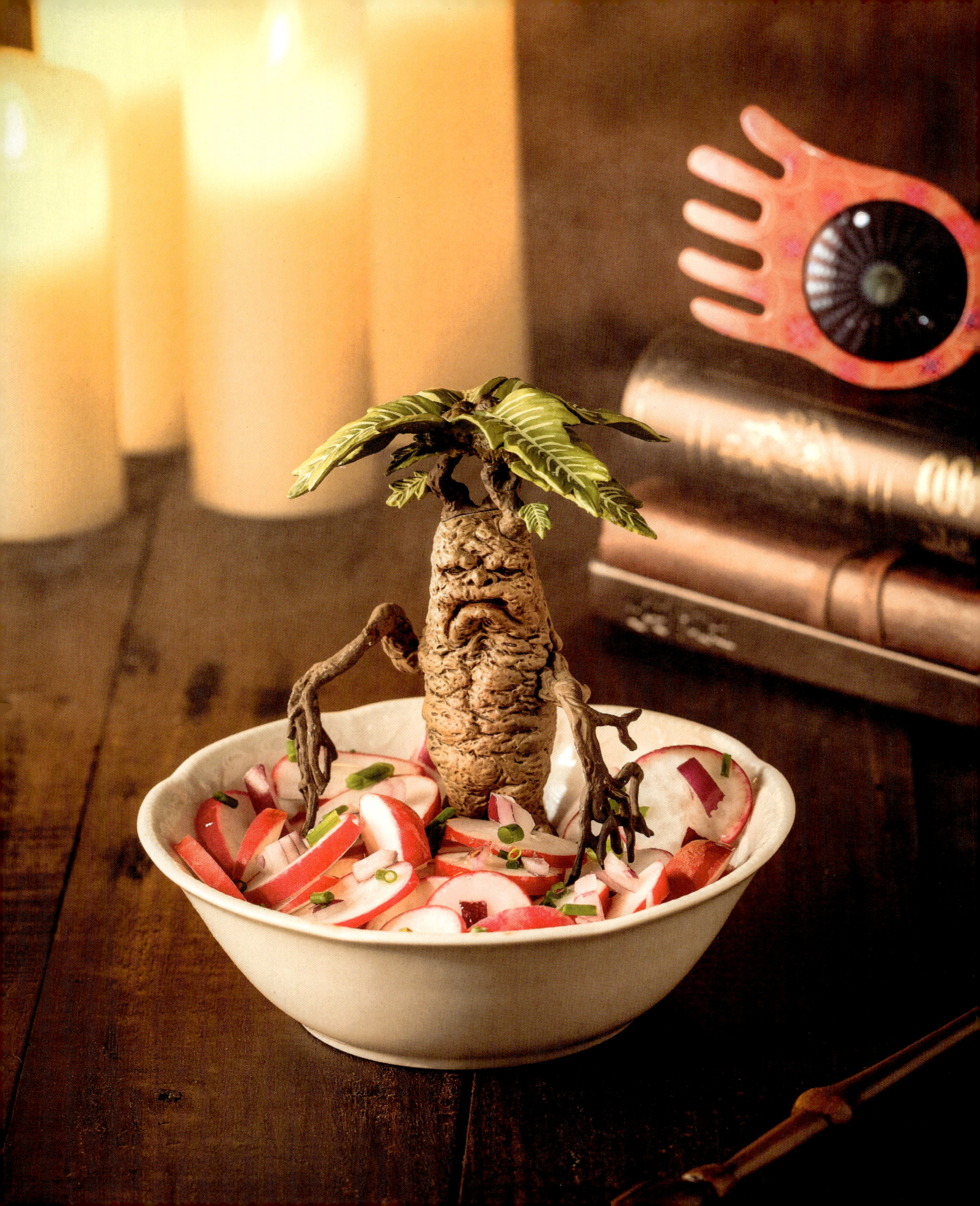

Luna Lovegood's Radish Salad

INGREDIENTS
SERVES 2–3

3 tbsp sour cream
3 tbsp herbal white vinegar
2 tbsp olive oil
1 tbsp mustard (medium-spicy)
Salt and freshly ground black pepper
2 bunches of radishes, thinly sliced
1 small red onion, finely chopped
Fresh chives, finely chopped

1. In a small bowl, mix the sour cream, the vinegar, the olive oil, and the mustard. Season to taste with salt and pepper, lightly cover with plastic wrap, and leave in the refrigerator for 15 minutes.

2. Meanwhile, in a separate, larger bowl, mix the radishes and the finely chopped onion.

3. Put the dressing on the radishes and onions, and mix thoroughly. Let infuse a few minutes. Then mix again, sprinkle with finely chopped chives, and serve.

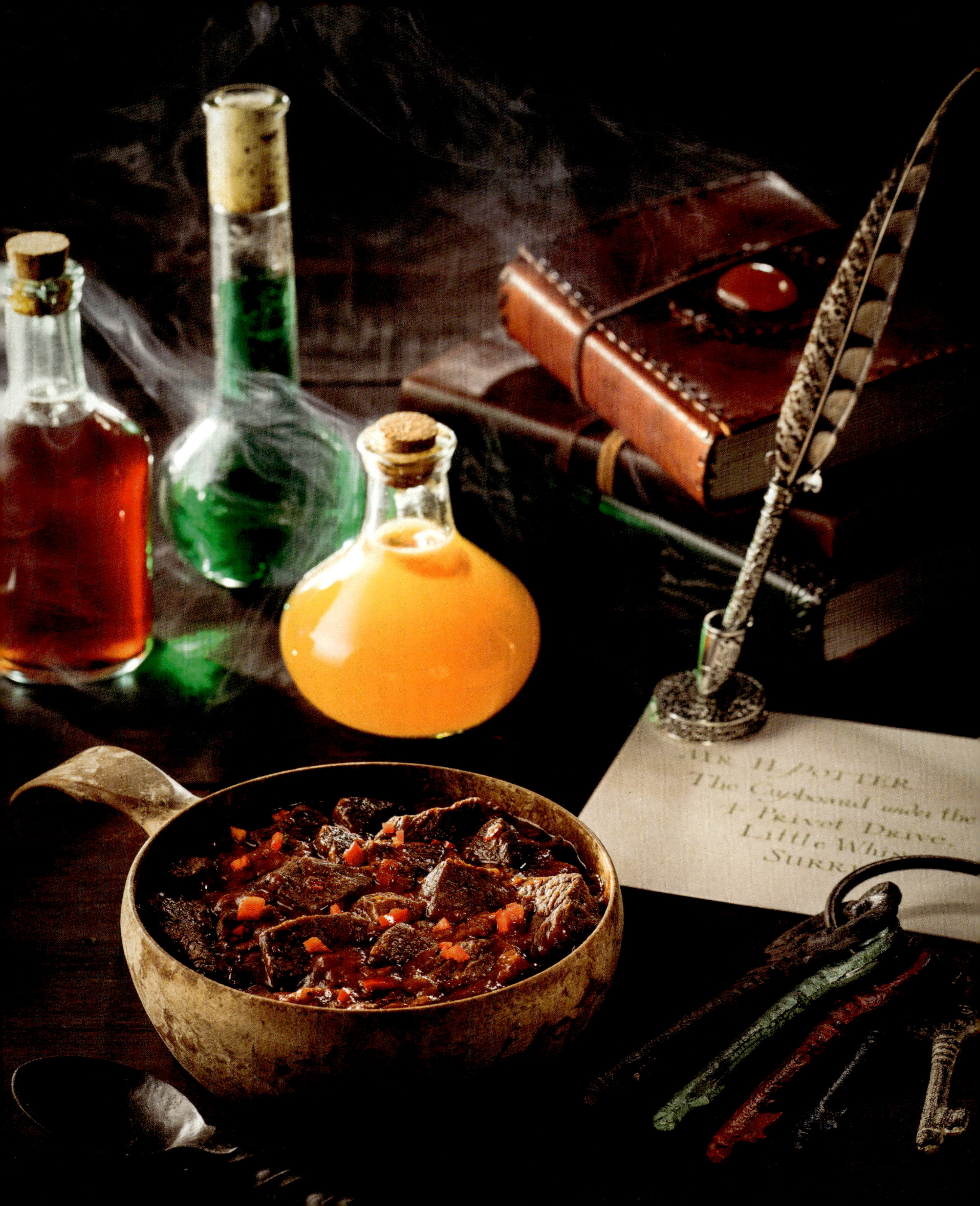
MR H. POTTER
The Cupboard under the
4 Privet Drive.
Little

Beef Goulash

CONTAINS ALCOHOL

INGREDIENTS
SERVES 4

2¼ lb beef (shoulder)
2 tbsp clarified butter
6½ cups onions, finely chopped
1 tbsp tomato purée
2 cups red wine (dry)
2 cups beef stock
2 garlic cloves, finely chopped
3 tbsp caraway seeds
1 tbsp dried marjoram
½ tsp sugar
1 tbsp lemon zest
3 tbsp paprika (sweet)
3 tbsp paprika (hot)
⅓ cup sour cream
salt, freshly ground black pepper

1. Remove any fat and tendons from the beef and cut it into about 1.25-in. cubes.

2. Heat up the clarified butter in a large casserole. Brown the cubes of beef on all sides over a medium heat, then remove from the casserole. Fry the onions in the beef fat until they are translucent. Stir in the tomato purée and sauté gently along with the onions. Return the beef to the casserole and deglaze with a little red wine. Let the contents of the casserole boil down a little, then pour in the beef stock and the rest of the red wine. The meat must be completely covered by the liquid! Instead of using a lid, cover the casserole with a weighted-down piece of baking parchment. Turn down the temperature and leave the goulash to braise over a gentle heat for 4 hours, stirring it occasionally. Note: Do not let the goulash boil!

3. While the goulash is braising, mix the garlic, caraway, marjoram, sugar, and lemon zest together in a small bowl. Add both kinds of paprika, combine thoroughly, then mix with a little water to form a smooth paste. Stir this mixture into the goulash towards the end of the cooking time. After turning off the heat, leave the goulash to stand for 5–10 minutes, then add the sour cream, season the goulash to taste with salt and pepper, mix everything together well, and serve either on its own or with boiled potatoes.

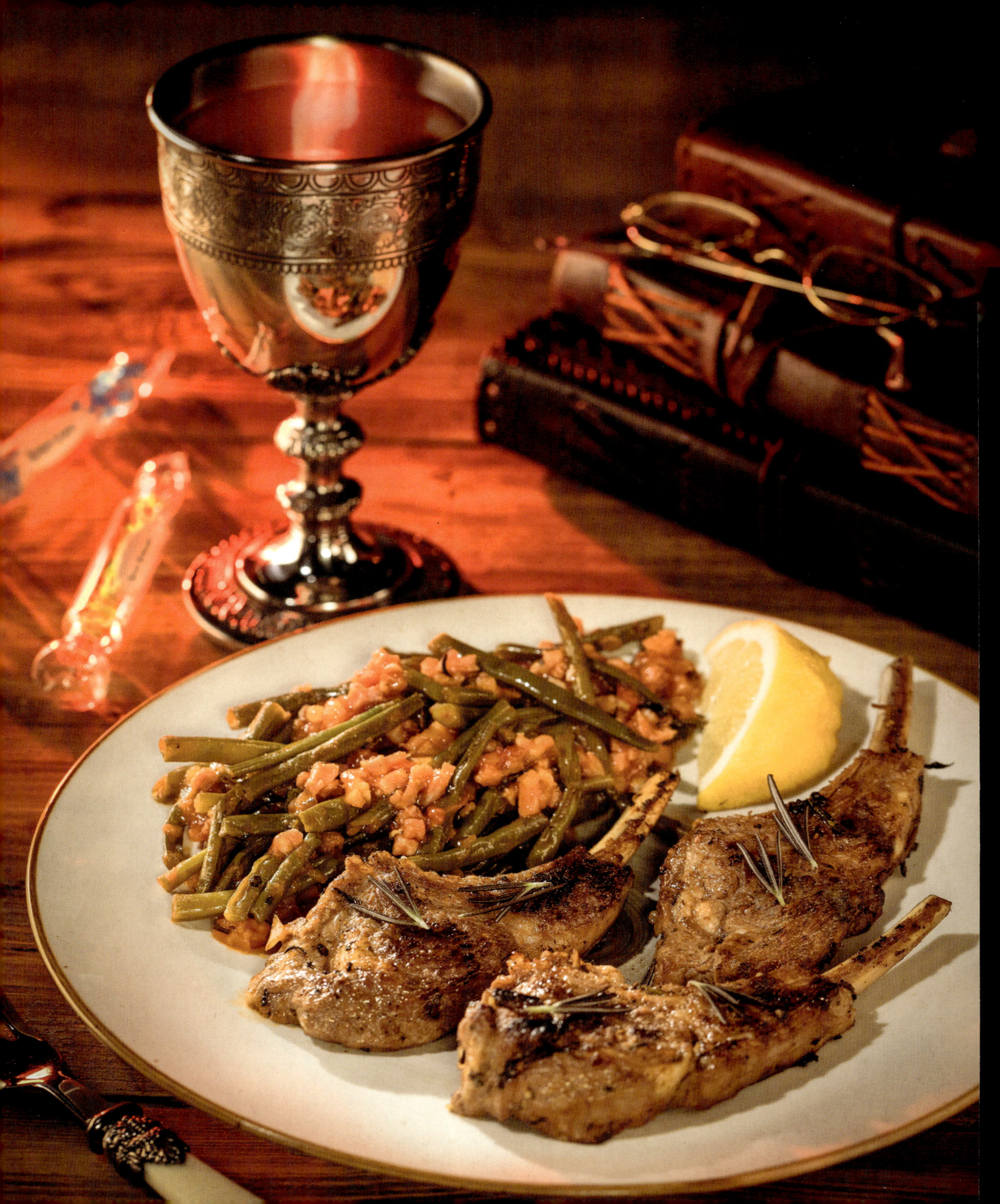

Braised Lamb Chops with Green Beans

INGREDIENTS
SERVES 4

For the lamb chops:
8 lamb chops (about 2 oz each)
1 garlic clove, finely chopped
8 sprigs of thyme, stripped and finely chopped
2 sprigs of rosemary, stripped and finely chopped
1 tbsp Dijon mustard
3 tbsp olive oil, plus a little extra for frying
salt, pepper

For the green beans:
1 lb green beans
2 tbsp olive oil
1 large onion, finely chopped
3½ oz streaky bacon, finely chopped
1 garlic clove, finely chopped
2 tomatoes, finely diced
1¾ cups vegetable stock
3 tbsp savory
salt, pepper

1. Wash the lamb chops and pat dry.
2. In a small bowl, mix the garlic, thyme, rosemary, mustard, and olive oil together thoroughly. Decant the marinade into a freezer bag, add the chops, and seal the bag firmly. Massage the marinade thoroughly into the meat and leave it in the refrigerator for at least 2 hours, ideally overnight.
3. Wash the beans, snip off the ends and cut into 2 or 3 pieces of equal size.
4. Heat up the oil in a pot and fry the chopped onions until they are glassy and translucent. Add the bacon and garlic and sauté, stirring constantly, until the bacon is slightly browned. Then stir in the beans, tomatoes, vegetable stock, and savory, season with salt and pepper, cover the pot, and cook over a medium heat for 30–35 minutes.
5. Meanwhile, take the lamb chops out of the refrigerator and let them get back to room temperature. Take the meat out of the marinade, heat a little olive oil in a non-stick frying pan, and sear the chops for 2-3 minutes on each side over a high heat. Season generously with salt and pepper and serve with the green beans.

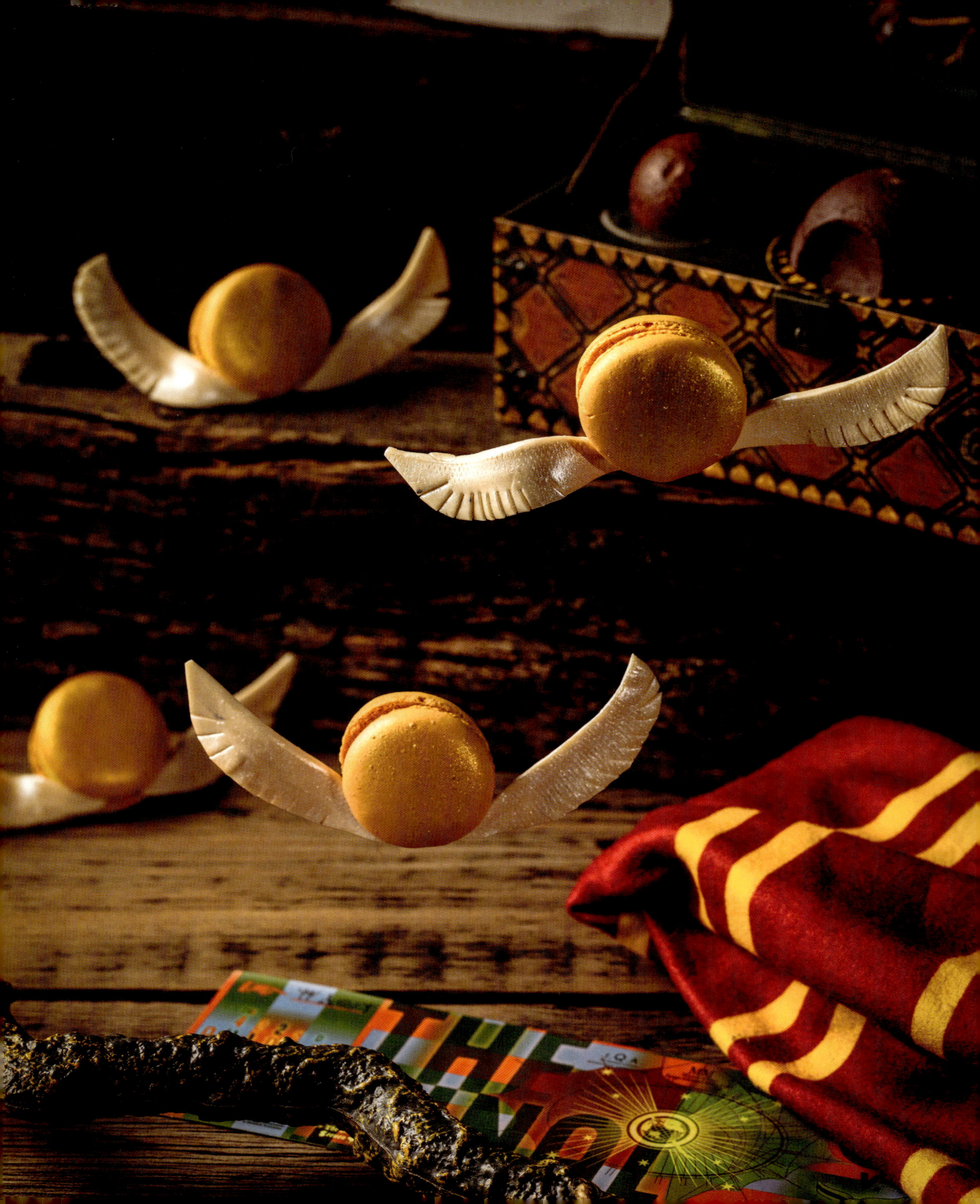

Golden Snitches

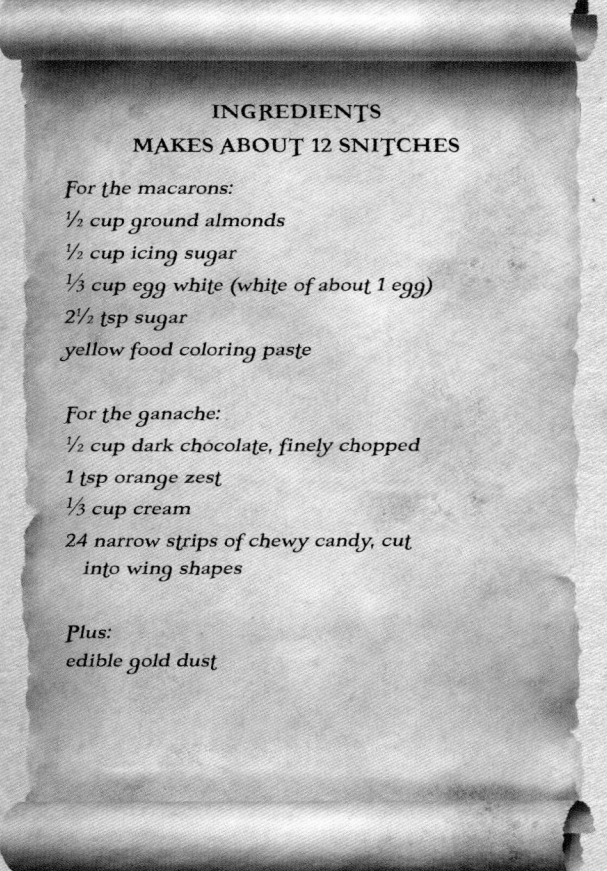

INGREDIENTS
MAKES ABOUT 12 SNITCHES

For the macarons:
½ cup ground almonds
½ cup icing sugar
⅓ cup egg white (white of about 1 egg)
2½ tsp sugar
yellow food coloring paste

For the ganache:
½ cup dark chocolate, finely chopped
1 tsp orange zest
⅓ cup cream
24 narrow strips of chewy candy, cut into wing shapes

Plus:
edible gold dust

1. Put the ground almonds and icing sugar in a tall mug, mix together with a spoon, then grind as finely as possible in a food processor. Sift thoroughly into a bowl to remove any larger bits.

2. Weigh out the egg white exactly, then beat it with a mixer. As soon as the egg white turns frothy, sprinkle in the sugar and keep beating until it forms stiff peaks. Now add the yellow food coloring and beat for another 1 minute.

3. Transfer the beaten egg whites into a large bowl, gradually add the ground almond and icing sugar mixture, carefully folding it in all the while with a pastry spatula. Keep folding the mixture until it runs off the spatula. Pour it into a piping bag with a nozzle.

4. Line a baking sheet with baking parchment. Use the piping bag to pipe about blobs of macaron mixture just under 1 inch wide onto the baking sheet, leaving some space between them. Carefully tap the underside of the baking sheet twice against the countertop so that any air bubbles can escape. Leave to stand for 30 minutes.

5. Meanwhile, preheat the oven to 300°F. Put the baking sheet in the oven, turn down the heat to 145°F and bake for about 12–14 minutes. When the baking time is up, take the sheet out of the oven, transfer the baking parchment with the macarons still on it to the cool countertop and leave to cool down.

6. Meanwhile, put the chocolate for the ganache in a bowl. Put the orange zest and cream in a small saucepan and bring to a boil over a medium heat, stirring constantly, then pour the hot mixture over the chocolate. Leave to stand for 2 minutes, then stir the mixture until there are no more lumps. Leave the ganache to cool a little, then transfer it to the refrigerator for at least 1 hour.

7. Stir the cold ganache thoroughly, then transfer it to a piping bag. Loosen the macaron halves from the baking parchment and lay half of them out on the countertop, with their flat sides facing up. Pipe a dollop of ganache onto the top of each one, add a chewy candy wing on either side so that they are held in place by the ganache, then place another macaron half on top of each and press down lightly. Leave to chill in the refrigerator overnight, so that the filling sets properly. Finally, brush the macarons all over with the edible gold dust. Store in a cool place and consume within 5–7 days!

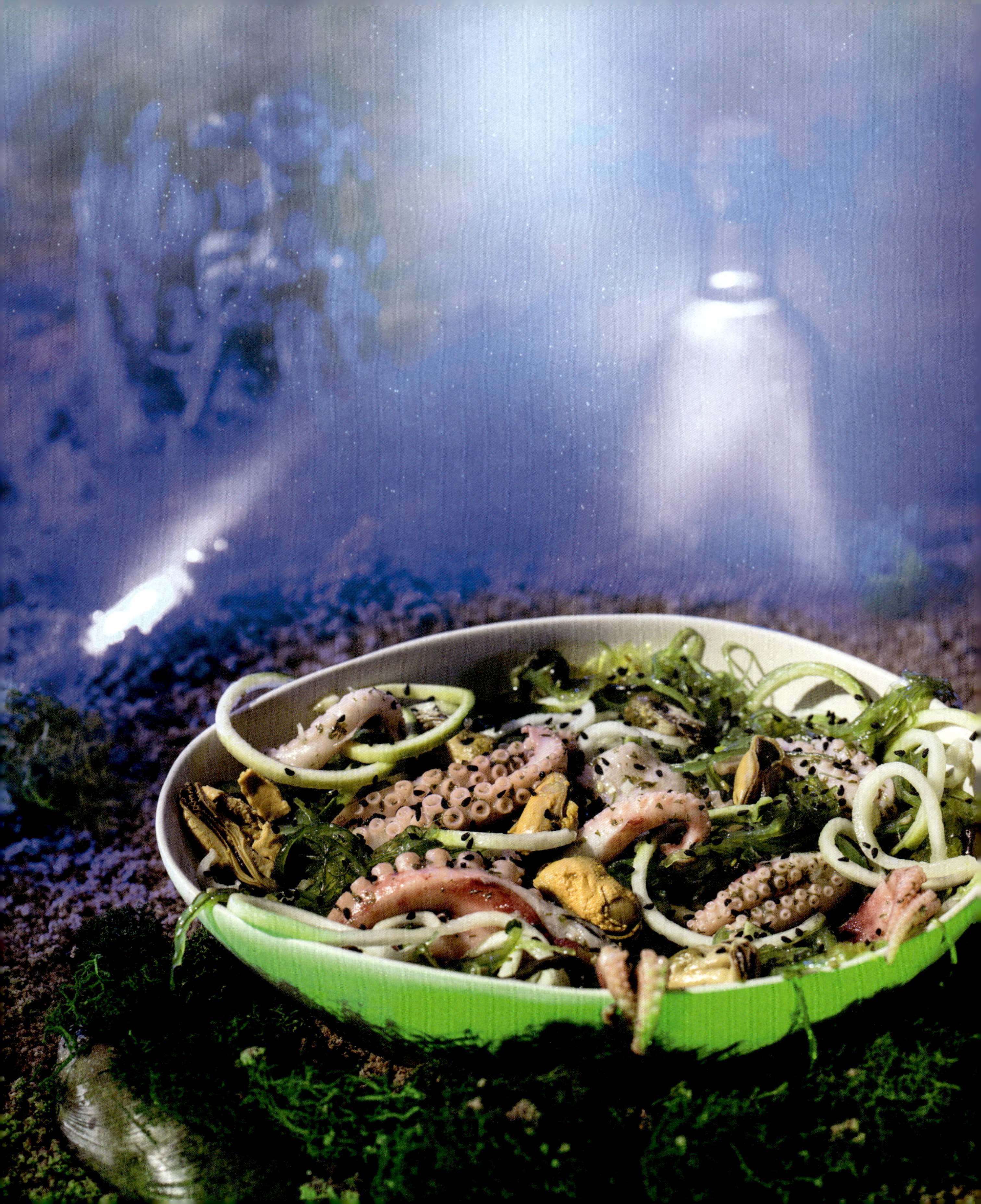

Harry's Gillyweed Salad

INGREDIENTS
SERVES 4

1 small octopus (about 1⅓ lb), or fresh octopus salad from a fishmonger
freshly ground black pepper, salt
juice of 1 lemon
2 garlic cloves, finely chopped
a little parsley, finely chopped
6 tbsp olive oil
2 tbsp rice vinegar
1 cucumber
1 cup seaweed salad (wakame)
¼ oz pickled mussels, drained
a sprinkling of black sesame seeds

Plus:
a spiralizer

1. Bring some water to a boil in a large pot. Add a generous pinch of pepper and steep the octopus in the water over a low heat for about 30–40 minutes, or until a knife slides into the flesh easily. Remove the pot from the heat, season with plenty of salt, and leave the octopus to cool in the liquid.

2. Meanwhile, mix the lemon juice, garlic cloves, and parsley together in a large bowl. Mix in a generous pinch of salt, then fold in the olive oil and vinegar.

3. Use the spiralizer to shred the cucumber into thin lengths of "spaghetti."

4. Remove the octopus from its stock, cut into bite-sized pieces, then add it to the marinade. Toss it thoroughly with the cucumber, seaweed salad and drained mussels. Cover the bowl tightly with clingfilm and leave to stand in the refrigerator for at least 2 hours, or preferably overnight.

5. Just before serving, stir it thoroughly once again and sprinkle with the black sesame seeds. The salad goes beautifully with fresh, crusty white bread.

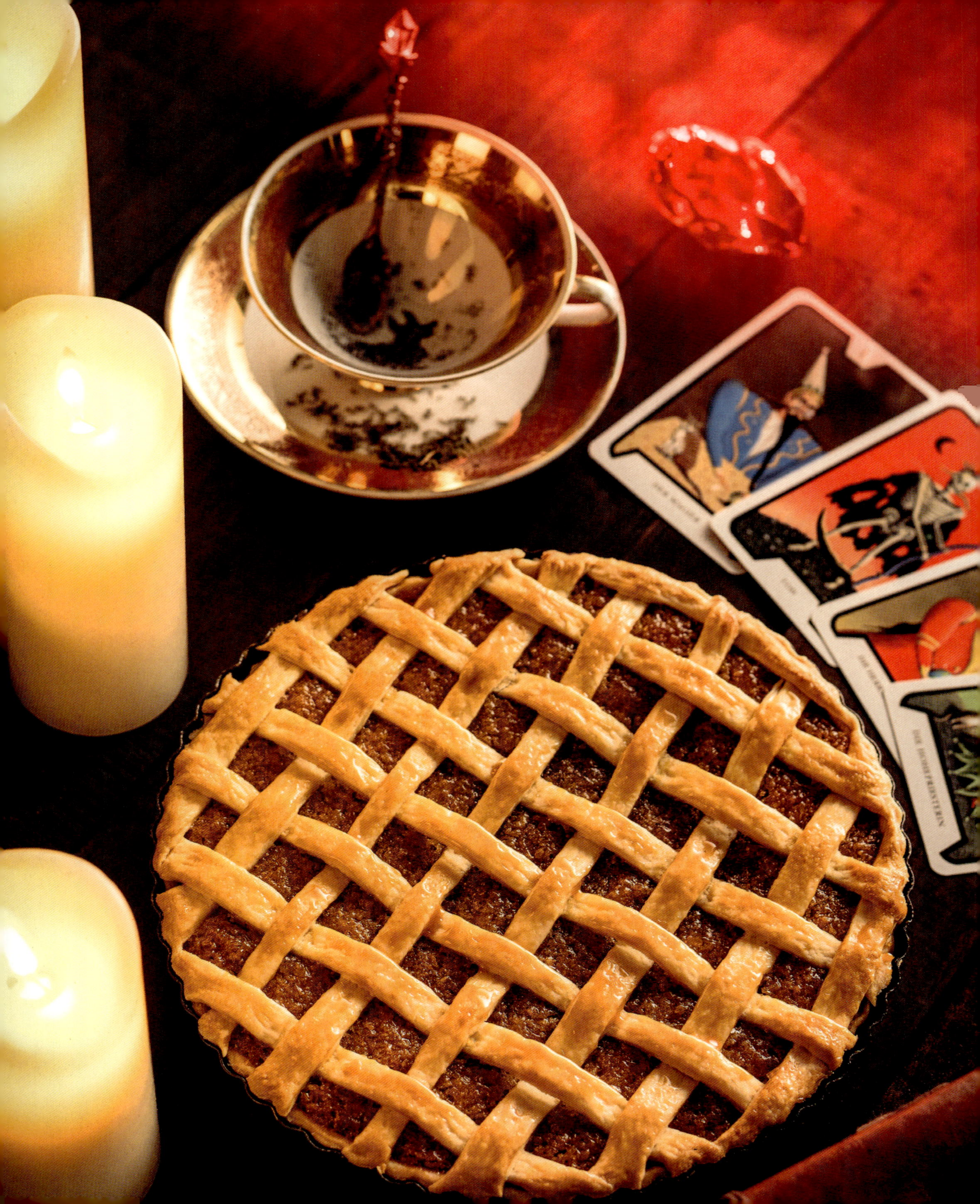

Treacle Tart

INGREDIENTS
MAKES 1 TART

For the tart base:
2½ cups flour plus a little more for dusting the countertop
2 tbsp icing sugar
zest of 1 lemon
pinch of salt
¾ cup cold butter, cubed
1 egg yolk
1–2 tbsp very cold water

For the filling:
2½ cups sugar syrup
pinch of ground ginger
2½ cups fresh breadcrumbs
zest and juice of 1 lemon
1 egg, beaten

Plus:
tart tin (diameter about 10 in.), dried beans or other baking beans

1. Mix the flour, icing sugar, lemon zest, and salt together in a bowl. Work in the cubes of cold butter until the mixture has a breadcrumb-like consistency. Add the egg yolk and 1-2 tbsp of very cold water. Knead the mixture with your hands to form a dough, then turn out onto a lightly floured countertop. Form the dough into a ball, wrap it in clingfilm, and chill it in the refrigerator for 30 minutes.

2. Take off ⅓ of the dough, wrap it in clingfilm again and put it back into the refrigerator. Roll the remaining dough out on a lightly floured countertop to form a circle measuring 12 in. across and about ¼ in. thick. Drape the pastry over the tart tin and press it down on the base and against the sides, making sure that it goes into all of the corners. Prick the pastry base a few times with a fork, then put it into the refrigerator to chill for 30 minutes.

3. Meanwhile, preheat the oven to 375°F and put a baking sheet in there to warm up.

4. Line the chilled tart base with baking parchment and fill it with baking beans or other blind baking weights. Bake it in the preheated oven for 15 minutes, then remove the baking parchment and weights and bake for another 5 minutes or so until the tart base is golden.

5. Roll out the remaining dough as thinly as possible (about ⅛ in.) to form a circle measuring about 10 in. across. Cut this into ¼-in.-wide strips and set aside. Heat the sugar syrup and ground ginger in a saucepan over a low heat until the mixture is hot but not boiling. Stir in the breadcrumbs, lemon zest, lemon juice, and one beaten egg, and mix everything together thoroughly. Pour the mixture onto the tart base and spread it evenly.

6. Place the pastry strips over the top to form a lattice pattern. To do this, start on a piece of baking parchment at each corner, then weave the pastry strips under and over each other. Carefully lift the lattice onto the tart and gently pull the paper away.

7. Bake the tart for about 30–35 minutes, until the filling has set and the pastry is golden. Take out of the oven and leave to cool on a wire rack for about 15 minutes. Carefully remove the tart from its tin and serve while still warm.

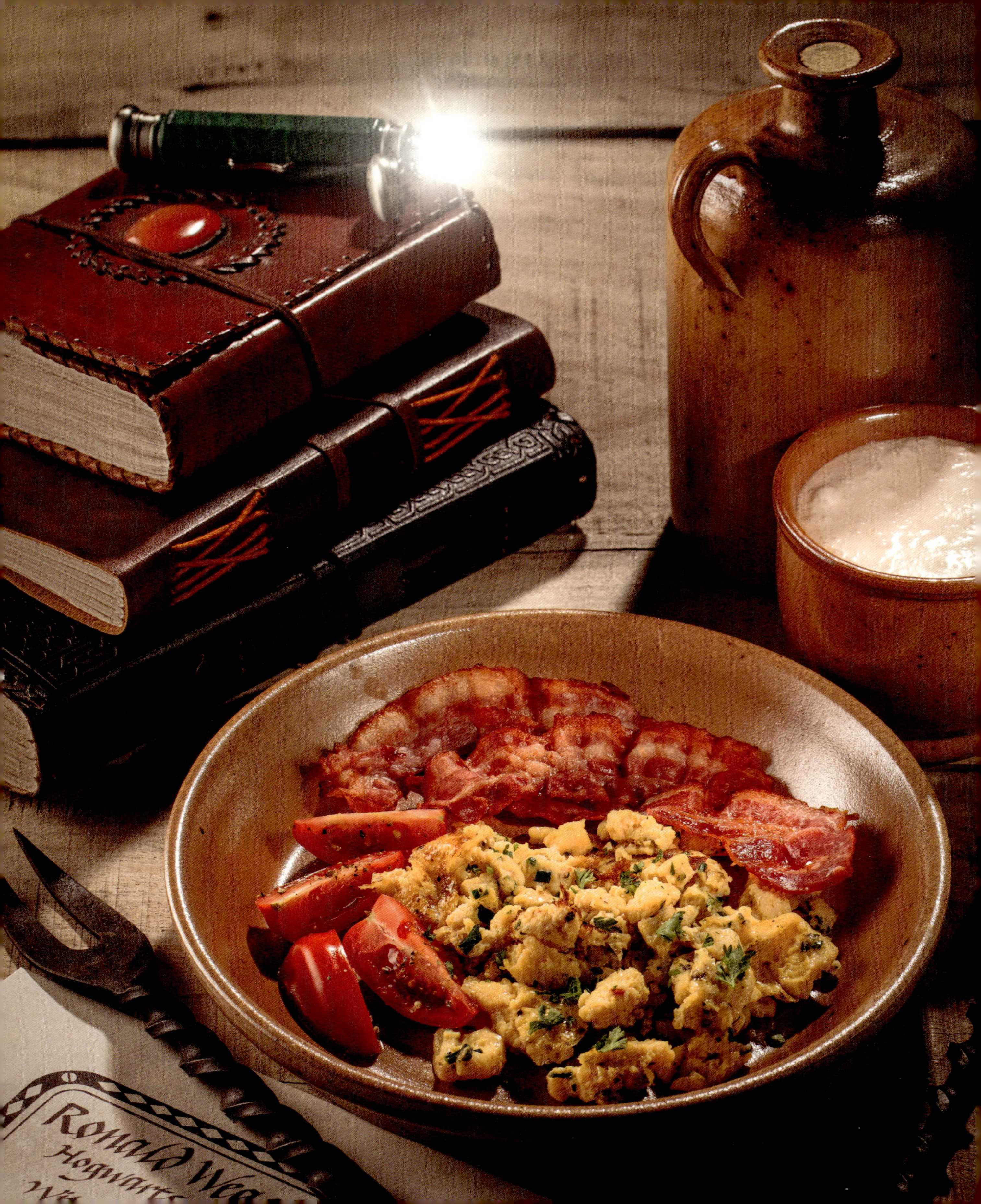
Ronald

Scrambled Eggs with Bacon

INGREDIENTS
SERVES 2–3

4 eggs
8 tbsp cream
salt, freshly ground black pepper
4 tsp butter
6–8 bacon rashers
chives, freshly chopped

1. Break the eggs into a high-rimmed bowl, add the cream, season generously with salt and pepper, and whisk until the entire mixture is relatively thick, but still nice and creamy.

2. Melt half the butter in a non-stick frying pan over a low heat. Add the whisked eggs and let them set slowly. Every now and then, carefully stir the mixture, running your spatula over the base of the frying pan to make sure that the eggs don't burn.

3. Meanwhile, melt the remaining butter in a separate frying pan over a high heat. Lay the bacon rashers in the frying pan, leaving a little space between them, and fry for 1-2 minutes on both sides, depending on how crispy you want them to be.

4. Once the scrambled eggs are as firm or runny as you prefer them, remove from them from the heat, spoon onto places and sprinkle with the freshly chopped chives. Arrange the bacon alongside and serve immediately!

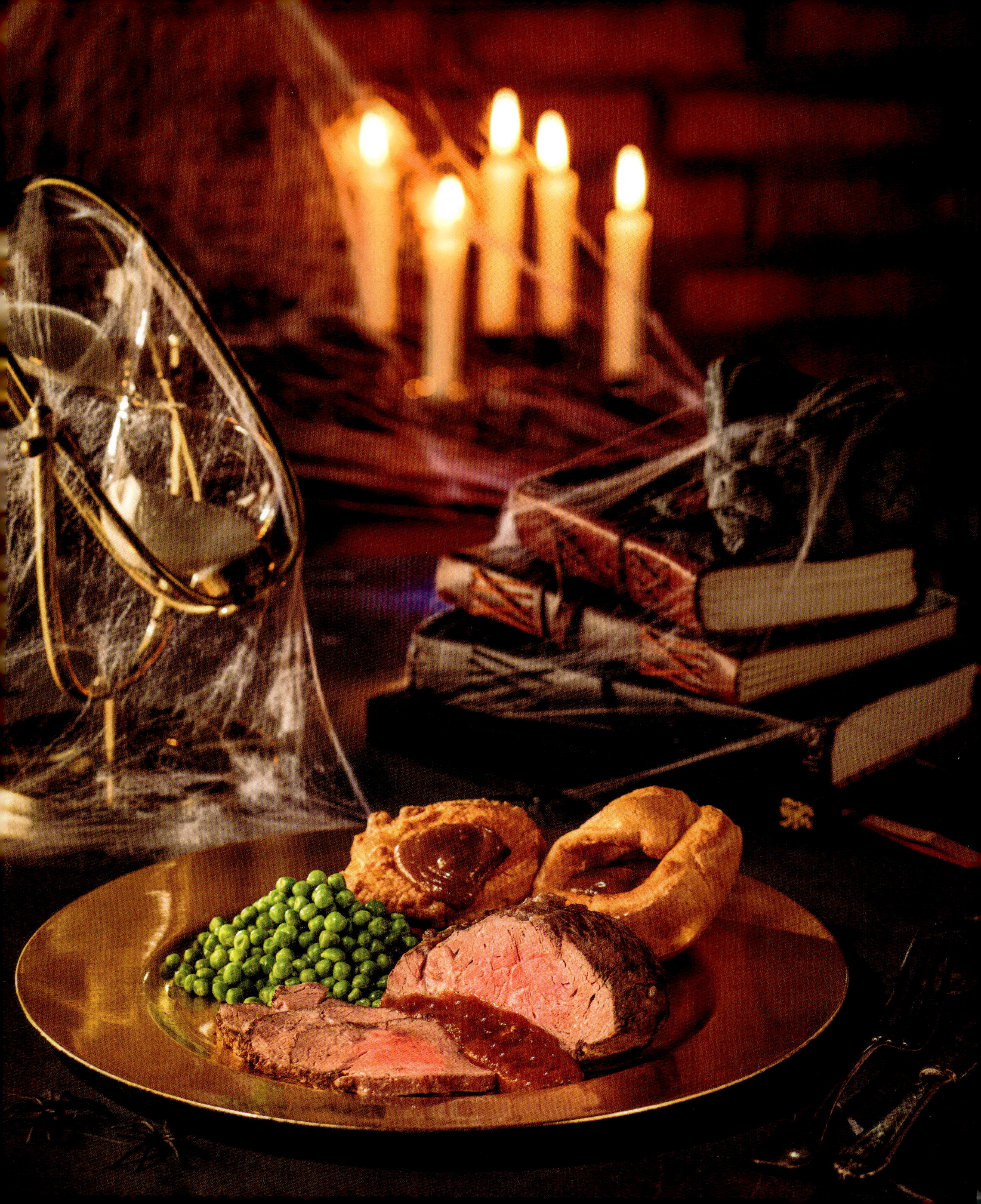

Roast Beef with Yorkshire Pudding and Buttered Peas

INGREDIENTS
SERVES 4

For the roast beef:
¼ cup clarified butter
1¾ lb beef sirloin or fillet
2 garlic cloves, crushed
rosemary, finely chopped
4 sprigs of fresh thyme, finely chopped
2 sage leaves, finely chopped
pepper, salt
6 tbsp mustard (medium-hot)
1 pinch of coarse sea salt

For the Yorkshire pudding:
2½ cups flour
salt, pepper
⅔ cup milk
⅔ cup water
4 eggs
3 tsp lard

For the buttered peas:
1½ cups frozen peas
3 tbsp butter

Plus:
A muffin pan with 6 molds

To make the roast beef:
1. Preheat the oven to 175°F (fan).
2. Melt the clarified butter in a large casserole over a high heat and sear the roast beef on all sides. Add the garlic, rosemary, thyme, and sage and sweat for 3 minutes. Place the beef in the center of a large piece of aluminum foil, season with salt and pepper, spread thinly with mustard, and pour the warm herbs all over. Wrap the beef tightly in the foil and roast for 2½ hours on the middle shelf of the oven.
3. Once the time is up, switch off the oven and leave the beef to stand in there, with the door open, for 5 minutes. Unwrap the foil, cut the beef into slices about the width of a finger, sprinkle over a pinch of coarse sea salt, and serve with the Yorkshire puddings and the buttered peas (see below). Keep the meat warm until then if necessary.

To make the Yorkshire puddings:
4. Mix the flour with the salt and pepper in a large bowl. Mix the milk and water together in a separate bowl. Make a well in the middle of the flour and add the eggs to it. Little by little, add the milk and water mixture, working it in with your hands until you have a creamy dough. Leave to stand for 15 minutes.
5. Meanwhile, preheat the oven to 430°F. Grease the molds of the muffin tin with the lard and place the tin in the oven to warm. Carefully take the hot tin out of the oven again, place it on a heat-resistant countertop, spoon the batter into the molds, and put the tin back in the oven. Bake for 15–20 minutes until the Yorkshire puddings are crispy and golden brown. Take the tin out of the oven, leave the puddings to cool, then turn them out carefully.

To make the buttered peas:
6. Boil the frozen peas in a pot of salted water for about 12 minutes until done. Remove from the heat, carefully strain through a sieve, leave to drain, then transfer back into the pot. Add the butter, put the lid on, and rock the pot back and forth until the butter is melted and the peas are coated in it. Salt the peas well, give them one more shake, and serve immediately if possible.

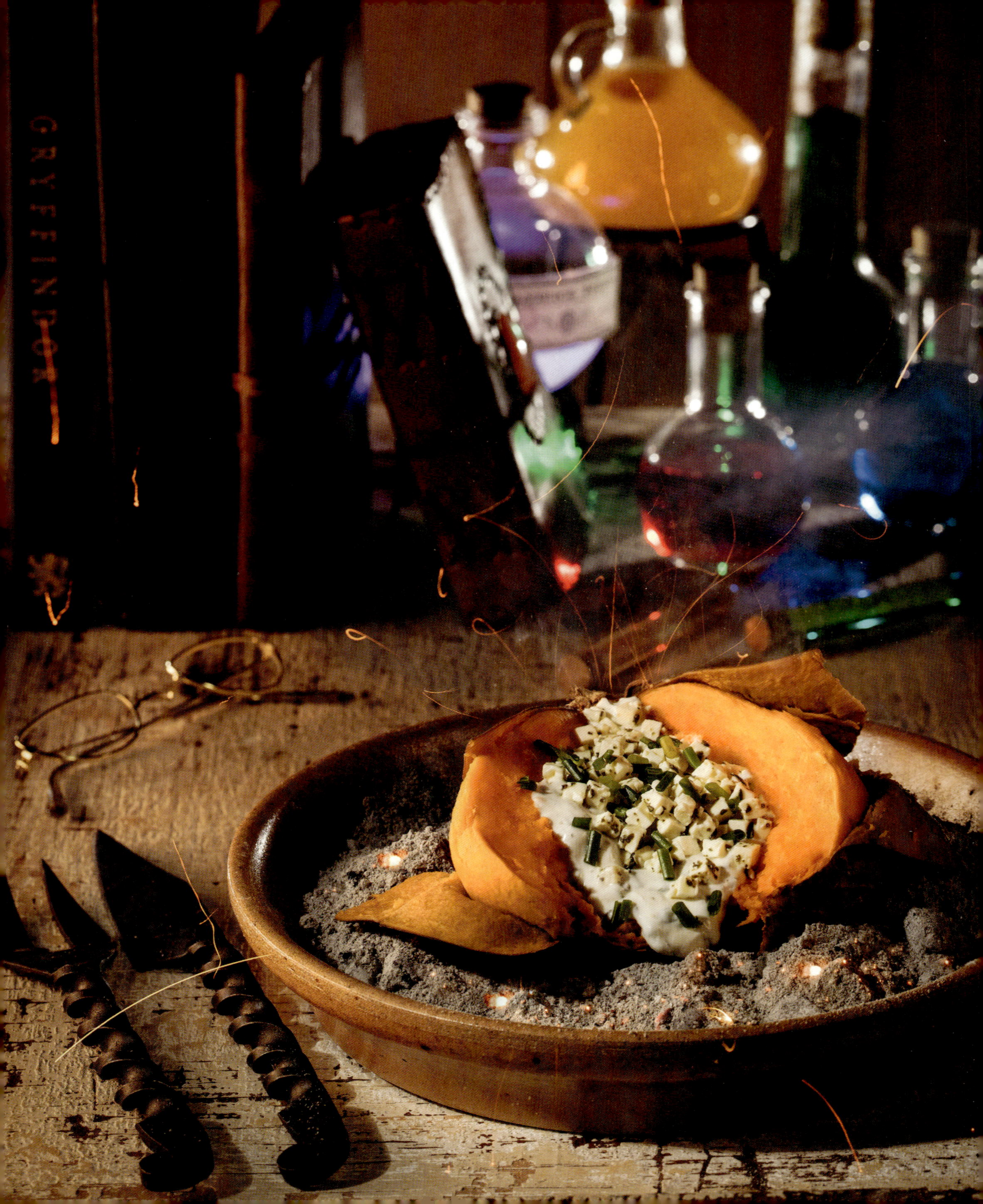
GRYFFINDOR

Oven-roasted sweet potatoes

INGREDIENTS
SERVES 4

1½ cups crème fraîche
1 tbsp lemon juice
salt, pepper
4 large sweet potatoes
¼ cup crumbled goat's cheese
chives, finely chopped.

1. Preheat the oven to 390°F.
2. In a small bowl, mix the crème fraîche with the lemon juice and season with salt and pepper to taste.
3. Wash the sweet potatoes and dry them thoroughly, then prick them several times all over with a knife. Wrap each potato in aluminum foil and place them on a grill rack on the middle oven shelf. Place a baking sheet underneath to catch any roasting fat or other liquids. Roast for about 45–60 minutes, or until your knife slides into them easily, then take them out of the oven.
   Be careful: they will be very hot!
4. Leave the sweet potatoes to cool for a few minutes. Take them out of their foil, score a big X across the top of each of them, then push both sides away from the center so that they open evenly. Spoon a generous dollop of the crème fraîche onto each one. Scatter the crumbled goat's cheese over the top and garnish with the finely chopped chives. Serve immediately.

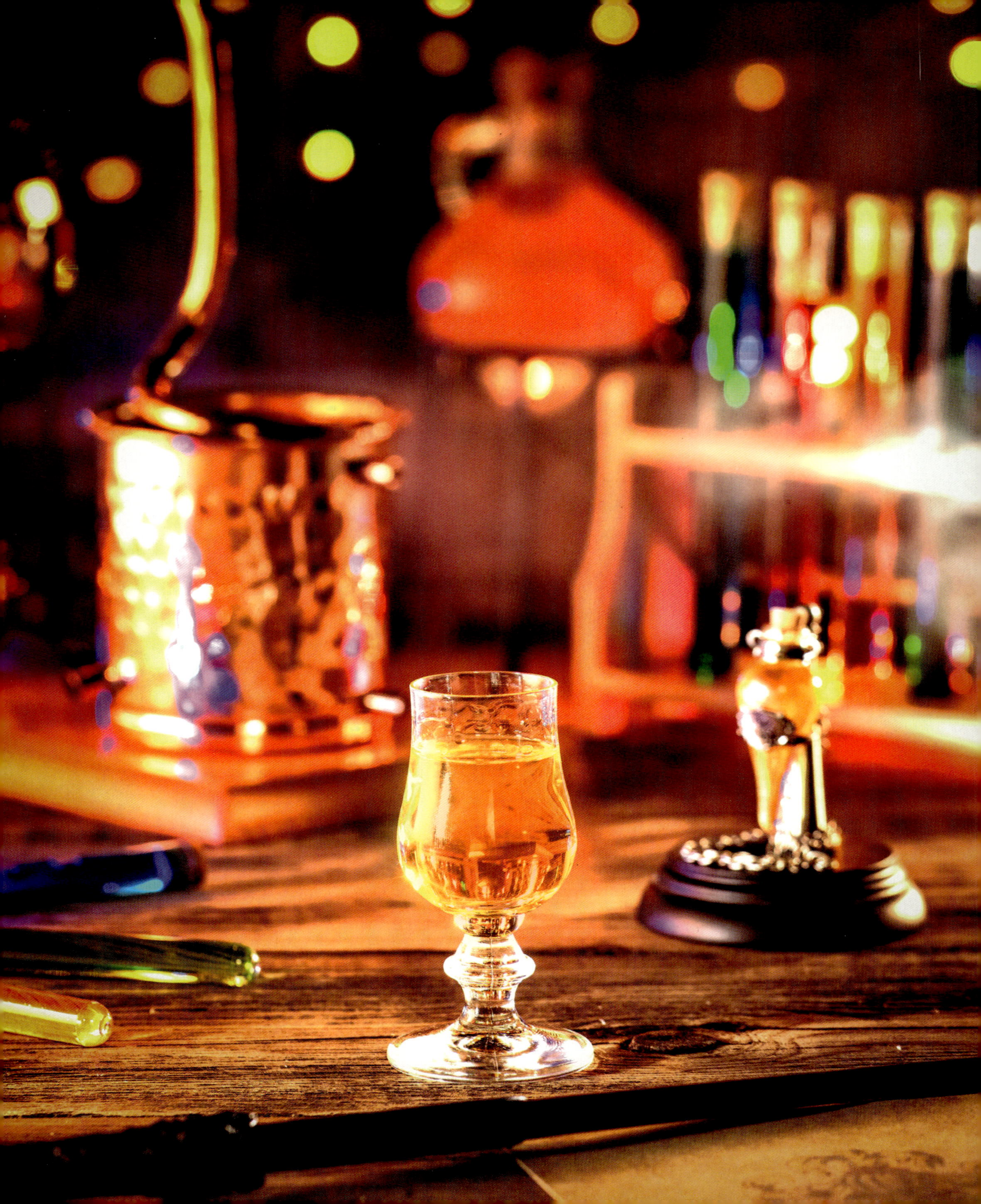

Felix Felicis

CONTAINS ALCOHOL

INGREDIENTS
MAKES ABOUT 1 QT LIQUID LUCK

1½ cups blossom honey
3 cups grain alcohol
1 cinnamon stick
1 vanilla pod
1 cardamom pod
dried cinnamon flower buds
1–2 cloves

Plus:
2–3 small or 1 large magic potion bottle, edible glitter or gold leaf, and a large mason jar with a lid

1. Drizzle the honey into the mason jar. Pour over the grain alcohol and stir it until the honey has completely dissolved. Now add all of the spices, screw the lid onto the jar, and leave to stand in a cool, dark place for 3–4 weeks. Shake it vigorously every couple of days.

2. Once this time has elapsed, strain the liqueur through a fine-mesh sieve and pour into the potion bottles, having washed them out with hot water. Add some edible glitter or small flakes of edible gold leaf to make the finished drink look utterly magical. Close the bottles tightly and shake them well.

3. You could also adorn them with a pretty label (optional).

DOBBY THE HOUSE-ELF'S TIP: The longer you leave this honey liqueur to stand, the better it will taste!

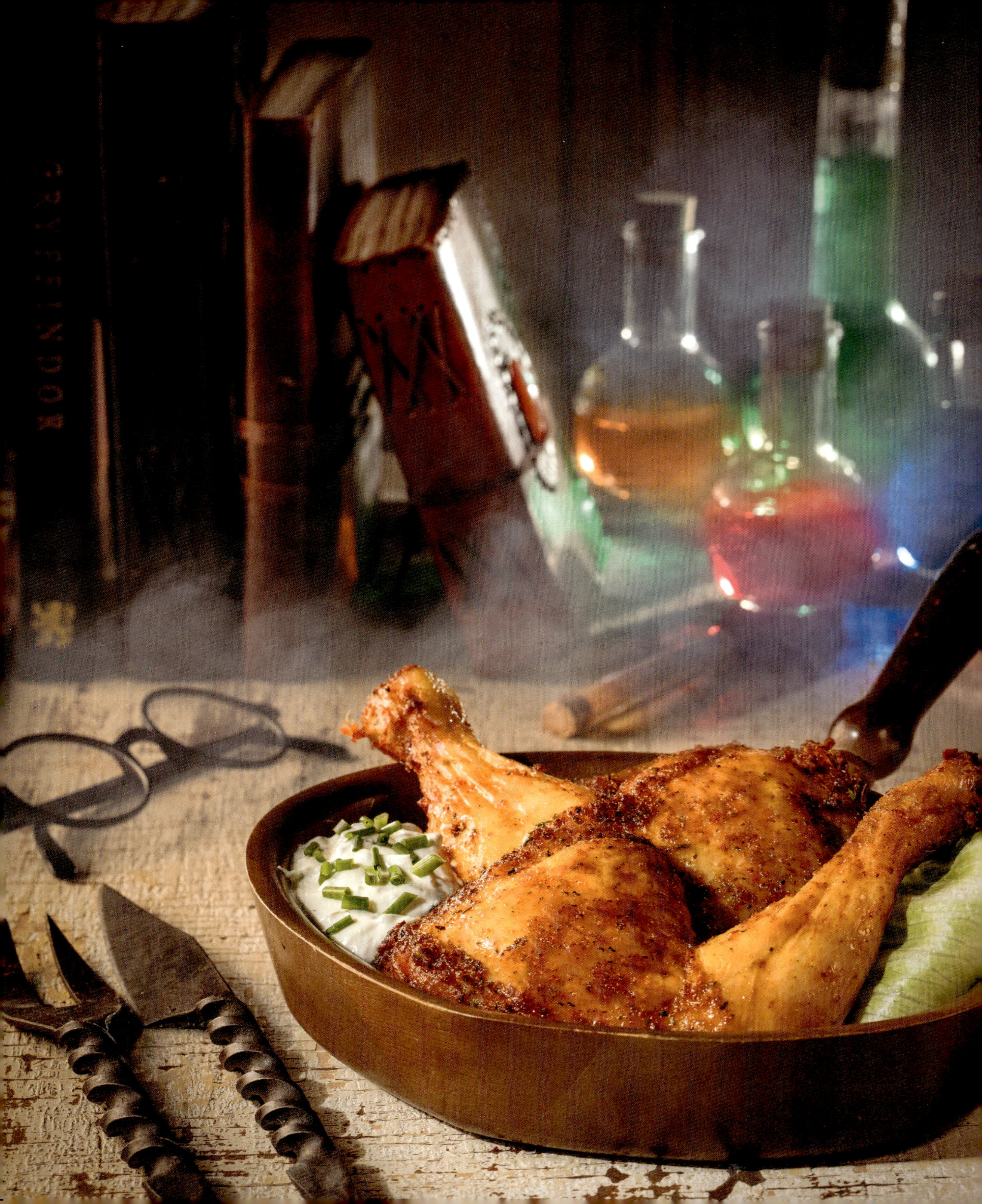
GRYFFINDOR

Succulent roast chicken legs

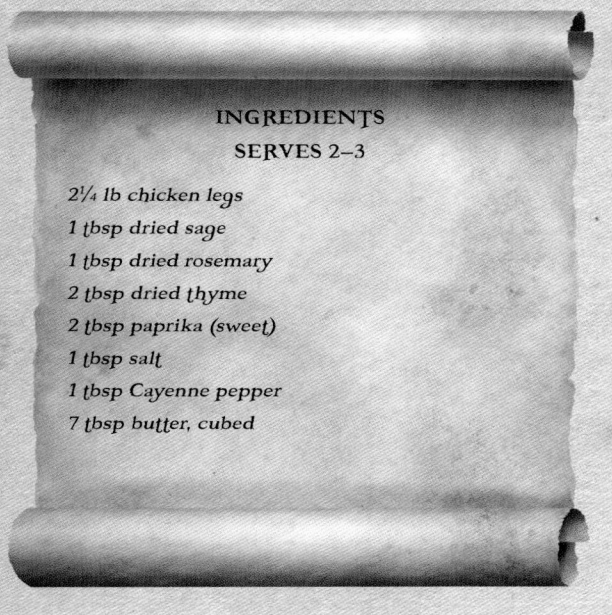

INGREDIENTS
SERVES 2–3

2¼ lb chicken legs
1 tbsp dried sage
1 tbsp dried rosemary
2 tbsp dried thyme
2 tbsp paprika (sweet)
1 tbsp salt
1 tbsp Cayenne pepper
7 tbsp butter, cubed

1. Preheat the oven to 320°F (fan). Slide an oven rack onto the middle rail of the oven and place a large bowl containing about a finger's depth of water to catch any dripping fat.

2. Rinse the chicken legs briefly and pat dry with kitchen paper.

3. Mix the sage, rosemary, thyme, paprika, salt, and Cayenne pepper together in a small bowl. Melt half of the butter in the microwave and mix it in with the spices to form a paste. Brush the chicken legs all over with half of the spiced butter, then place them on the oven rack. Loosely cover them with aluminum foil and roast in the oven for 40 minutes, turning and basting them with the spice mixture halfway through.

4. Once the cooking time is up, brush the chicken legs with the rest of the spice mixture, remove the aluminum foil, and turn up the heat to 430°F to crisp up the skin. Remove the chicken legs from the oven, arrange in a large dish and serve immediately.

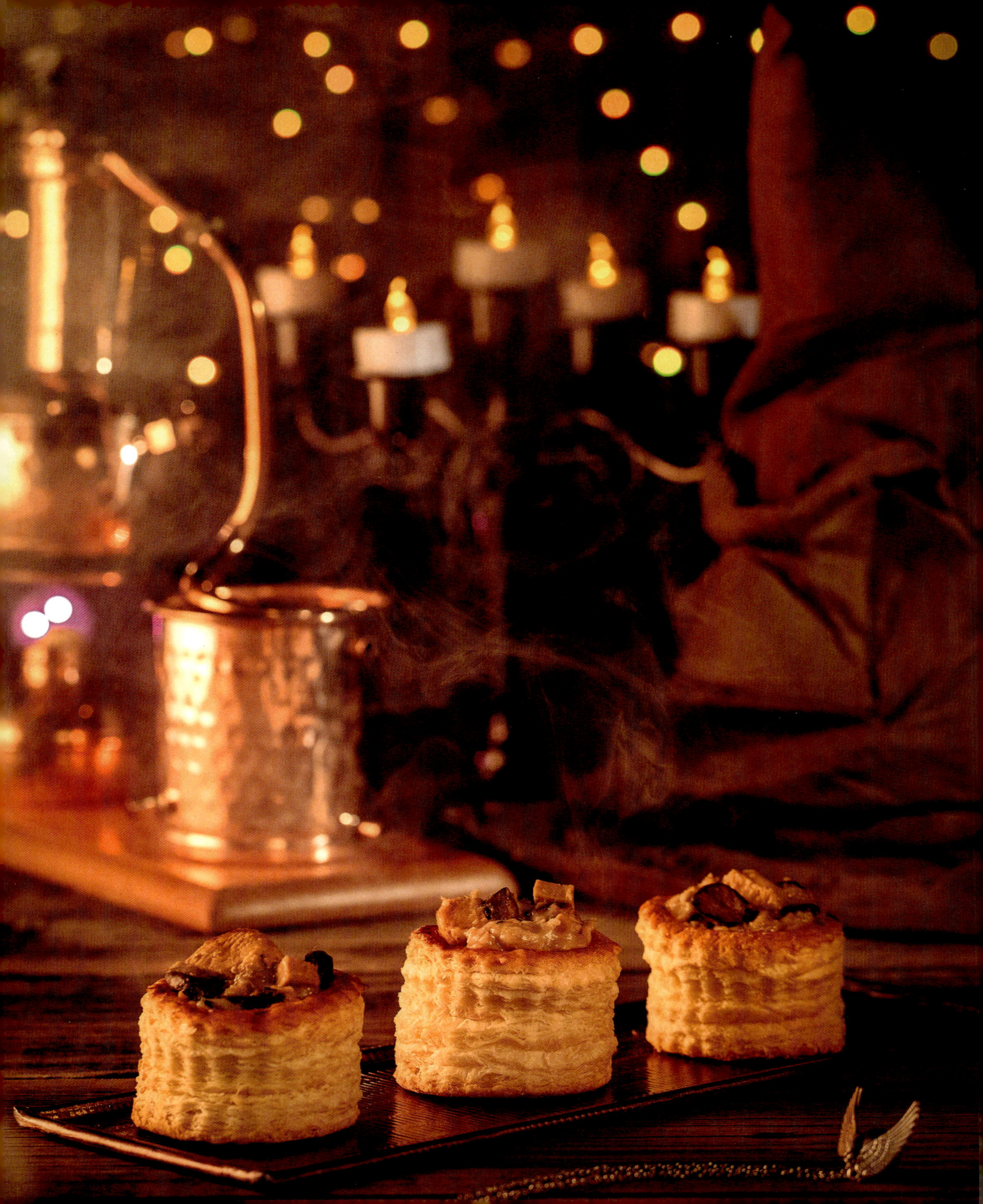

Vol-au-vents

INGREDIENTS
SERVES 4

2 tbsp olive oil
1 onion, finely diced
2 garlic cloves, crushed
1⅓ LB chicken breast, roughly diced
1 tbsp butter
4 oz button mushrooms, sliced thinly
6½ tbsp flour
4 tbsp dry white wine
2 cups chicken stock
1 oz crème fraîche
⅓ cup frozen peas
1 tbsp freshly squeezed lemon juice
1 pinch of sugar
salt, pepper
4 large puff pastry cases (ready to cook)
fresh parsley, finely chopped
cranberry jam (optional)

1. Warm the olive oil in a frying pan over a medium heat. Sauté the onion and garlic until soft (about 3–4 minutes). Then add the chicken and slightly browned all over. Transfer the chicken to a bowl and set aside.

2. Now add the butter and mushrooms to the pan, turn the heat down low, and fry gently for 5 minutes. Little by little, sprinkle the flour over the mushrooms and continue cooking, stirring well so that everything is mixed together thoroughly. After another 5 minutes, stir in the white wine, the stock, and the crème fraîche, and simmer gently until the content of the pan have noticeably thickened. Add the frozen peas, lemon juice, and a pinch of sugar, and season to taste with salt and pepper. Now return the chicken to the pan and add more seasoning if required. Let everything simmer over a low heat until the meat is warmed through.

3. Meanwhile, preheat the oven to 345°F (fan). Remove the "lids" of the pastry cases (cutting them with a knife if necessary) and bake the vol-au-vents in the oven for about 6–8 minutes until golden brown. Put them on plates and spoon in the chicken stew. Garnish with a little fresh parsley and serve with a dollop of cranberry jam (optional).

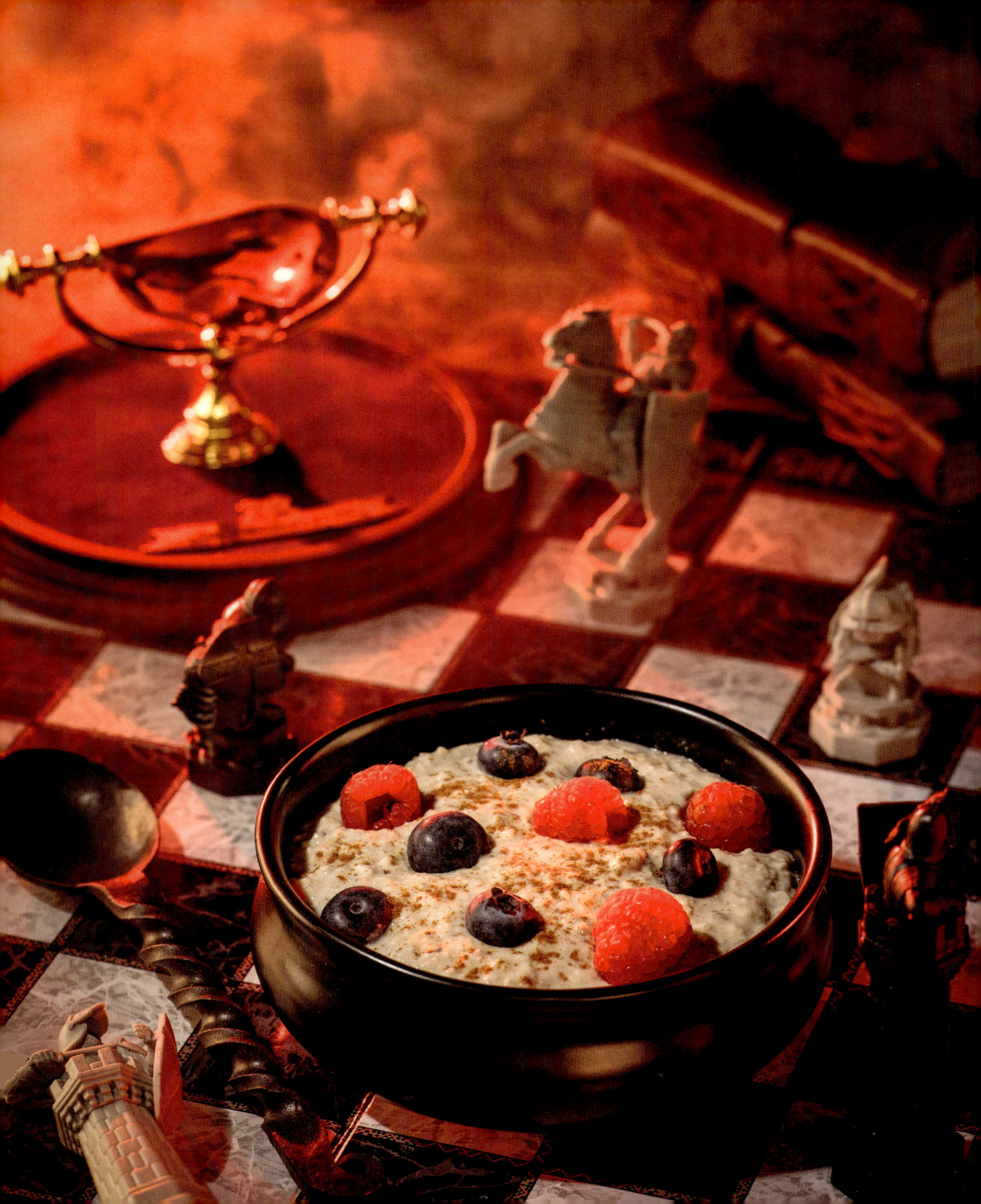

Oatmeal with fresh fruit

INGREDIENTS
SERVES 2

½ cup coarse oatmeal
1 cup milk
3 tbsp sugar
1 banana, cut into bite-size pieces
2 handfuls of fresh blueberries, raspberries (or other berries of your choice)
2 pinches of cinnamon

1. Put the oatmeal, milk, and sugar in a small pan and bring to a boil over a medium heat, stirring constantly. Simmer until the oatmeal has boiled down enough to give you the consistency you want. Make sure that it doesn't burn!

2. Remove the pan from the stove, add the banana pieces, and crush them roughly. Leave to cool for 5 minutes.

3. Divide evenly between two bowls, scatter the fresh berries over the top, sprinkle each with a pinch of cinnamon, and serve immediately.

> **DOBBY THE HOUSE-ELF'S TIP:** Of course, you can also eat this oatmeal cold—especially in summer!

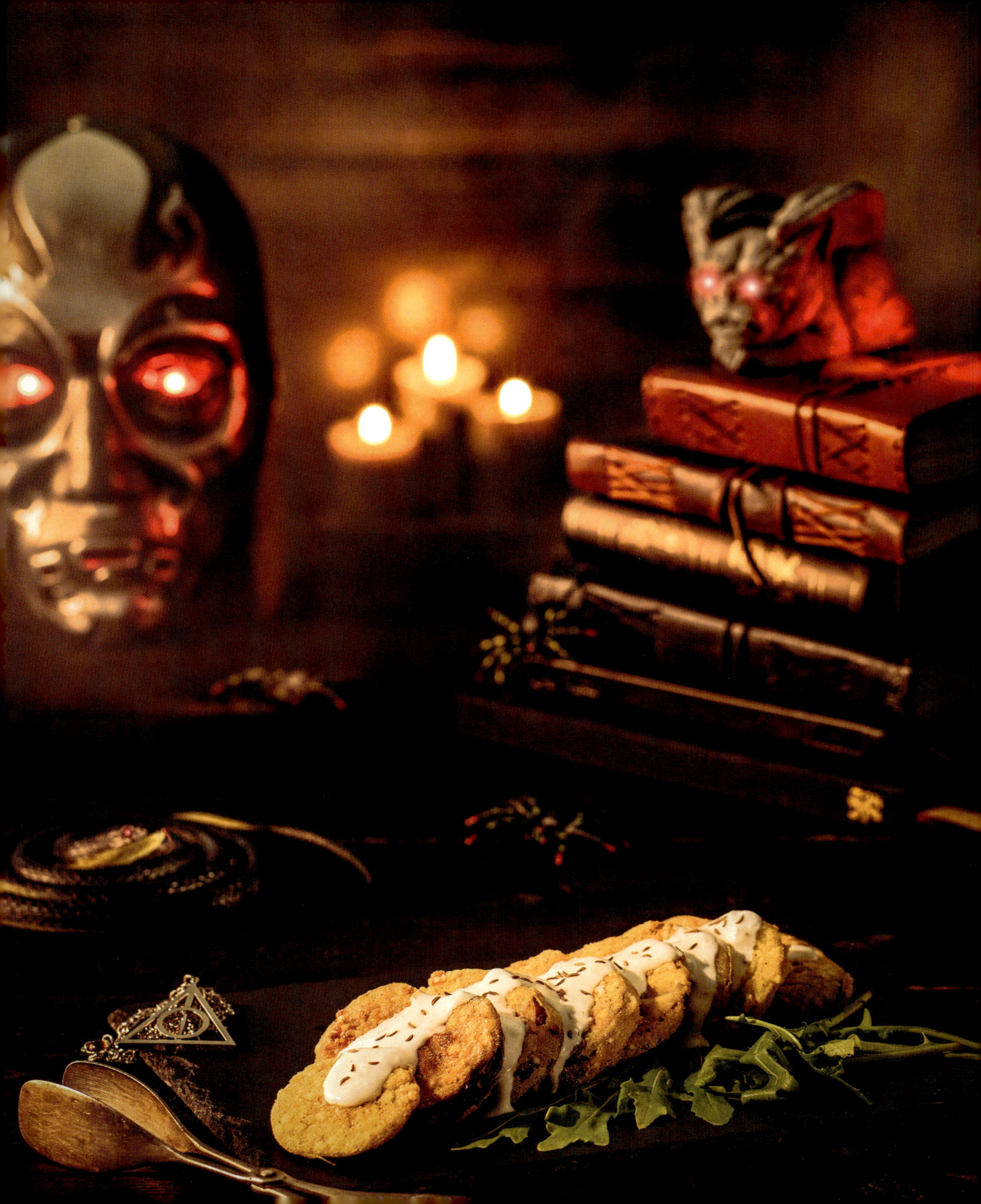

Fried green tomatoes

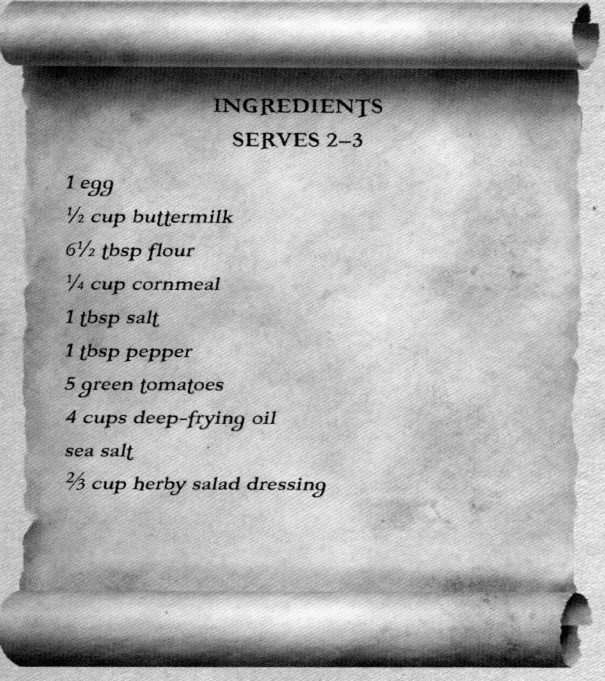

INGREDIENTS
SERVES 2–3

1 egg
½ cup buttermilk
6½ tbsp flour
¼ cup cornmeal
1 tbsp salt
1 tbsp pepper
5 green tomatoes
4 cups deep-frying oil
sea salt
⅔ cup herby salad dressing

1. Whisk the egg and buttermilk together in a deep-sided dish. Mix the flour, corn meal, salt, and pepper together in a separate deep-sided dish.

2. Wash the tomatoes, pat them dry, and cut into about ⅓-in.-thick slices. Turn them first in the egg and buttermilk mixture, and then in the flour mixture. Make sure that the slices of tomato are completely covered in the flour coating.

3. Put the deep-frying oil in a high-sided pot and warm over a high heat to 320°F. To test whether the oil is hot enough, test it by lowering one of the flour-covered tomato slices into it using a slotted spoon. If bubble rise, hissing, the oil is hot enough. Now deep-fry a few slices at a time for about 2-3 minutes until crispy, leaving enough of a gap between them. Use the slotted spoon to stir the oil every now and then. Remove the deep-fried tomato slices and place them on a dish lined with kitchen paper so that any excess oil can drain off. Repeat this process with all of the tomatoes.

4. Arrange the deep-fried tomatoes on a serving dish, sprinkle with sea salt, and serve with the herby salad dressing as a dip.

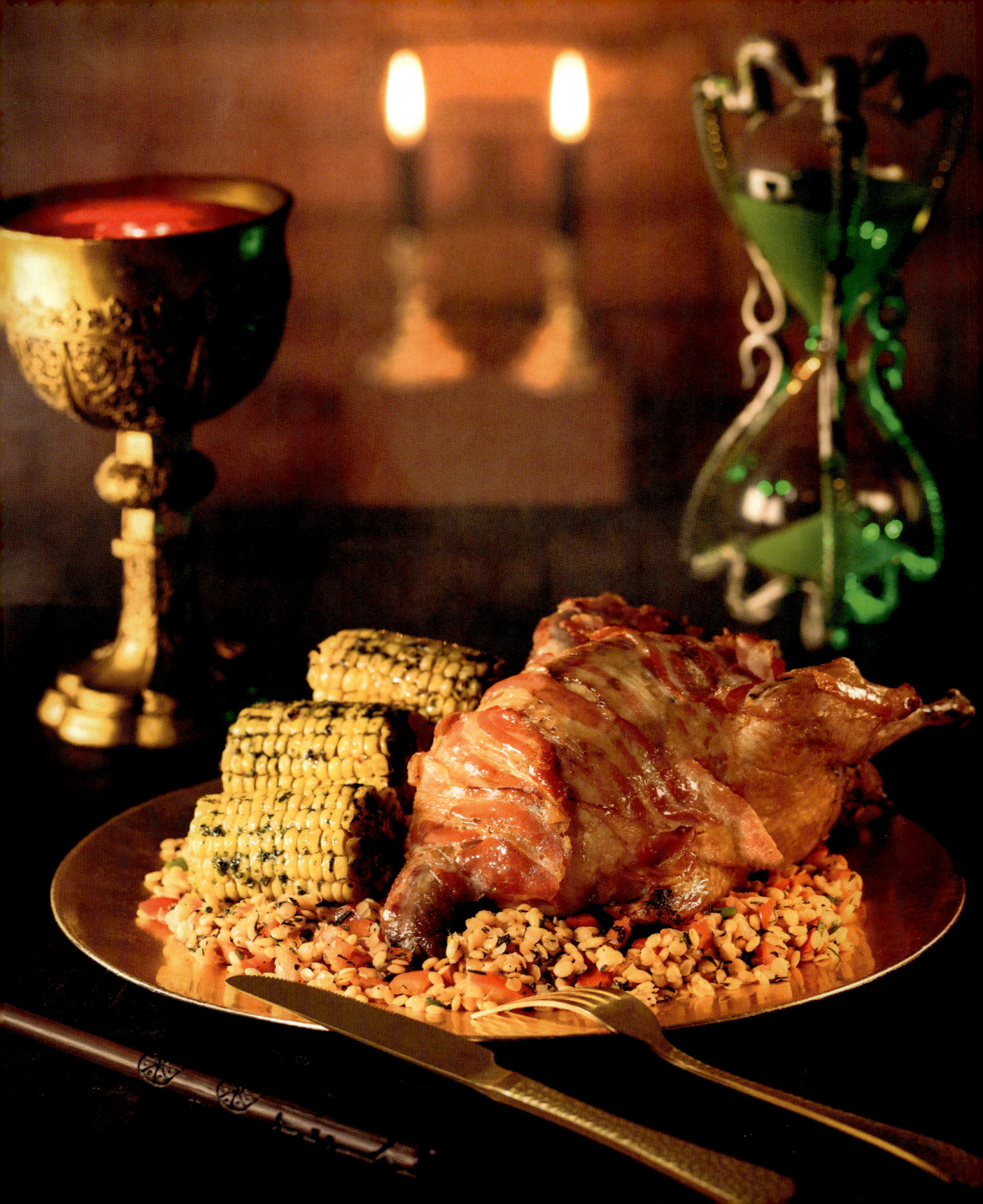

Pheasant with Lentils and Roasted Corn on the Cob

INGREDIENTS
SERVES 2–3

For the pheasant:
1 pheasant, ready to cook (about 2 lb)
salt, pepper
1½ tbsp butter, plus a little more for brushing the pheasant
10–15 bacon rashers

For the lentils:
2 tbsp oil
1 onion, finely chopped
1 red pepper, finely diced
1 cup dry white wine
1¼ cups chicken stock
¾ cup red lentils
2 tbsp fruit vinegar
salt, pepper, thyme
fresh parsley, finely chopped

For the corn on the cob:
1 tbsp butter
1 tbsp sugar
4 sweetcorn cobs, without leaves or strings
2 garlic cloves, peeled
7 tbsp soft butter
1 bunch of mixed herbs (e.g. rosemary, thyme, oregano), finely chopped
salt
6 tbsp oil, for brushing

For the pheasant:
1. Soak the red lentils overnight in a bowl of water. Drain them the next day.
2. Preheat the oven to 345°F (fan).
3. Wash the pheasant, pat it dry inside and outside, rub with salt and pepper, and put the butter into the bird. Place the pheasant breast-side up in a small stewing pan or casserole dish, cover with the rashers of bacon so that there are no gaps, and roast for about 50–60 minutes on the middle rack of the oven. Baste with melted butter every 10 minutes.

For the lentils:
4. Meanwhile, warm the oil in a large pan over a medium heat. Sauté the onion, the add the diced pepper and sauté briefly. Deglaze the pan with white wine, pour in the rest of the wine and the chicken stock, and simmer for 5 minutes. Add the lentils, season with the vinegar, salt, pepper, and thyme, and cook for another 10–15 minutes, until the lentils are done. Fold in freshly chopped parsley.

For the corn:
5. Fill a large pot with water and bring to a boil over a medium heat. Add the butter and sugar, then parboil the corn cobs the pot for about 10 minutes.
6. Meanwhile, press the garlic cloves. Mix the butter, herbs, and a pinch of salt together in a bowl. Loosely cover with clingfilm and chill in the refrigerator for 15 minutes.
7. Drain the corn and pat dry. In a large pan, heat the oil and sear the corn cobs all over for about 8–10 minutes, brushing generously with the herb butter every now and then.

CONTAINS ALCOHOL

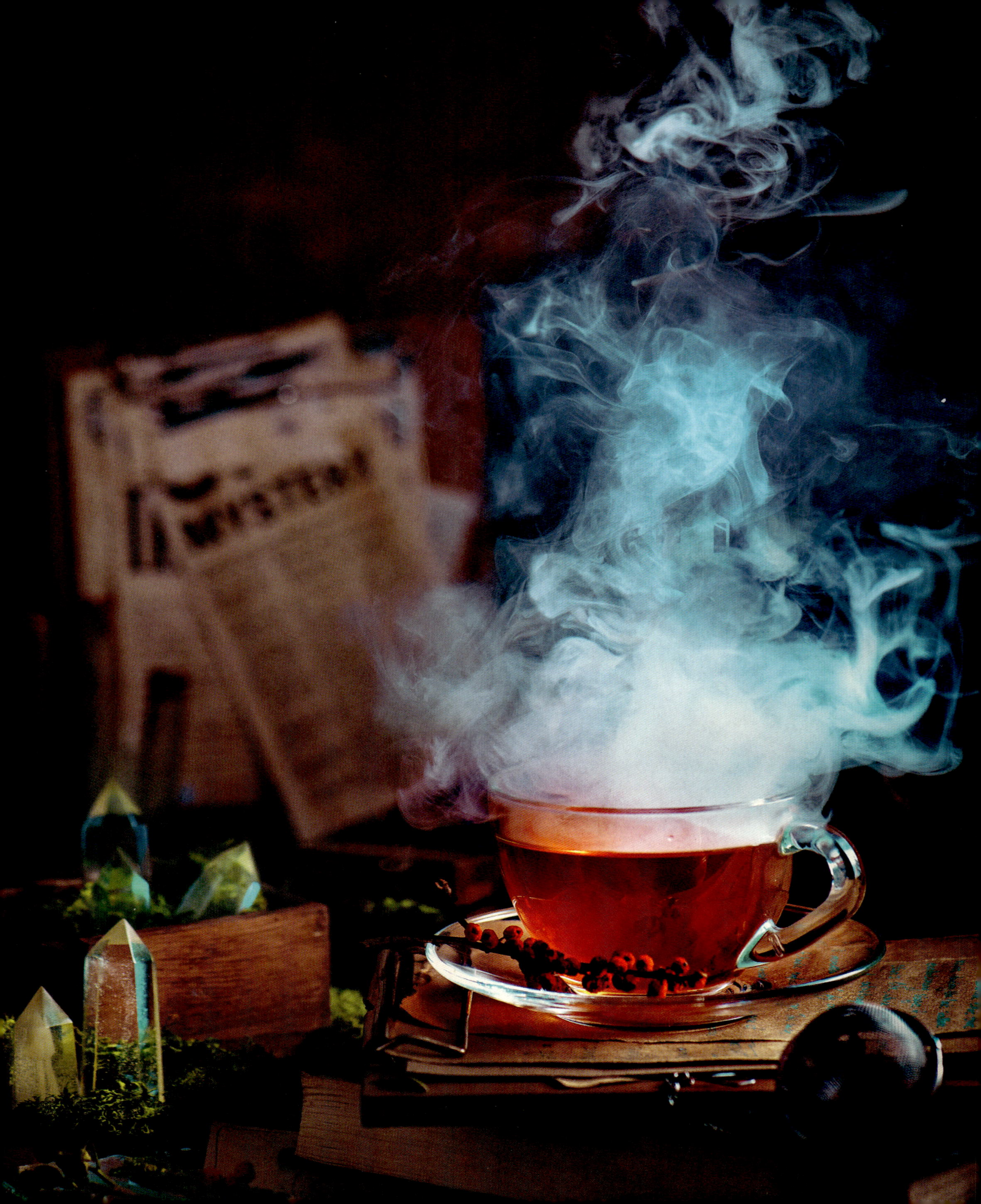

Dumbledore's Favorite Tea

**INGREDIENTS
FOR 4 5 POTS OF TEA**

10 tbsp peppermint
5 tbsp lemon verbena
5 tbsp oregano (flowers and leaves)
5 tbsp mixed flowers (e.g. elder, mallow, marigold)
1 tbsp grated licorice
1 vanilla pod, in small pieces
1⅓ cup black tea
honey (optional)

1. Line a baking sheet with baking parchment. Arrange the peppermint, lemon verbena, oregano, and mixed flowers on the tray. Either leave the tray in a warm, dry place for several days or dry the leave and flowers in the oven at 140°F for about 3 hours. Once they're dry, carefully strip the sprigs of their leaves and flowers, and discard the rest.

2. Coarsely grid the dried herbs with a pestle and mortar.

3. In a small bowl, mix the grated licorice and vanilla pod with the black tea. Add the ground herbs and mix everything together.

4. To make the tea, but 4–5 tsp of the herbal tea mixture into a tea infuser, hang it in a teapot, pour in boiling water, and leave to steep for no more than 5 minutes.

5. Then remove the tea infuser and serve immediately. It is best to strain the tea through a fine-mesh sieve to make sure that no residue gets into the cups. Sweeten with a little honey (optional).

DOBBY THE HOUSE-ELF'S TIP: If stored in a small tin, this tea will keep for several months!

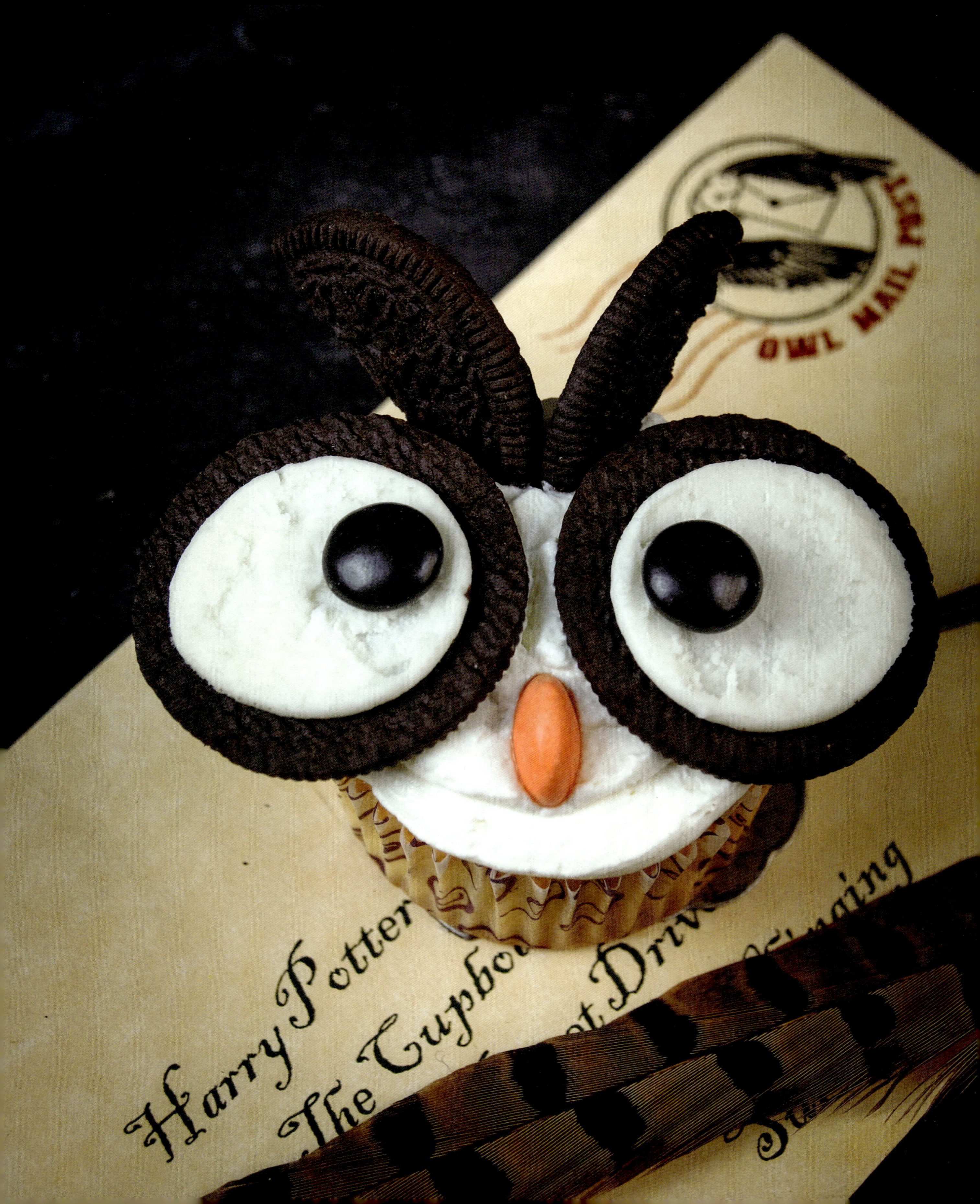
OWL MAIL POST
Harry Potter

Hedwig Muffins

INGREDIENTS
MAKES 12 OWL MUFFINS

For the muffin mixture:
2 tbsp soft butter
8 tbsp peanut butter
2 tsp of vanilla sugar
⅔ cup cane sugar
2 eggs
pinch of salt
1 tsp baking powder
1 cup flour
⅓ cup milk

For the buttercream:
9 tbsp butter, at room temperature
1 cup icing sugar
½ cup cream cheese, at room temperature

For the decoration:
24 Oreo cookies or other chocolate cookies with a vanilla filling
24 black (or dark brown) M&Ms
12 orange M&Ms

Plus:
12-mold muffin tin, 12 paper muffin cases

1. Preheat the oven to 355°F. Put paper cases into the hollows of a 12-mold muffin tin.

2. Beat the butter, peanut butter, vanilla sugar, and cane sugar together in a bowl until fluffy. Stir in the eggs one by one, add the salt, and mix everything together thoroughly.

3. In a separate bowl, mix the baking powder with the flour, then sieve it. Then add the flour and baking powder mixture and the milk alternately to the butter and sugar mixture and keep stirring until you have a creamy muffin mixture. Divide the mixture evenly between the muffin cases and bake them for 20 minutes on the middle shelf of the oven. Leave to cool on a wire rack, while still in the tin.

4. Meanwhile, beat the butter and icing sugar together in a separate bowl until pale and fluffy. Stir in the cream cheese and put the mixture in the refrigerator for 30 minutes to chill.

5. Carefully remove the muffins in their cases from the tin. Transfer the chilled buttercream to a piping bag or a freezer bag with the corner cut off and pipe them evenly onto the muffins.

6. Carefully pull the two halves of the cookies apart, ideally with a twisting motion, so that all of the vanilla filling remains sticking to one half. Cut the other halves in half with a sharp knife. Place the cookie halves that still have the filling towards the top of each muffin as the eyes, carefully pressing them into the buttercream. Add a black (or dark brown) M&M to each as the pupil. Press the cut cookie halves into the buttercream at the very top to make the eyebrows. Place an orange M&M vertically in the center of the buttercream as the beak. Leave to set for a few minutes.

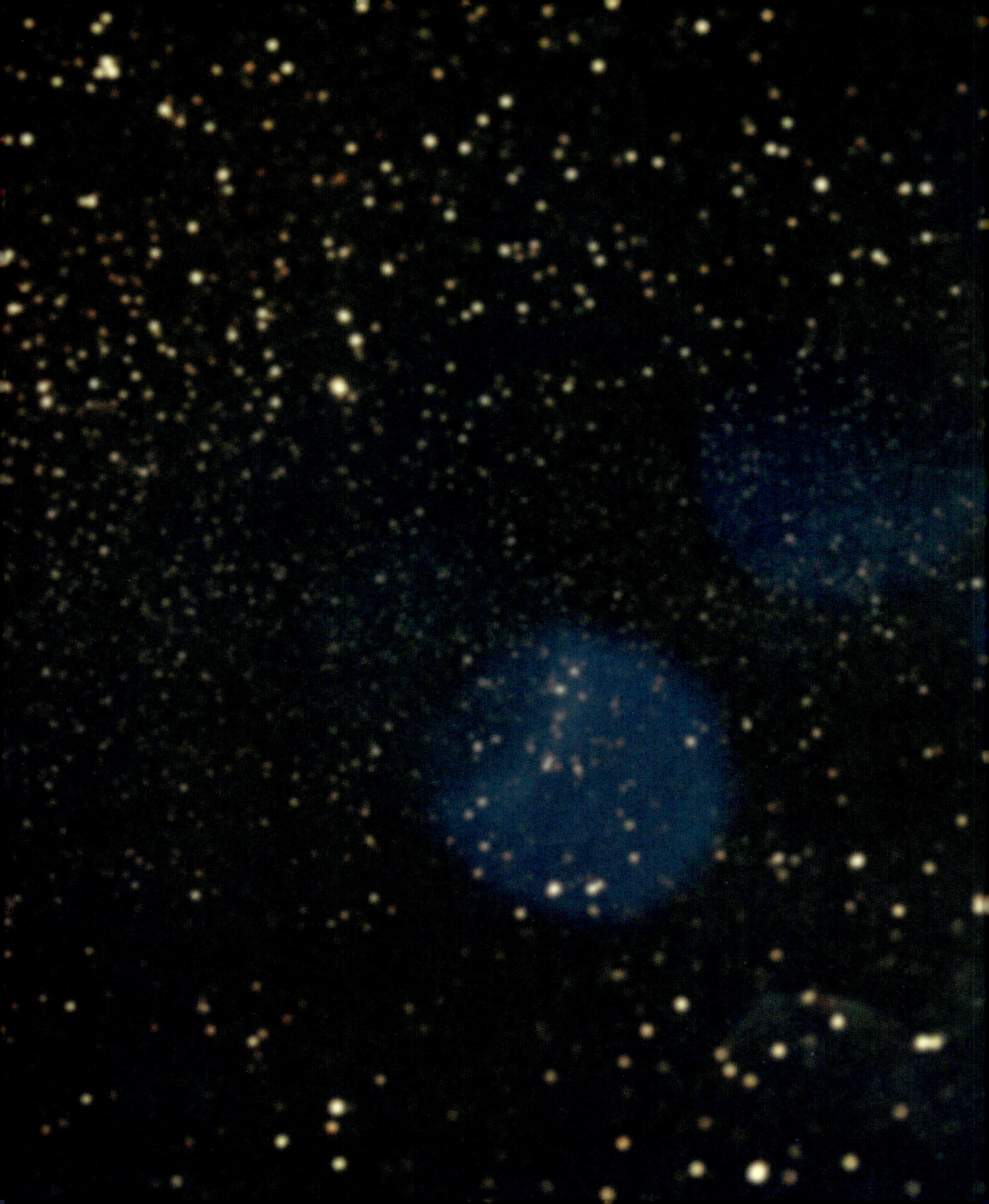

Hagrid's kitchen efforts

Half-giant Rubeus Hagrid may seem a bit scary at first glance, what with his shaggy mane and untamed beard, but despite his rugged appearance, the Hogwarts gamekeeper is a kindhearted soul and one of Harry's best friends. It is he who frees "the Boy Who Lived" from his quasi-imprisonment with the Dursleys and opens his eyes to the wizarding world, and he, too, who presents Harry with the very first birthday cake of his life. His generosity is such that he's always eager for Harry and the others to taste his attempts at cooking. It's just a shame that Hagrid's talents don't really extend to knowing his way around the kitchen. His rock cakes, for instance, are exactly as their name describes: bite into them, and you could lose a few teeth ... But as with everything he takes on, the good-natured half-giant really throws himself into cooking and baking with gusto, and ultimately that's what it's all about!

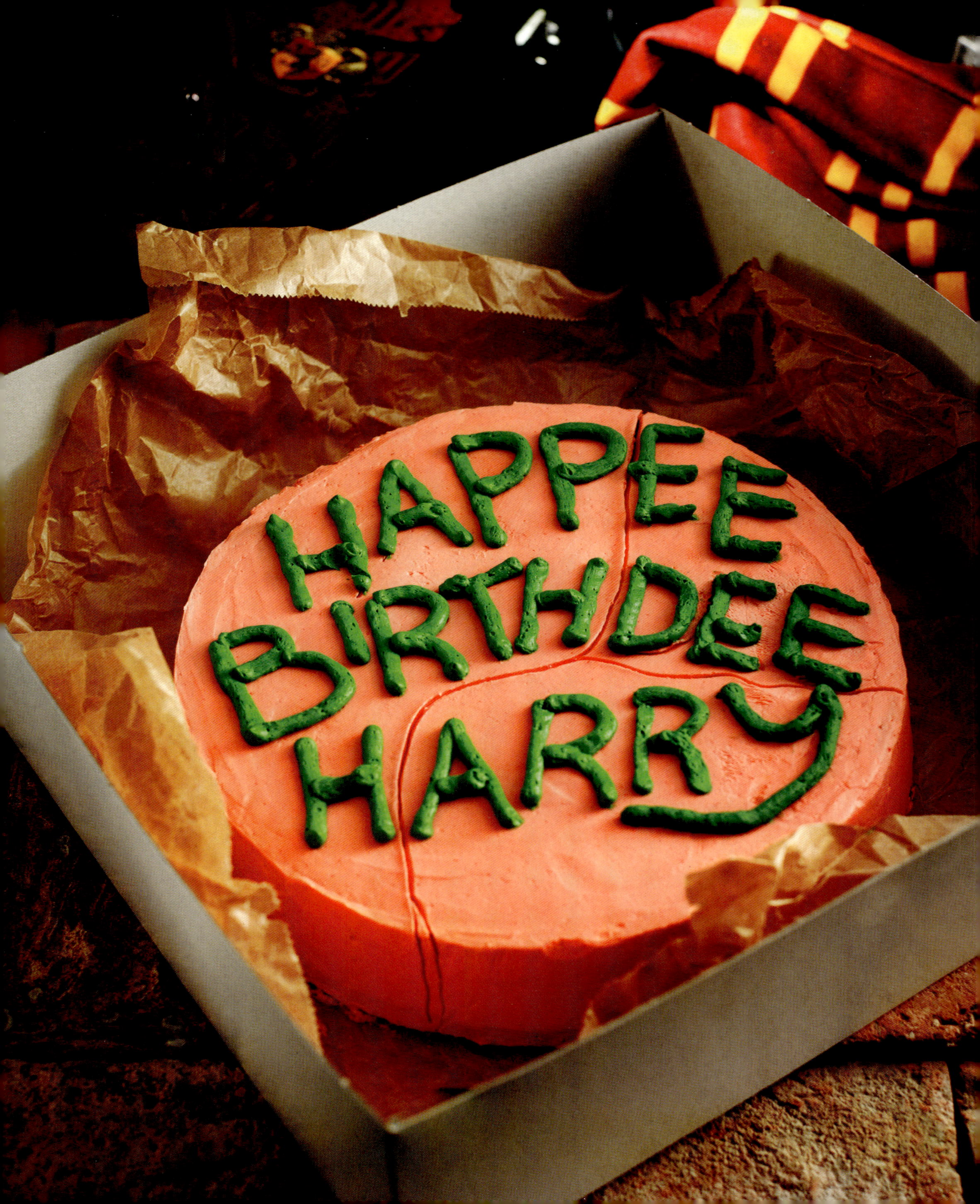
HAPPEE
BIRTHDAE
HARRY

Harry's Birthday Cake

INGREDIENTS
MAKES 1 CAKE

For the chocolate cake:
1⅓ cups butter
1¼ cups dark chocolate, roughly chopped
8 eggs
1¼ cups sugar
1 tsp vanilla extract
pinch of salt
¼ cup cocoa powder
2 level tsp baking powder
1½ cups flour

For the buttercream:
2 tsp of custard powder
1¾ cups milk
2½ cups sugar
13 tbsp butter at room temperature
6 tbsp icing sugar
green food coloring
red food coloring

Plus:
springform pan (diameter about 10 in.)

1. Preheat the oven to 320°F. Line the base of the springform pan with baking parchment.

2. Melt the butter in a pan over a low heat. Add the chocolate and melt it into the mixture. Now leave the chocolate mixture to cool for a few minutes.

3. Mix the eggs, sugar, vanilla extract, and salt together in a bowl. Add the cooled chocolate mixture, stirring vigorously.

4. In a separate bowl, mix the cocoa powder and baking powder with the flower, add to the wet ingredients, and work everything together to form a smooth cake batter. Pour this into the springform pan, then bake in the preheated oven for about 30–35 minutes, until a toothpick inserted into the middle of the cake comes out clean. Turn the cake out onto a plate and leave it to cool down completely. Pull off the baking parchment and slice the cake in two horizontally through the middle.

5. Make the custard according to the packet instructions, but only bring it to a boil with 1¾ cups milk and 2 tbsp sugar (i.e. less than specified). Cover the custard with clingfilm and set it aside to cool down to room temperature. Note: The butter and the custard must be at the same temperature when you come to use them!

6. Put the butter (at room temperature) and the sifted icing sugar into a bowl and beat until frothy with a mixer. Add the custard in spoonfuls and continue mixing at the highest speed. Set aside a quarter of the buttercream for the filling. Take out a small amount of the remaining buttercream for the writing, and color it with the green food coloring. Use the red food coloring to color the rest of the buttercream pink.

7. Place the bottom half of the cake on a cake plate and spread it evenly with the non-colored buttercream. Place the other half of the cake on top, press down lightly, and spread the entire cake with the pink buttercream.

8. Put the green buttercream into a piping bag with a nozzle or a freezer bag with the corner cut off and pipe the birthday greeting HAPPEE BIRTHDEE, HARRY! onto it, or another message of your own. For an even more authentic look, carve a distinctive crack into the cake.

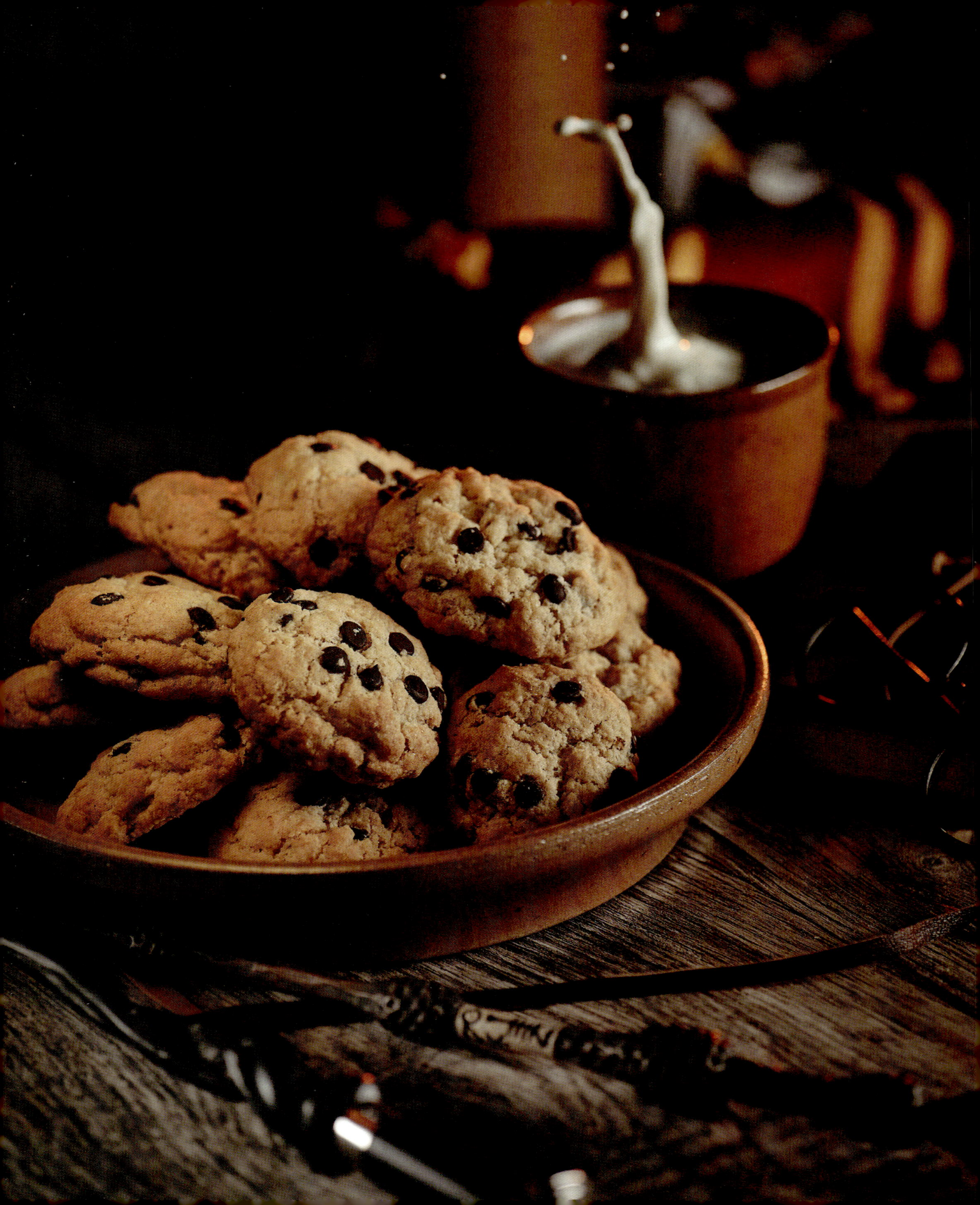

Rock Cakes

INGREDIENTS
MAKES ABOUT 12 ROCK CAKES

1¾ cups flour
2 tsp of baking powder
½ cup butter, very cold
½ cup sugar
1 level tsp cinnamon
1 pinch of nutmeg
pinch of salt
1 egg
1–2 tbsp milk
½ cup chocolate chips

1. Preheat the oven to 355°F. Line a baking sheet with baking parchment.

2. Sieve the flour finely and mix it with the baking powder in a bowl. Cut the butter into small pieces and knead it into the flour until the mixture looks smooth. Add the sugar and spices and work them in roughly.

3. Whisk the egg and add it to the mixture, with a little milk if necessary. Mix everything with a spatula until the dough is reminiscent of coarse breadcrumbs. Now carefully work in the chocolate chips.

4. With a tablespoon, put tennis-ball-sized dollops of dough onto the baking sheet, leaving about 5 cm gaps between the cakes. Bake in the preheated oven for 17–20 minutes, or until the rock cakes are golden. Take them out of the oven and leave to cool on a wire rack.

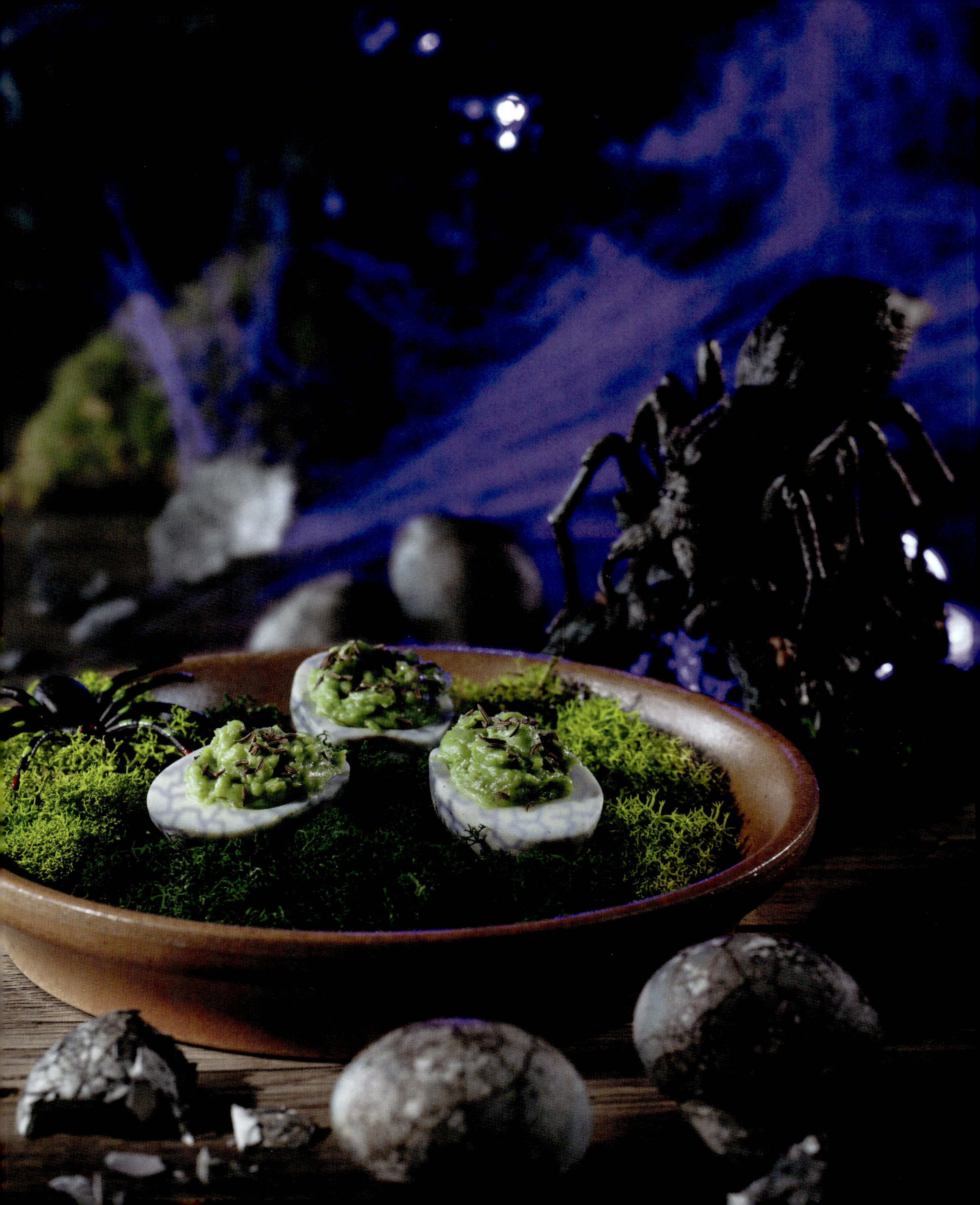

Spider Eggs

INGREDIENTS
SERVES 8

2 avocados
2 tsp lemon juice, freshly squeezed
2 tbsp cream cheese
3 tsp wasabi paste
8 large eggs
2 cups blueberry juice
salt, pepper
black sesame seeds

1. Halve the avocados lengthways and scoop out the flesh with a spoon. Put the avocado flesh, lemon juice, cream cheese, and wasabi in a medium-sized bowl and set it aside to stand for 10 minutes.

2. In the meantime, bring a medium-sized pot of water to a boil. Add the eggs and hard-boil them for 8–10 minutes. Take the eggs out of the water and refresh them in icy water.

3. Do not peel the hard-boiled eggs, but simply tap them lightly with a tablespoon so that cracks form all over the shell. Put the blueberry juice in a bowl and carefully lower the eggs into it so that they are completely covered with the juice. Put them in the refrigerator for at least 3 hours, ideally overnight, so that the juice can really soak into the eggs.

4. Remove the eggs——which will now be completely covered in dark "veins"—from the juice and peel them carefully. Cut them in half and carefully remove the yolks with a spoon. Add the egg yolks to the bowl with the avocados, wasabi and the rest of the ingredients, and process them to a purée with a handheld blender. Season to taste with salt and pepper.

5. Transfer the avocado cream to a piping bag and pipe it into the egg halves. Scatter a few black sesame seeds over the filling. Serve immediately.

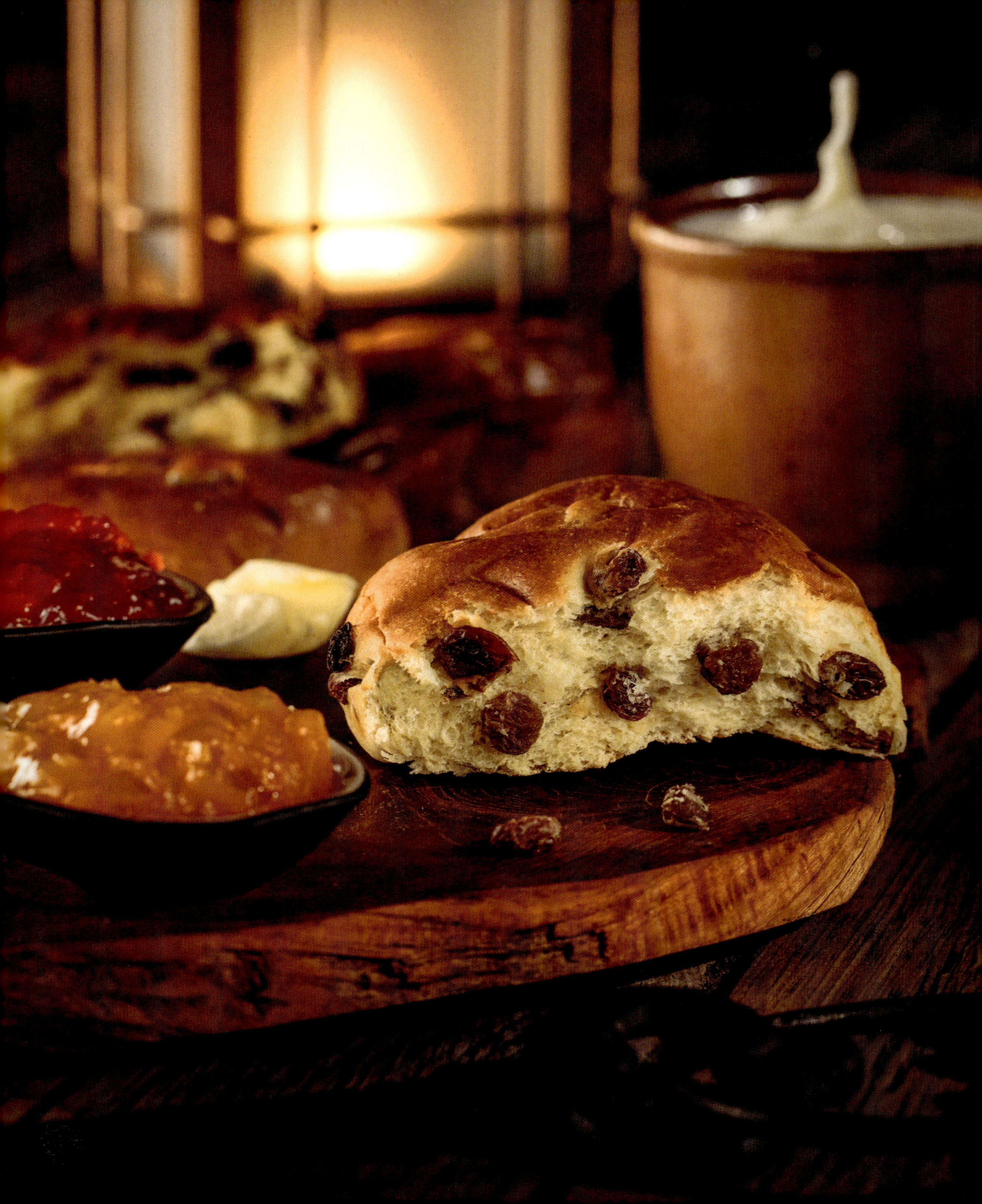

Raisin Buns

INGREDIENTS
MAKES 12 BUNS

1 cup raisins
3 tbsp milk plus 1 tbsp for brushing
½ cup butter
3¼ cup flour
2 tsp of dried yeast
½ cup low-fat curd cheese
⅓ cup sugar
1 egg
1 egg white
1 pinch of salt
1 egg yolk

1. Put the raisins in a bowl, cover with water, and soak for about 1 hour. Strain them through a sieve and leave to drain.
2. In a small pan, warm the milk over a medium heat. Add the butter and let it melt.
3. Mix the flour and dried yeast together in a mixing bowl. Add the low-fat curd cheese, sugar, egg, egg white, and salt and mix with an electric mixer with dough hooks to form a smooth dough. Cover with a clean tea towel and leave in a warm place for 40 minutes to rise.
4. Transfer the dough to a lightly floured countertop and knead it briefly with you hands. Work in the raisins evenly, shape the dough into a roll, and cut it into 12 equal-sized slices. Shape these pieces of dough into round rolls, place them on the baking sheet, cover, and leave to rise in a warm place for 30 minutes.
5. Meanwhile, preheat the oven to 320°F and line a baking sheet with baking parchment.
6. In a small bowl, mix the egg yolk with 1 tbsp milk, brush this mixture over the teacakes, then bake them for about 20 minutes or until they are golden. Take the teacakes out of the oven and leave them to cool down for a few minutes before eating them!

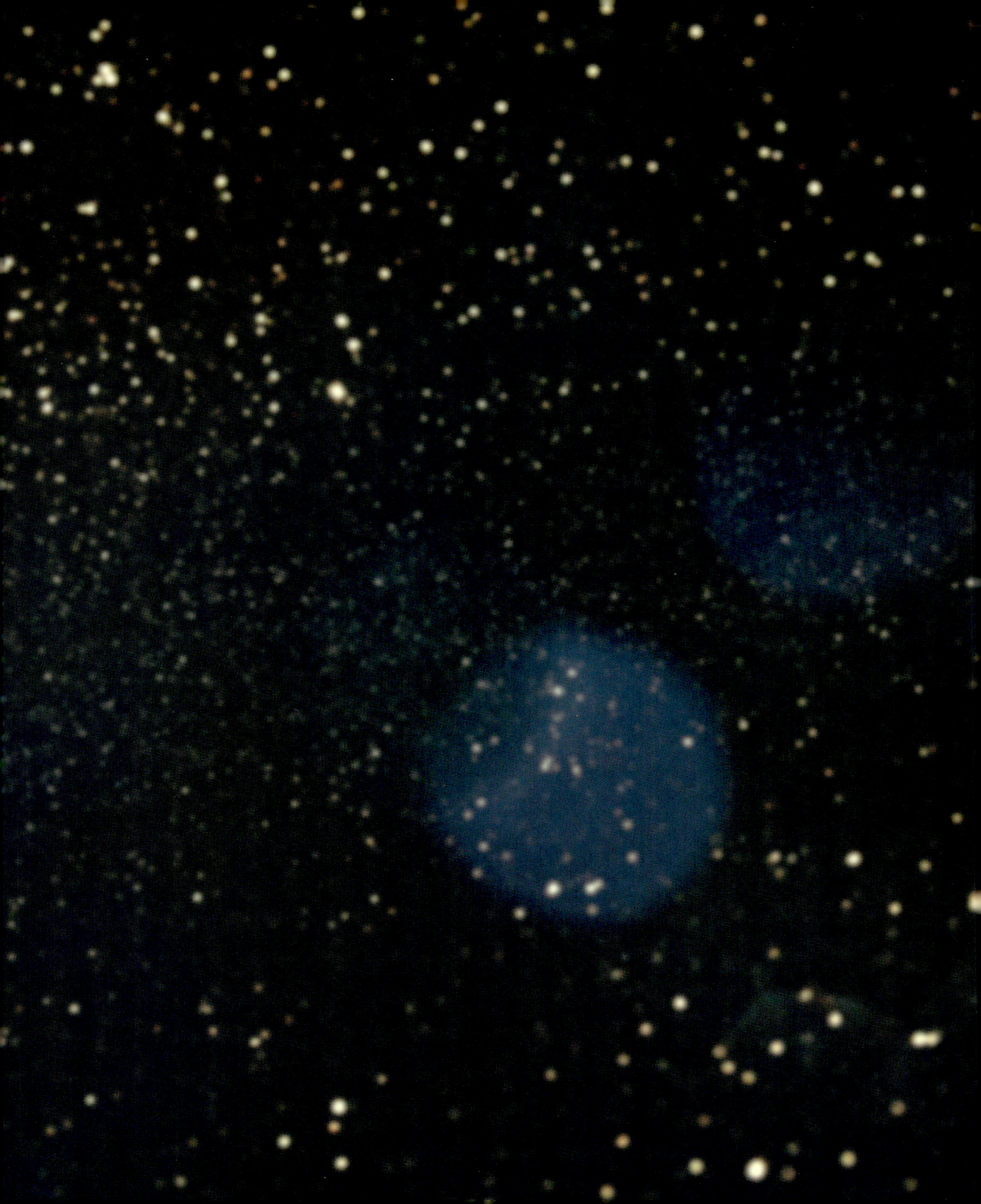

Dobby's House-Elf Cuisine

Since time immemorial, much of the more menial work in the wizarding world has been carried out by house-elves. Dobby is one of them. This lovable little elf with the saucer-sized eyes had been under the thumb of the tyrannical Malfoy family for many years, but Harry played a trick to free him from slavery. He gave Dobby a sock, a gesture that granted Dobby the freedom for which he had yearned for so long. Dobby does everything he can to show his appreciation, from supporting Harry in his fight against You-Know-Who to making sure that Harry and Dumbledore's Army are always well nourished and ready to head into battle. Remember, too, that all of those sumptuous dishes on the groaning banquet tables in the Great Hall at Hogwarts are prepared by house-elves, so you can be sure that Dobby knows his stuff!

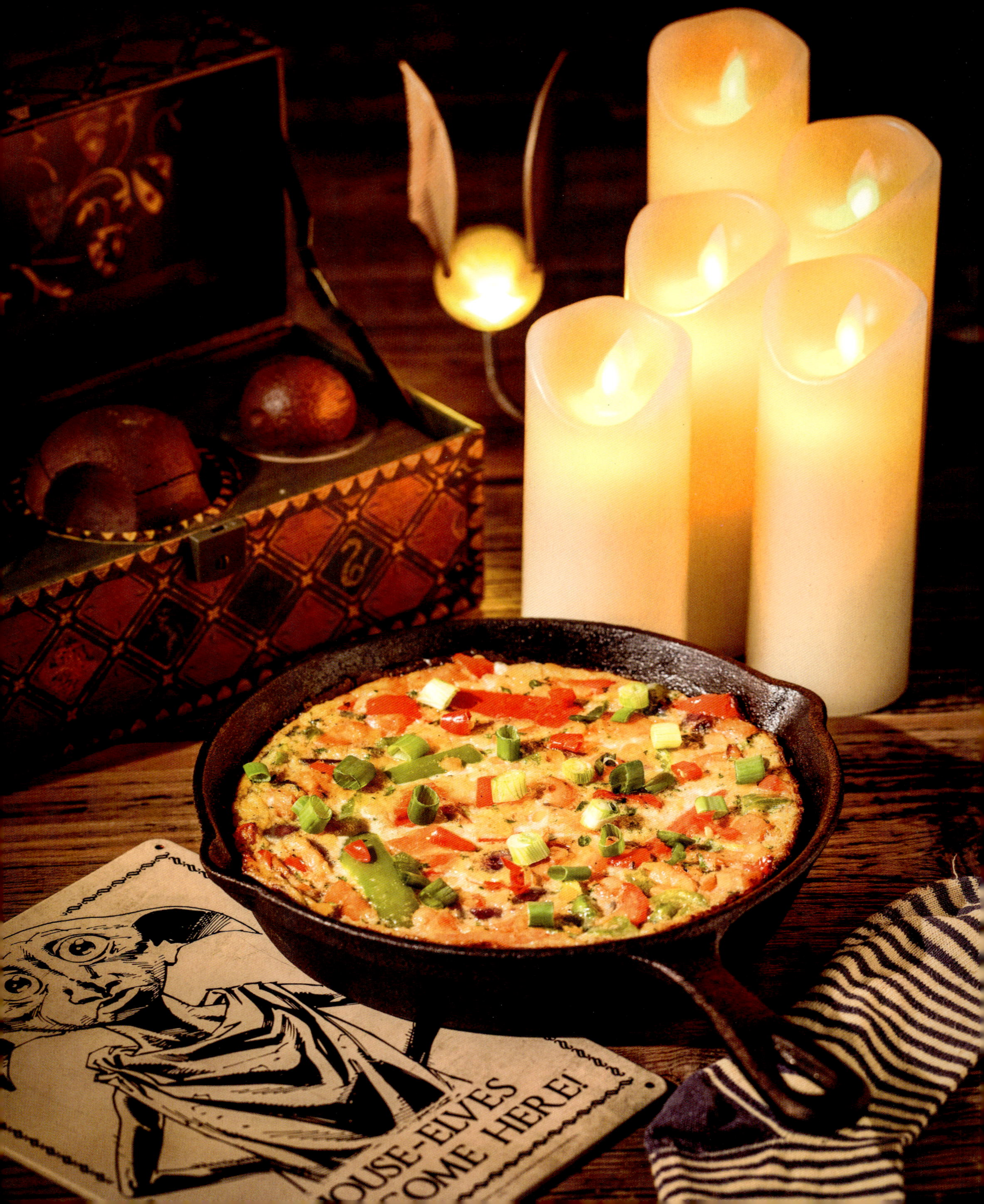
OUSE-ELVES
COME HERE!

Dobby's Veggie Frittata

INGREDIENTS
SERVES 2–3

5 tbsp red lentils, soaked
2 tsp olive oil
1 large red onion, finely chopped
2 carrots, finely chopped
1 red pepper, finely sliced
1 green pepper, finely sliced
1 cup vegetable stock
6 eggs
⅓ cup cream
salt, pepper, nutmeg
2 scallions, white parts only, finely sliced
1 small chile, finely sliced

1. Put the lentils in a bowl, cover them completely with water, and soak overnight. Strain through a sieve.

2. Warm the olive oil in a medium-sized coated frying pan over a medium heat. Tip in the onion and sauté until glassy and translucent. Add the carrots and pepper and sweat for 5 minutes, stirring regularly. Deglaze the pan with a little vegetable stock, then pour in the rest of the stock, cover, and simmer gently for about 5 minutes.

3. Add the soaked lentils. Cover and cook for about 5 minutes, until all of the liquid has been absorbed.

4. Meanwhile, whisk the eggs and cream together in a high-sided bowl. Season with salt, pepper, and a little nutmeg, pour over the vegetable mixture in the frying pan, stir everything thoroughly, cover and leave to set over a low heat until the frittata is as firm as you want it.

5. Serve the frittata immediately in its pan. Garnish with finely sliced scallions and scatter sliced red chile over the top, (optional).

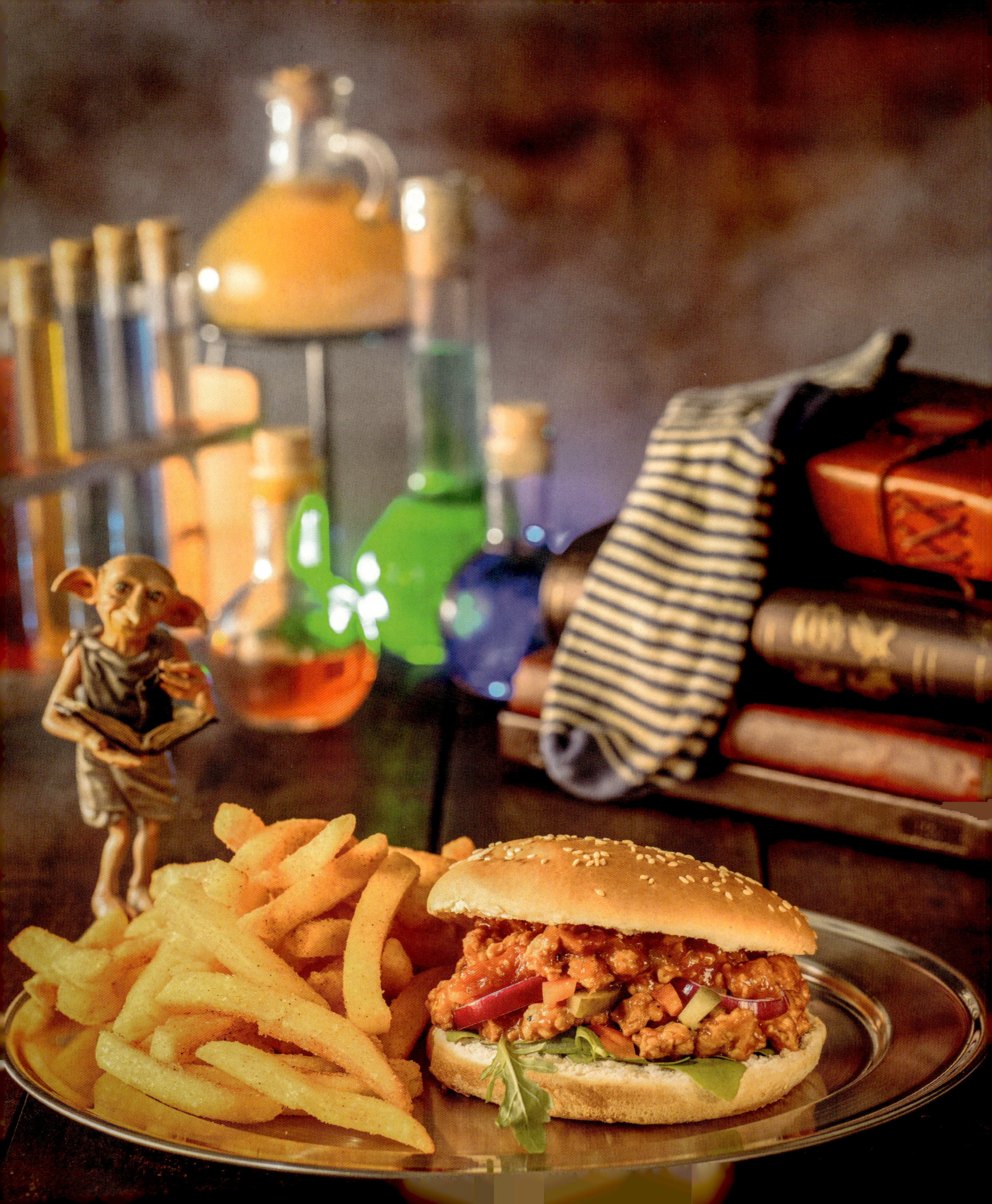

Dobby's Turkey Sloppy Joes

INGREDIENTS
SERVES 4

For the sloppy Joes:
2 tbsp olive oil
2 large red onions, finely chopped
18 oz minced turkey
1 green pepper, finely chopped
2 pickles, finely diced
2½ tsp cane sugar
1 tbsp vinegar
⅔ cup ketchup
2 tbsp mustard
1 pinch of ground cloves
salt, freshly ground black pepper
4 burger buns

For the fries:
2¼ lb floury potatoes
1 qt oil for deep-frying
coarse sea salt

1. Warm the olive oil in a large pan over a medium heat. Add and sauté the onions. Add the minced turkey and sear, stirring constantly, until the meat has browned a little. Drain off the excess fat, add the pepper pieces and the diced gherkins, mix everything together well, and braise for another 3–4 minutes. Finally, add the cane sugar, vinegar, ketchup, mustard, and ground cloves, season with salt and pepper, and simmer with the lid off for 30 minutes, stirring occasionally.

2. Peel the potatoes and cut them into batons roughly 1 cm thick. Place the potato batons in ice-cold water to remove the starch.

3. Meanwhile, put the deep-frying oil in a high-sided pot and bring to 320°F over a high heat. To test whether the oil is hot enough, drop in one of the potato batons. If bubbles rise hissing to the top, you know it's ready. Remove the potato batons from the icy water, pat dry thoroughly with kitchen paper, and deep-fry in batches (depending on the size of your pot) for about 4–5 minutes, until the chips are a pale yellow. Lift the chips out with a slotted spoon and place in a dish lined with kitchen paper for any excess oil to drip off. Pre-fry all of the chips like this, heating up the oil in between if you need to.

4. Now heat the oil to 375°F. Deep-fry the chips in batches a second time until they are crispy and golden brown. Lift the finished chips out of the oil, drain again in a dish lined with kitchen paper, and sprinkle with coarse sea salt.

5. Toast the burger buns briefly, cut them in half and fill them with the thick mince mixture. Arrange on large flat plates with the chips and serve with mayonnaise or ketchup.

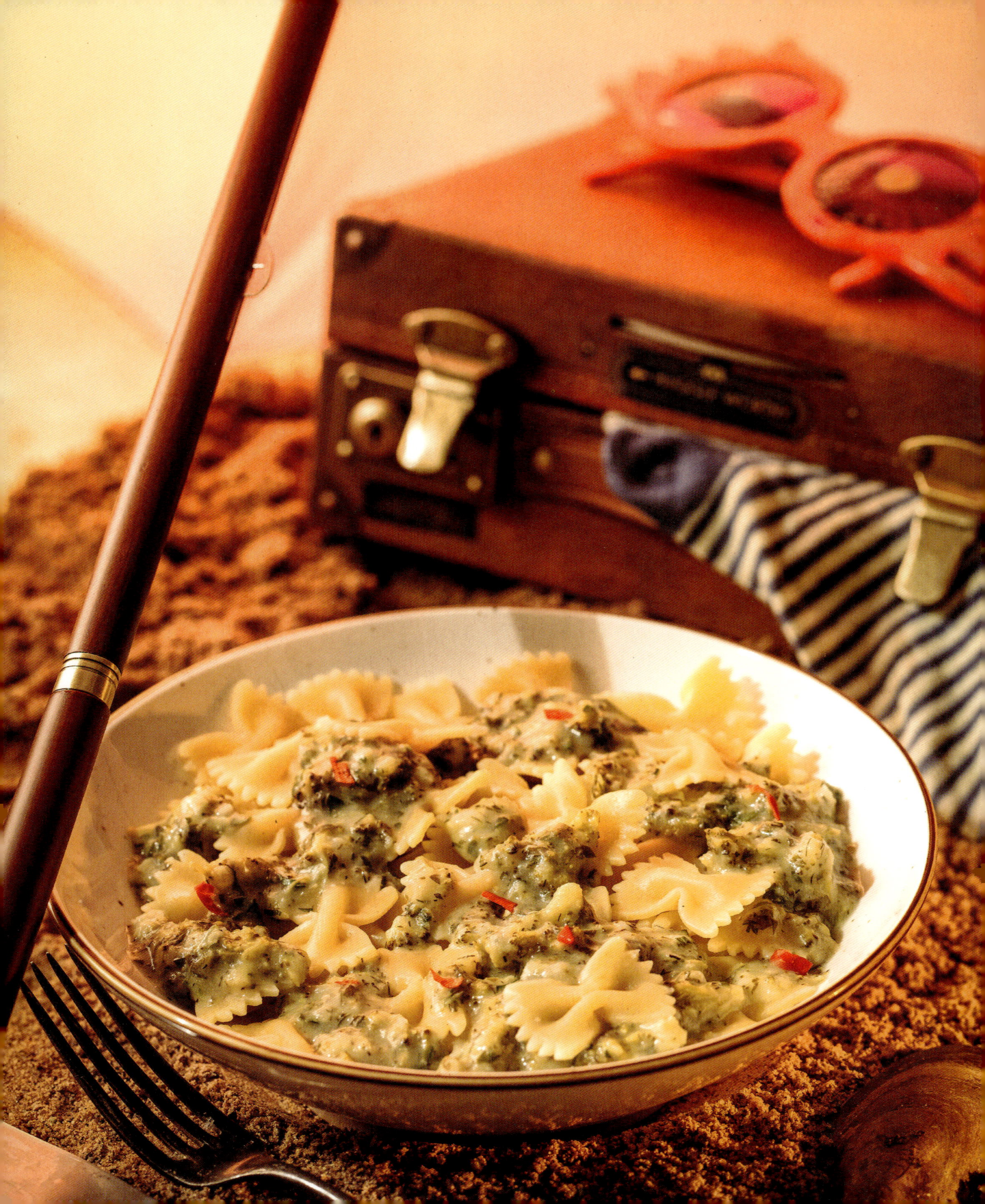

Dobby's Bowtie Pasta with Broccoli Sauce

INGREDIENTS
SERVES 2–3

1 tbsp butter
1 shallot, finely chopped
1 garlic clove, finely chopped
4¼ cups frozen broccoli
⅓ cup vegetable stock
1¾ cups mini farfalle
½ bunch of parsley, finely chopped
13 tbsp crème fraîche
salt, pepper
nutmeg, freshly grated
¼ cup ricotta

1. Melt the butter in a pot and sauté the shallots and garlic until translucent. Add the frozen broccoli and the vegetable stock, bring to a boil briefly, then cover and simmer over a medium heat for 6–7 minutes.

2. Meanwhile, cook the mini farfalle in a pot with lots of generously salted water until al dente (firm to the bite).

3. Add ¾ of the finely chopped parsley and the crème fraîche to the broccoli sauce. Purée everything with a handheld blender until smooth, then process until the sauce goes frothy. Season with salt, pepper, and freshly grated nutmeg.

4. Drain the pasta and fold into the broccoli sauce. Arrange on deep-rimmed plates. Crumble the ricotta and sprinkle it over the top. Garnish with the rest of the parsley.

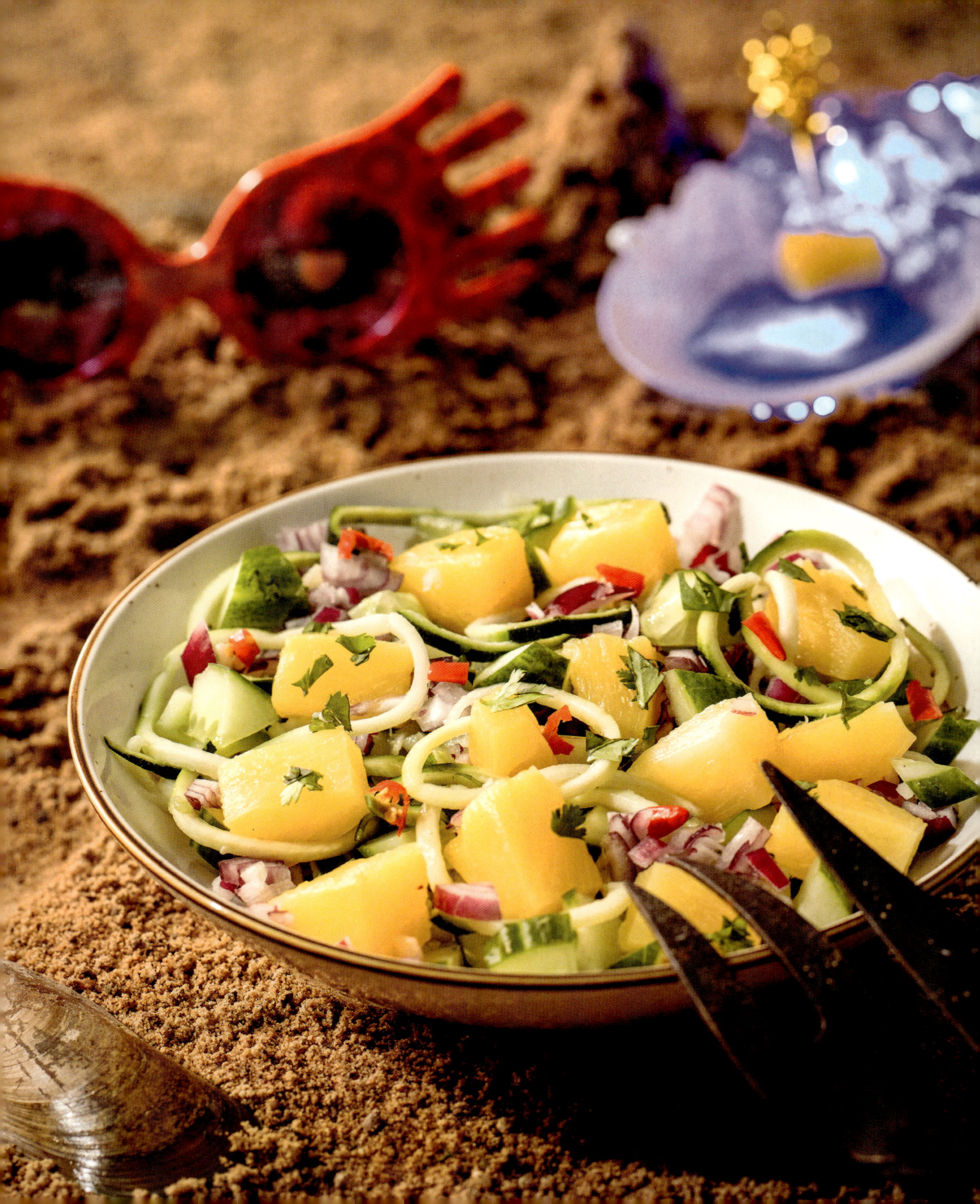

Dobby's spicy pineapple salad

INGREDIENTS
SERVES 4

2⅓ cups pineapple (ideally fresh, otherwise from a can)
1 zucchini
1 large red onion, finely diced
1 cucumber, diced
juice and zest of 1 lime
1 red chile, finely sliced
½ bunch of fresh cilantro, finely chopped
freshly ground black pepper

Plus:
A spiralizer

1. Peel the pineapple and remove the woody stalk. Cut the flesh into bite-size pieces and put them in a large bowl.

2. Use the spiralizer to cut the zucchini into thin spaghetti-like ribbons.

3. Add the zucchini ribbons, onion, and cucumber to the pineapple pieces and mix everything together carefully. Fold in the juice and zest of the lime, the chile, and the cilantro. Season with a little freshly ground pepper and leave to stand for 15 minutes. Pour off any excess liquid.

4. Mix everything through thoroughly once more immediately before serving. This is great served with fresh French bread.

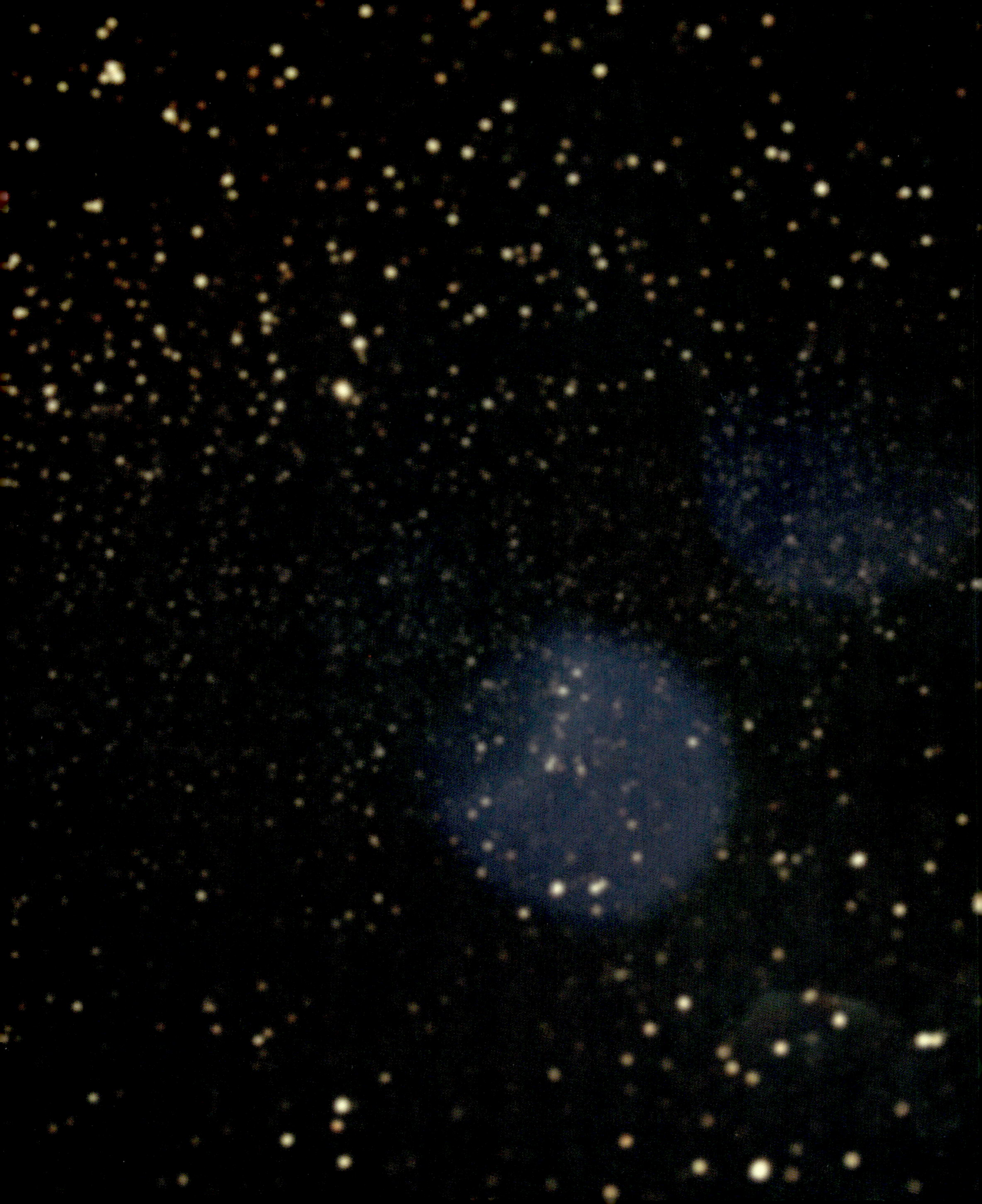

The Deathday Party of Nearly Headless Nick

Nearly Headless Nick—known in life as Sir Nicholas de Mimsy-Porpington—is the ghost of Gryffindor House. His unfortunate demise over 500 years ago was all down to a stupid misunderstanding. In 1492, he performed a teeth-straightening spell on a noblewoman, but it went awry, causing her to grow a pair of unsightly fangs in their place. Yet instead of allowing Sir Nicholas to rectify his mistake, he was abruptly sentenced to death. Alas, the executioner's axe was blunt, believe it or not, so that after some 45 blows he was very definitely dead, but only nearly decapitated. He has haunted Hogwarts ever since, and holds a celebration on his deathday, October 31, every year. In their first year at the school of witchcraft and wizardry, Harry, Ron, and Hermione are invited to attend—although they might have preferred to be spared this honor, due to the somewhat dubious selection of dishes served up by their host ...

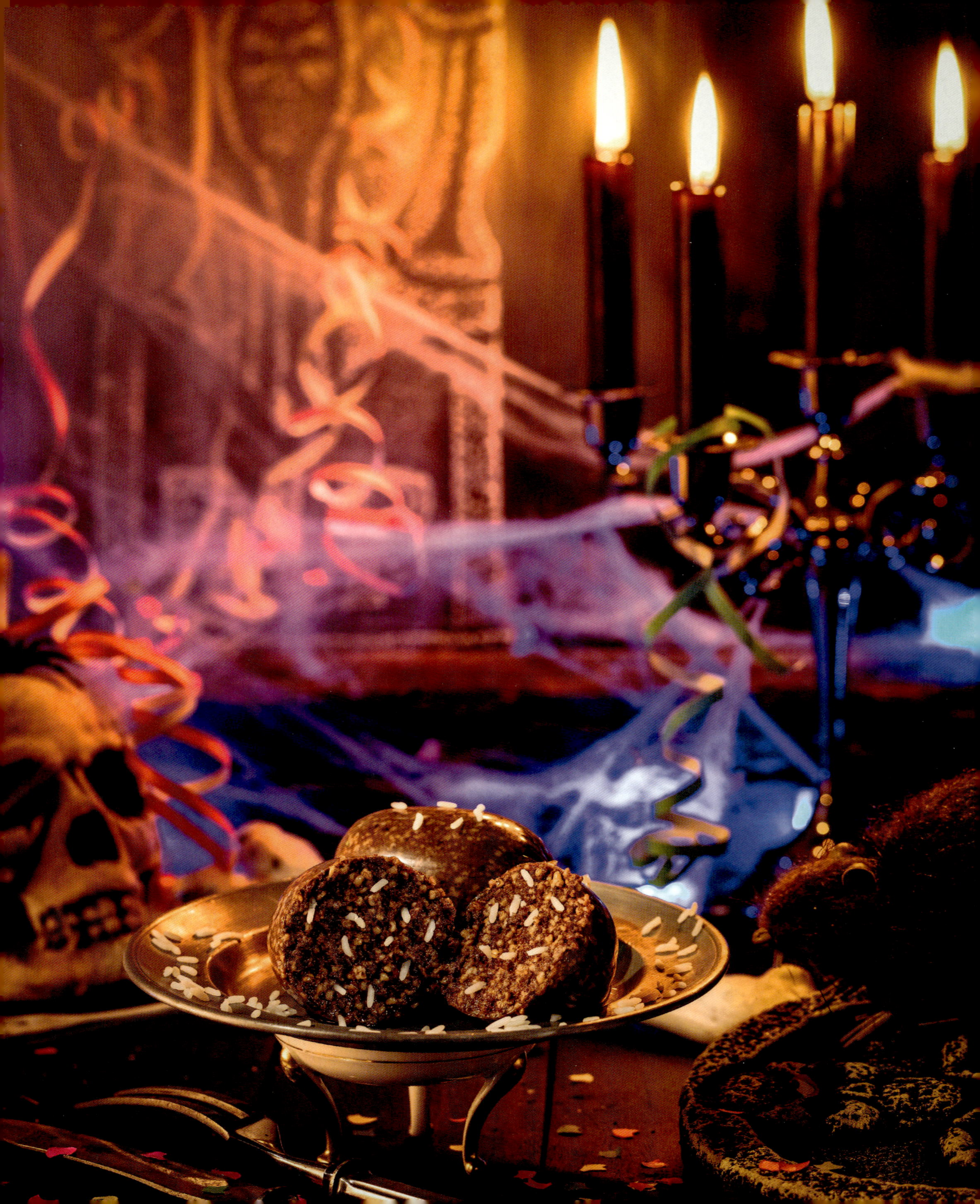

Maggoty Haggis

INGREDIENTS
SERVES 4

1 sheep's stomach
1 sheep's kidney
1 sheep's heart
1 sheep's lung
1 bay leaf
4 juniper berries
1 clove
2 onions, finely diced
3½ oz kidney fat
1 sheep's liver
2½ cups oatmeal
salt, pepper
1 pinch of nutmeg
1 pinch of Cayenne pepper

Plus:
sewing needle, kitchen string

1. Wash the sheep's stomach carefully. Remove the flaps of skin and fat and soak the stomach overnight in cold salted water. Now turn the stomach inside out, wash the inside of it thoroughly and carefully scrape off any residues with the blunt side of a knife.

2. Put the kidney, heart, and lung in a large pot and cover with cold, generously salted water. Add the bay leaf, juniper berries, and clove, bring to a boil over a medium heat, then simmer, with the lid off, for about 1½ hours. Remove from the stove, strain the cooking liquid through a sieve into another pot, then set the cooked offal aside.

3. Fry the onions and oatmeal in a dry pan over a medium heat until golden brown. Cut half of the liver, heart, and lung (having removed the windpipe, if necessary) into fine dice. Chop the rest of the liver and the kidney fat roughly and mix them together in a separate bowl.

4. Mix the cooked meat, liver and fat, and onion and oatmeal together in a large bowl and season with salt, pepper, nutmeg, and Cayenne pepper. Gradually pour in the reserved stock, stirring constantly, until you have a soft mixture.

5. Pour this into the cleaned sheep's stomach. Note: Only make the stomach ⅔ full, as the oatmeal will expand during cooking. Then carefully press the air out of the stomach, roughly sew it up with the needle and kitchen string, and prick it several times with a knife. Cook in a large pot over a medium heat, with the lid off, for about 3–4 hours, topping up the water as it boils off.

6. After the cooking time is up, remove the string and arrange on a platter with cooked white rice "maggots". Be careful: The stomach is liable to burst! Be careful when cutting it open so that you don't end up needing to redecorate!

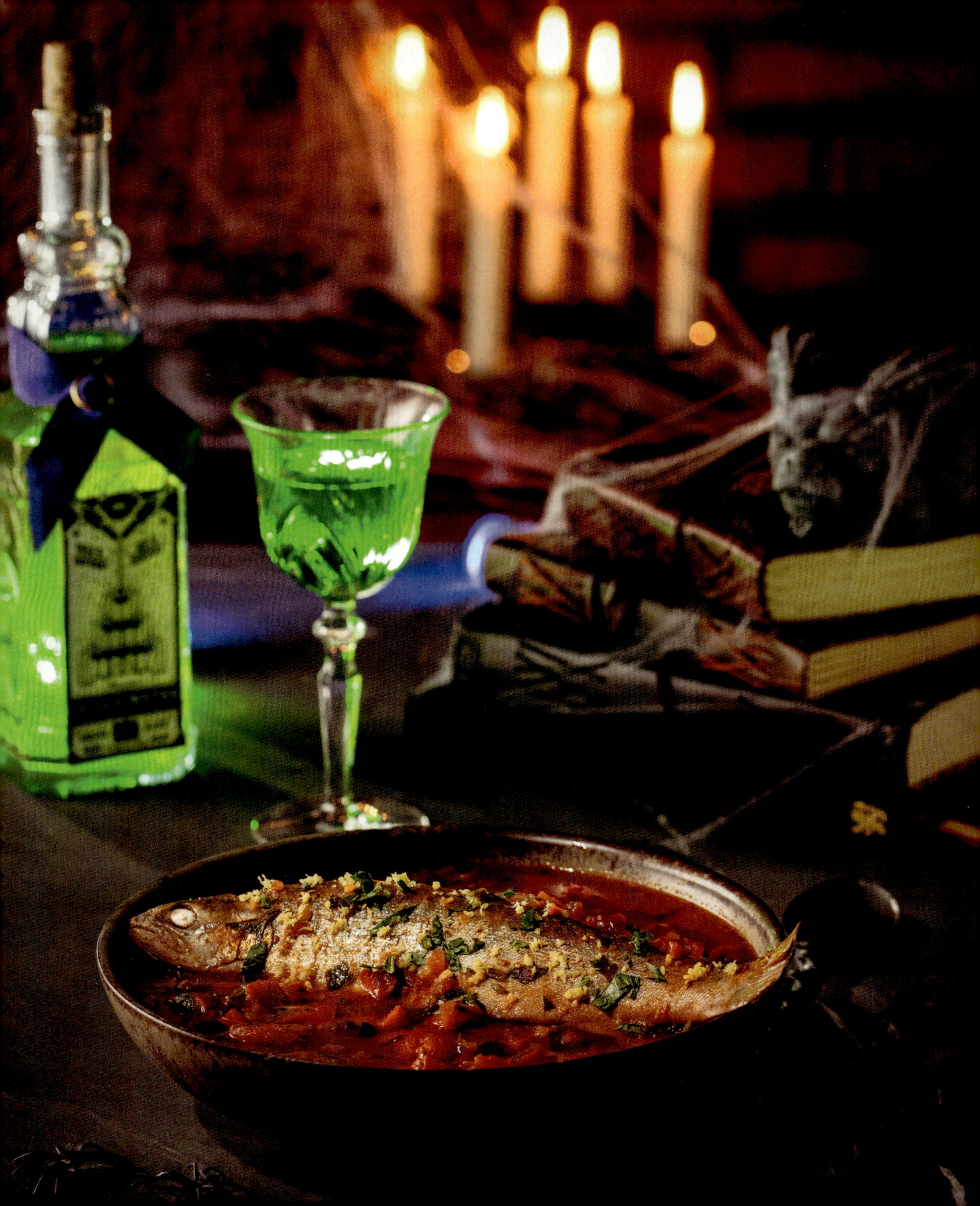

Rotten Fish

INGREDIENTS
SERVES 4

2 organic lemons
4–4½ lb red snapper, gutted, whole including head, or similar fish
⅓ cup olive oil
2 shallots, finely diced
4 garlic cloves, finely chopped
2 red peppers, thinly sliced
1 cup red wine (dry)
1½ cups tomatoes for pizza
2 bay leaves
1 tsp mild red paprika
½ tsp Cayenne pepper
salt
1 small pinch of pepper
1¼ cups fish stock
fresh parsley, finely chopped

1. Wash the lemons thoroughly. Zest one lemon and squeeze both of them. Brush the insides and outsides of the cleaned fish with the lemon juice. Set them aside.

2. Warm the oil in a large casserole over a high heat. Add the shallots and sauté until translucent. Add the garlic and diced pepper and briefly sauté along with the shallots. Deglaze the pan with the red wine. Add the tomatoes, bay leaves, and mild red paprika, then season with Cayenne pepper, salt, and a small pinch of sugar. Pour in the fish stock and simmer over a medium heat for 5 minutes.

3. Salt the fish inside and out, lay them in the sauce so that they are completely covered, and simmer for 25–30 minutes.

4. Season to taste, fold in some parsley, scatter over more freshly chopped parsley, and serve with bread or rice.

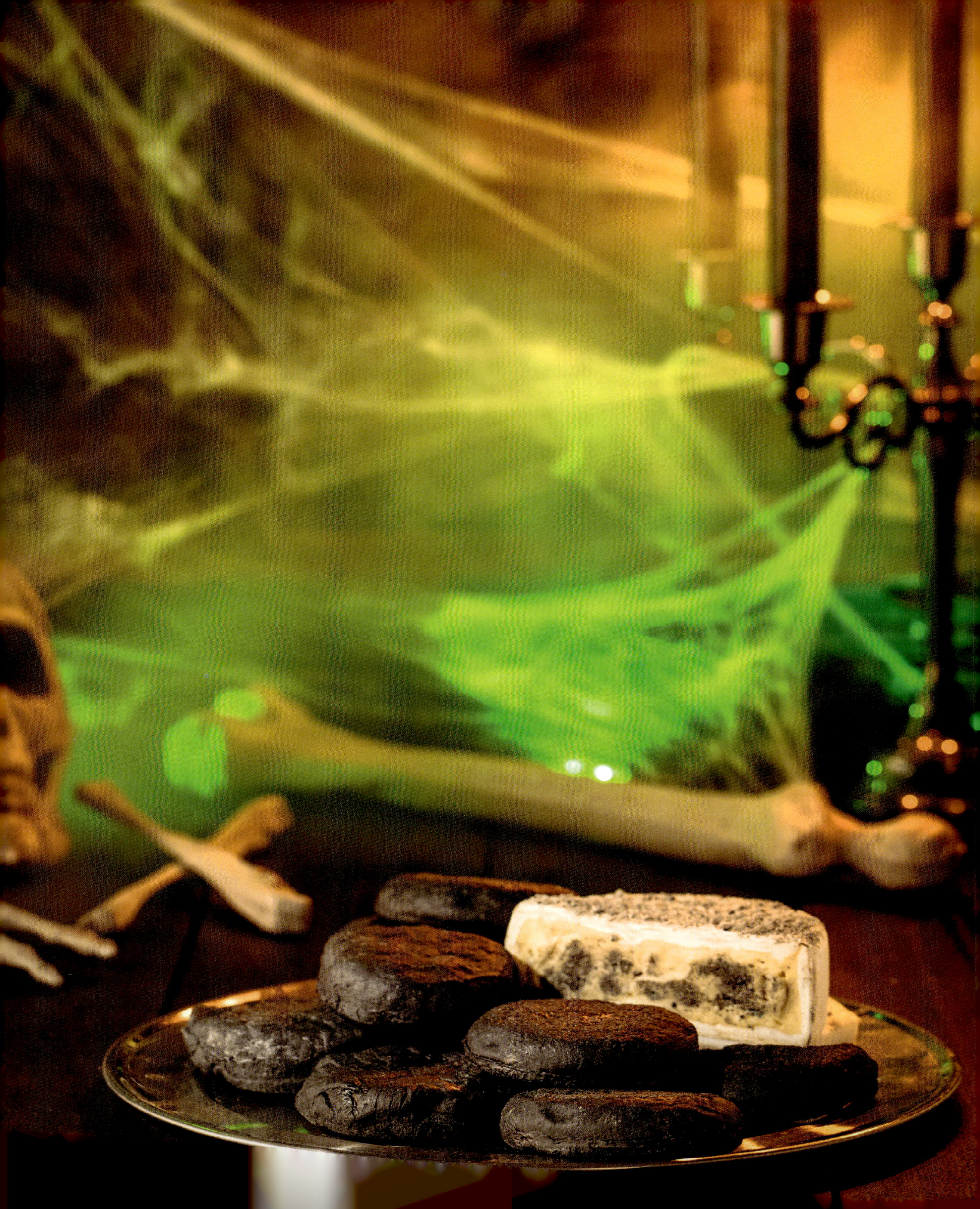

Cakes burned charcoal-black and moldy cheese

INGREDIENTS
SERVES 6–8

⅓ oz ground activated charcoal
2 tsp fine salt
⅔ cup full cream milk
5 cups pastry flour
2 tbsp clarified butter
2 tsp of dried yeast
⅓ cup sparkling mineral water
butter
8 oz good blue cheese, in one piece (e.g. Roquefort or Stilton)

Plus:
cookie cutters (diameter about 3 ½ in.)

1. Mix the activated carbon, salt, and milk together in a small bowl. Leave to stand for 10 minutes.

2. Mix the flour, clarified butter, and dried yeast in a separate bowl. Pour in the mineral water, stir thoroughly, then knead the mixture with your hands until you have a soft, stretchy dough. Shape the dough into a ball, cover with a clean tea towel, and leave to rise in a warm place for at least 1 hour.

3. Roll out the dough to about ½ in. thick on a lightly floured countertop. Use a cookie cutter to cut out as many pastry circles as possible. Knead the rest of the dough again, roll it out once more, and cut out more circles until all of the dough has been used up. Cover the pastry discs with a clean tea towel and leave to rise for another half an hour.

4. Brush a non-stick frying pan with a thin coating of butter, warm over a medium heat, and bake the discs for about 2-3 minutes on each side. Place the cakes on a dish lined with kitchen paper to get rid of any excess butter and repeat the process until all of the cakes are done.

5. The cakes are best served warm with a piece of good blue cheese and perhaps a little butter.

SIR NICHOLAS
DE MIMSY—PORPINGTON
† 31. 1 149

Tombstone cake with tar-like frosting

INGREDIENTS
MAKES 1 GRAVESTONE CAKE

½ cup dark chocolate, roughly chopped
1 cup soft butter plus a little extra for greasing the baking tin
¾ cup sugar
4 eggs
1½ cups sour cream
9 oz flour
2 tsp baking powder
1 pinch of salt
2 tbsp cocoa powder
2¼ cups sour cherries (from a jar), drained
icing sugar for dusting (optional)
1¾ cups whipping cream, chilled
4 tsp of cream stiffener
2 tsp vanilla sugar
black food coloring
dark chocolate sauce, to taste

Plus:
a rectangular baking tin (about 8 x 12 in.)

1. Preheat the oven to 355°F. Line a baking sheet with baking parchment and place the baking tin on top. Grease the baking tin generously with butter.

2. Melt the dark chocolate in a bowl over a saucepan with a little boiling water.

3. Mix the butter with the sugar in a separate bowl. Gradually add the eggs and mix them in. Add the sour cream and work it into the mixture.

4. In a third bowl, mix the flour with the baking powder, salt, and cocoa and add to the butter and sour cream mixture. Mix everything together well. Fold in the melted chocolate and the drained cherries.

5. Pour the batter into the baking tin and smooth over the top. Bake in the preheated oven for about 50–55 minutes, or until a toothpick inserted into the middle of the cake comes out clean. Then take the cake out of the oven and leave it to cool. Remove it from the baking tin. Dust it with a little icing sugar (optional). Now chill it in the refrigerator until you're ready to ice it.

6. In a mixing bowl, beat the cold whipping cream with the cream stiffener and vanilla sugar until it forms stiff peaks. Stir in a few drops of black food coloring until the cream turns a nice shade of tombstone gray. Tip the colored whipped cream over the cake and use a spatula to spread it evenly over the top and sides. Drip the dark chocolate sauce to look like the "tar" running down the "gravestone." Gryffindor's house ghost couldn't be happier!

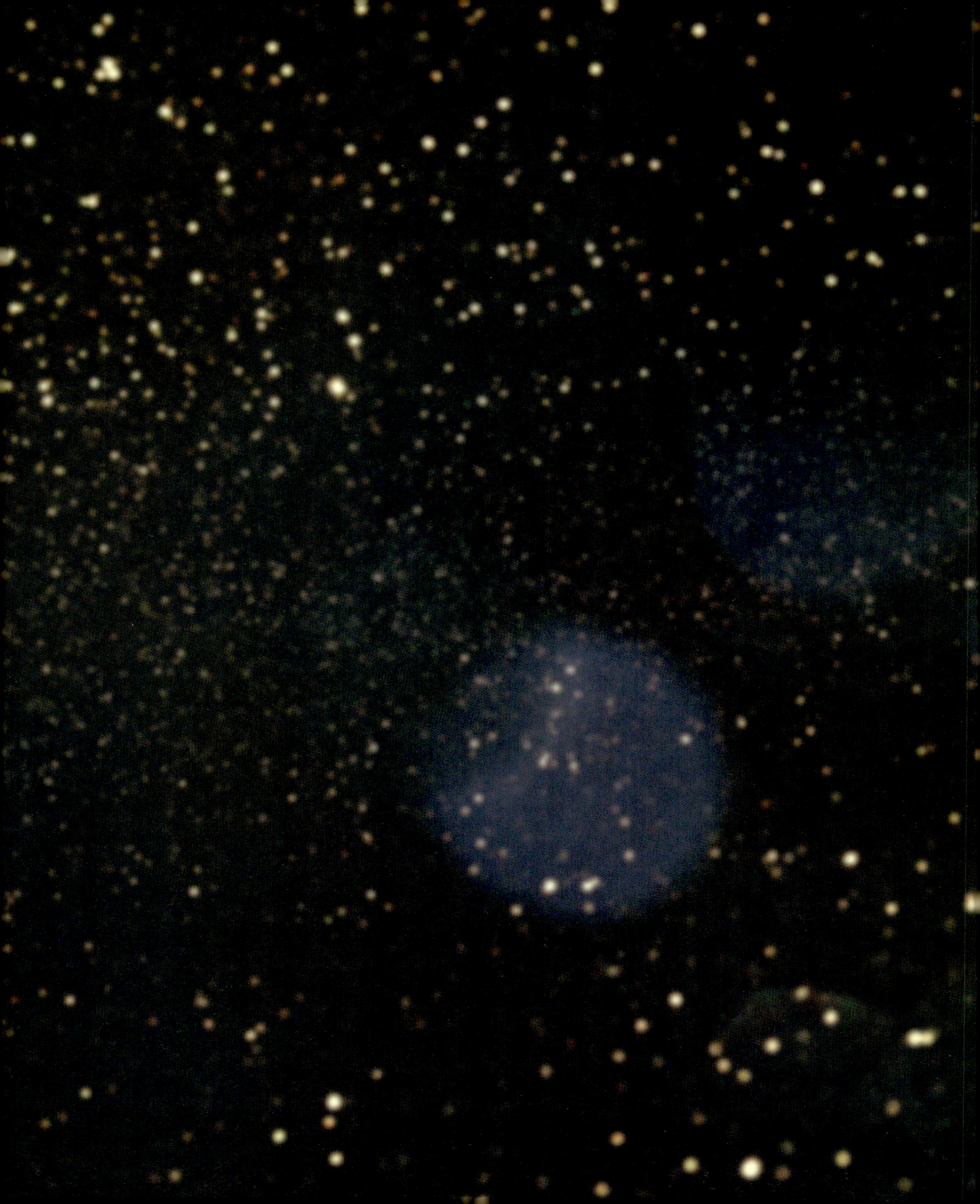

Magical Morsels from the Wizarding World

Beyond our drab and humdrum world, an entirely different realm lies hidden, where magic and witchcraft are as commonplace as taking out the trash, bad weather, and taxes; where mail is delivered by owls, felt hats break into song, and an affable giant with a pink umbrella might be spotted rattling through the air on his trusty motorcycle. Unfortunately, we Muggles are blind to that world and its wonders, large and small. But that's no reason to despair. We might not be able to go for a stroll down Diagon Alley, tuck into sweet treats at *Honeydukes*, or enjoy a butterbeer or two in pubs like the *Three Broomsticks* and the *Leaky Cauldron*, but with a little imagination and skill, we can conjure up our very own specialties from the wizarding world. No magic wands required—just original recipes and the right ingredients!

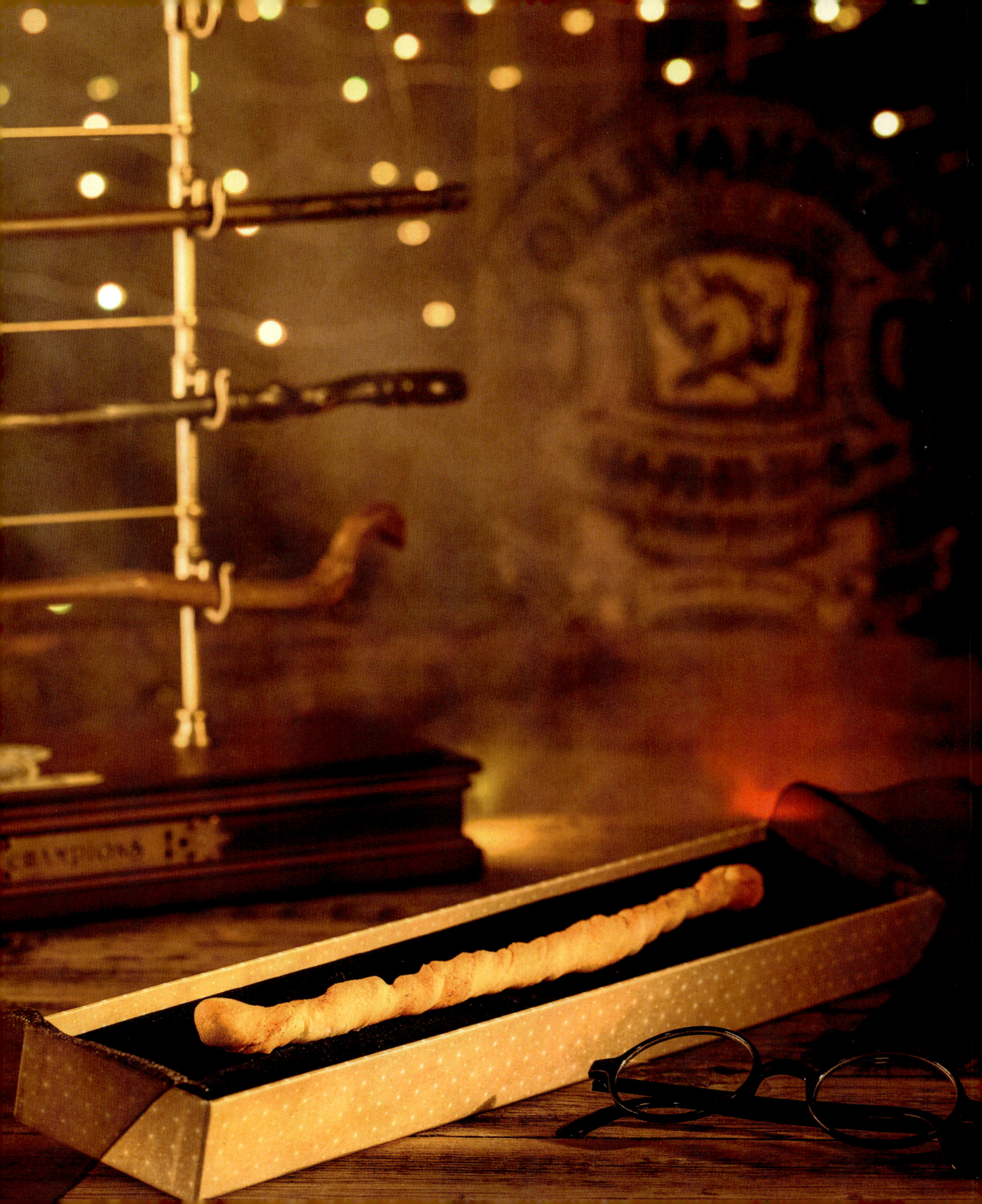

Magic Wands

INGREDIENTS
MAKES ABOUT 25 MAGIC WANDS

2 cups flour
1 tsp dried yeast
1 pinch sugar
½ cup lukewarm water
2 tbsp olive oil
1 tsp salt
dried herbs of your choice (e.g. basil, oregano, thyme)

1. Mix the flour and dried yeast together in a bowl. Knead together with all of the other ingredients until you have a smooth dough that is no longer sticky and pulls away from the sides of the bowl of its own accord. Add a little more flour if necessary. Cover the dough with a clean tea towel and put it in a warm place for 1 hour to rise.

2. Meanwhile, heat the oven to 355°F and line two baking sheets with baking parchment.

3. Once the dough has risen, knead it thoroughly once more with your hands and roll it out with a rolling pin as thinly as possible on a lightly floured countertop. Use a sharp knife or pizza cutter to cut it into thin strips about ½ in. wide. Now roll these into thin sticks approximately 10 in. long and place them on the lines baking sheets, leaving a little distance between them, and brush with a little water. Sprinkle them with dried herbs (optional).

4. Bake for about 12–15 minutes in the preheated oven, then take the magic wands and leave them to cool down completely, to get them as crispy as possible.

POLYJUICE POTION

FROM THE APOTHECARIUM OF HORACE E. F. SLUGHORN

Polyjuice potion

INGREDIENTS
FOR 1 TRANSFORMATION

a few ice cubes
½ fl oz Blue Curaçao syrup (non-alcoholic)
3 fl oz orange juice
3 fl oz mineral water (sparkling)
1 sprig of mint, as garnish (optional)

1. Place a few ice cubes in a tall glass. Add the Blue Curaçao and orange juice, the pour the mineral water on top. Stir slowly so that all of the liquids are well mixed and the drink takes on a rich green hue.

2. Garnish with a sprig of fresh mint (optional).

> **DOBBY THE HOUSE-ELF'S TIP:** Give this drink a little more oomph by replacing alcohol-free Blue Curaçao with the alcoholic version. Add 1 fl oz vodka and sparkling wine instead of mineral water.

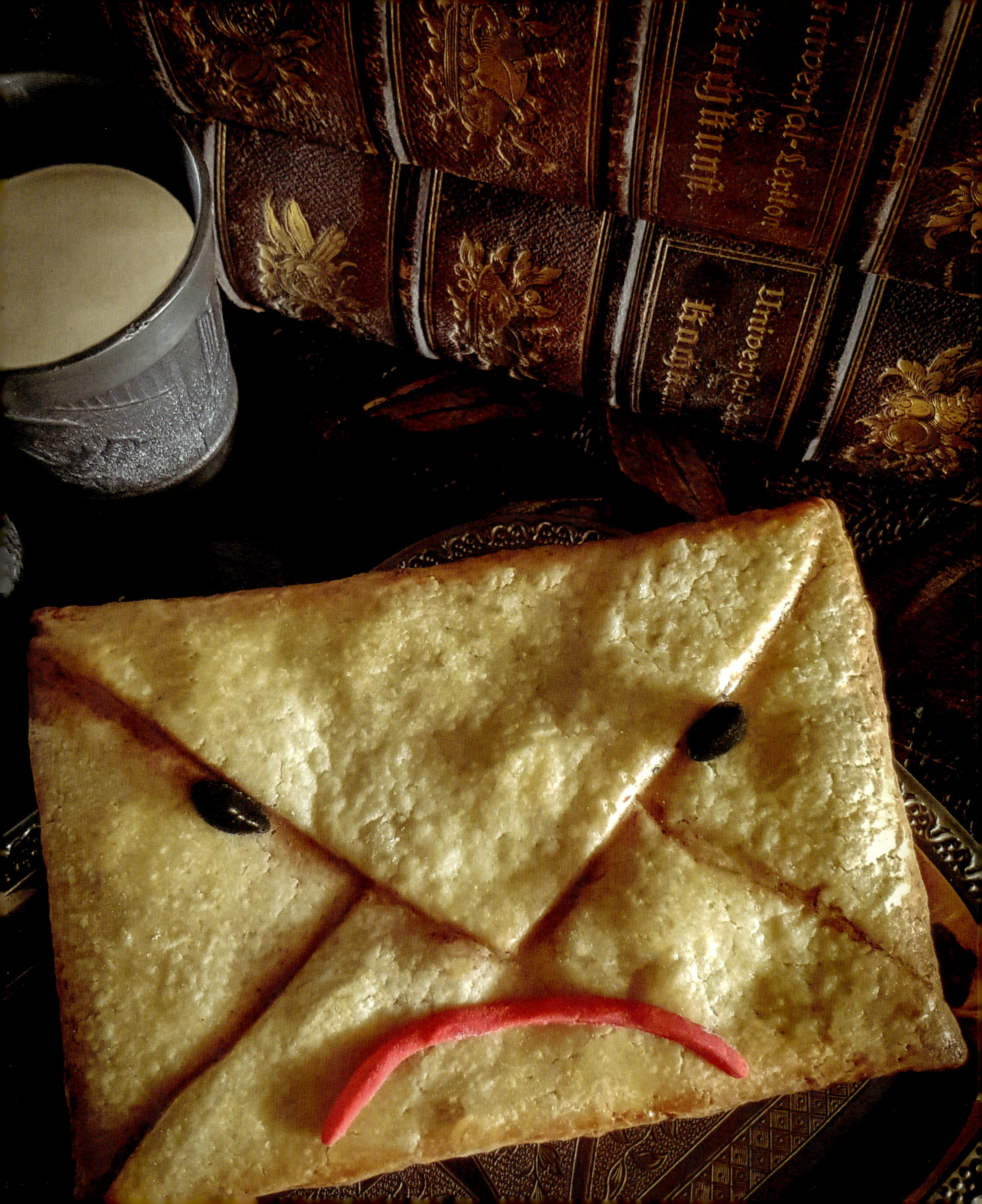

Shortcrust howlers

INGREDIENTS
MAKES 5 HOWLERS

For the mixture:
1 cup cold butter, in small pieces
½ cup sugar
1 dash of lemon juice
1 pinch of salt
1 egg
2⅓ cups flour
1 tsp of vanilla sugar
¼ cup sour cherry jam

For the decoration:
1 bar chocolate couverture
cocoa powder
5 black (or dark brown) M&Ms
1½ tbsp red fondant icing

Plus:
A6 envelope (4 ¾ x 6 ½") as a template

1. Put the butter, sugar, lemon juice, salt, egg, and vanilla sugar in a bowl and work it through with the dough hooks of a handheld mixer. Sieve the flour into the bowl and quickly work everything into a smooth dough, first with the dough hooks and then with your hands. Divide the dough into four pieces of equal size and shape them into flat tiles. Wrap each of them tightly in clingfilm and chill in the refrigerator for at least 3 hours.

2. Meanwhile, completely unfold an A6 envelope, unsticking all of the corners and seals until it can be laid out as a single sheet of paper. Place the unfolded envelope on a piece of cardboard, trace the outline with a felt tip pen, then cut it out. Now you have a sturdy template for your shortcrust envelopes.

3. Preheat the oven to 340°F. Line a baking sheet with baking parchment.

4. Take the dough out of the refrigerator 10 minutes before working with it again. Dust the countertop with a little flour, then roll out the dough as thinly as possible, to form a square. Place the template in the middle of the dough and cut around the edge with a sharp knife.

5. Use the back of a large knife or a dough scraper to press the edges of the envelope gently inwards, so that a postcard-sized rectangle appears in the middle. These indented edges will form the "bend points" and indicate exactly where the dough needs to be folded for everything to fit together properly at the end. Spread the rectangle in the middle with 1 tsp sour cherry jam, in an even layer. Now it's time to fold the envelope. First fold in the side corners, then the bottom one, and finally the top flap, which will slightly overlap all of the others.

6. Carefully place the pastry envelope on a lightly floured countertop and smooth it out with an angled palette knife. Fold the other envelopes in the same way. Knead the remaining scraps dough and use them to form one more envelope. Place the envelopes on the baking sheet, leaving enough of a gap between them, and bake for 15–20 minutes in a preheated oven. Take out of the oven and leave to cool down completely.

7. Once the envelopes are cool, melt a little chocolate couverture over a saucepan of boiling water. Cut the M&Ms in half with a sharp knife and stick them to the envelope with a little couverture to form the eyes. Make the mouth out of red fondant icing and fix it in place with chocolate, too. Finally, use a small brush to dust the edges with a little cocoa powder to emphasize the lines of the howler.

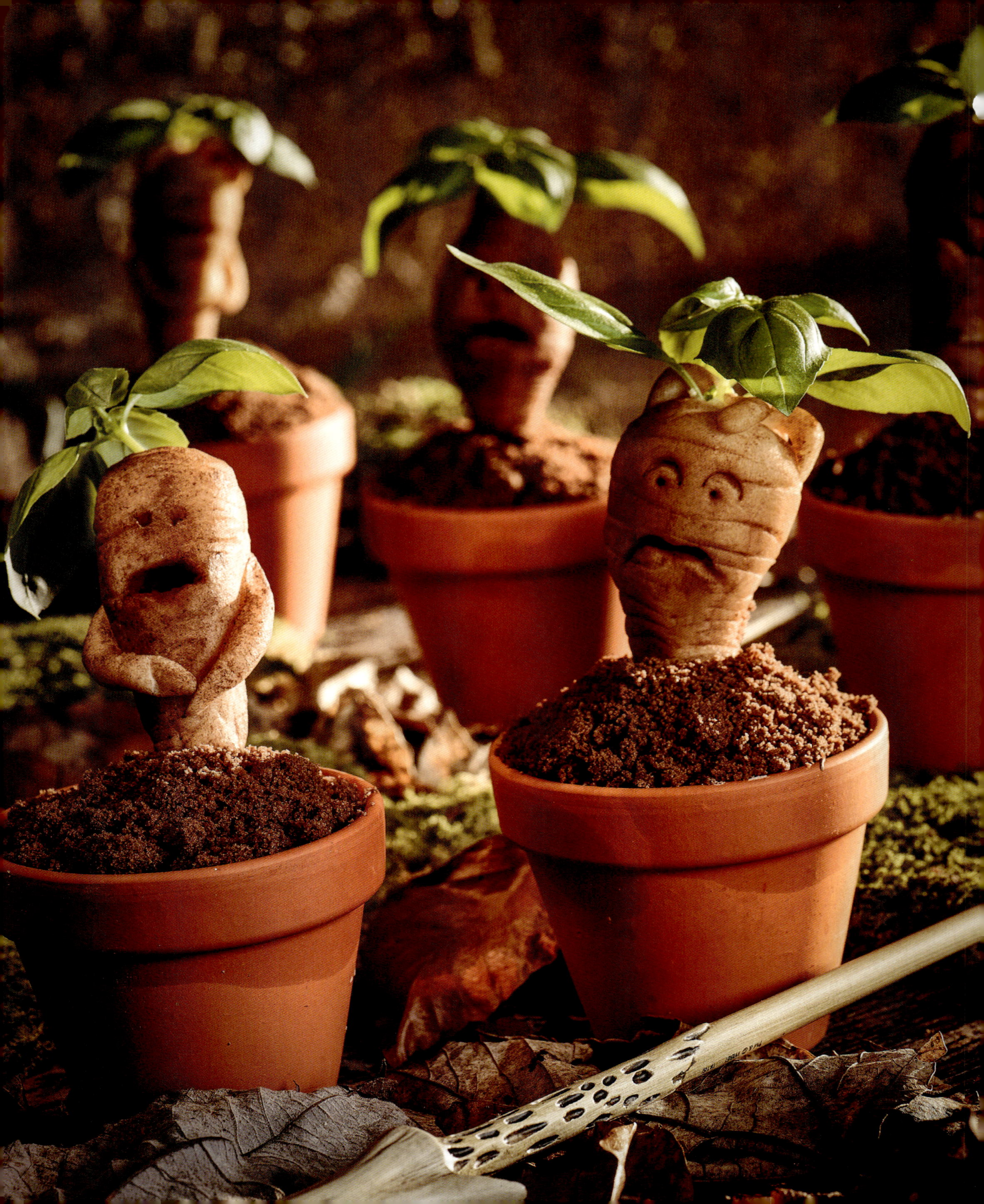

Baby Mandrakes

INGREDIENTS
MAKES 10 BABY MANDRAKES

For the muffins:
2 1/3 cups flour
2/3 cup cocoa powder
1 tsp baking powder
1 tsp baking soda
1 pinch of salt
7 tbsp soft butter
1 cup sugar
1 tsp vanilla extract
2 eggs
1 cup buttermilk
1 cup dark chocolate, chopped

For the baby mandrakes:
2 cups marzipan paste
cocoa powder, for dusting
20 herb leaves (e.g. basil, mint)

For the chocolate frosting:
2/3 cup cream cheese
2 tbsp icing sugar
1 heaped tbsp cocoa powder

Plus:
3 paper muffin liners,
10 small plant pots

1. Soak the clay pots in water for 1 hour. Cut circles of the right dimensions out of baking parchment and place them at the bottom of the pots to ensure that no dough can escape.

2. Preheat the oven to 390°F. Mix the flour, cocoa powder, baking powder, bicarbonate of soda, and salt together in a small bowl. In a larger bowl, beat the butter, sugar, and vanilla extract together with a handheld mixer. Add the eggs one by one and continue beating until you have a fluffy mixture. Mix in the buttermilk thoroughly.

3. Now fold the dry ingredients from the smaller bowl into the butter mixture. Remove enough of the mixture for three muffins and spoon it into the muffin liners. Fold the chopped chocolate into the rest of the mixture and spoon this into the clay pots. Put the pots and the filled muffin liners in the oven for 25 minutes, then take them out and leave to cool down completely. Once cool, remove the muffins from their cases and crumble them in a bowl.

4. Divide the marzipan into 10 pieces of equal size and shape each piece into a baby mandrake root, flattening the undersides a little. Give the mandrakes a bit of character by scoring them across with a knife to make little grooves, piercing eyes into them with a toothpick, and indenting them with a spoon to give them mouths. Then use a brush to dust them with cocoa powder. Finally, use the toothpick to pierce a hole in each mandrake head, into which you can later insert the edible leaves. Put them in the refrigerator to chill.

5. Mix the cream cheese, icing sugar, and 1 heaped tablespoon of cocoa powder together in a small bowl until smooth. Coat the top of the muffins in the pots generously with this frosting, "glue" the mandrakes to them, and decorate all around them with the crumbled "cake soil." Put the herb leaves into the holes at the tops of the mandrakes and enjoy the astonished faces of the Muggles when they come face to face with these magical creatures!

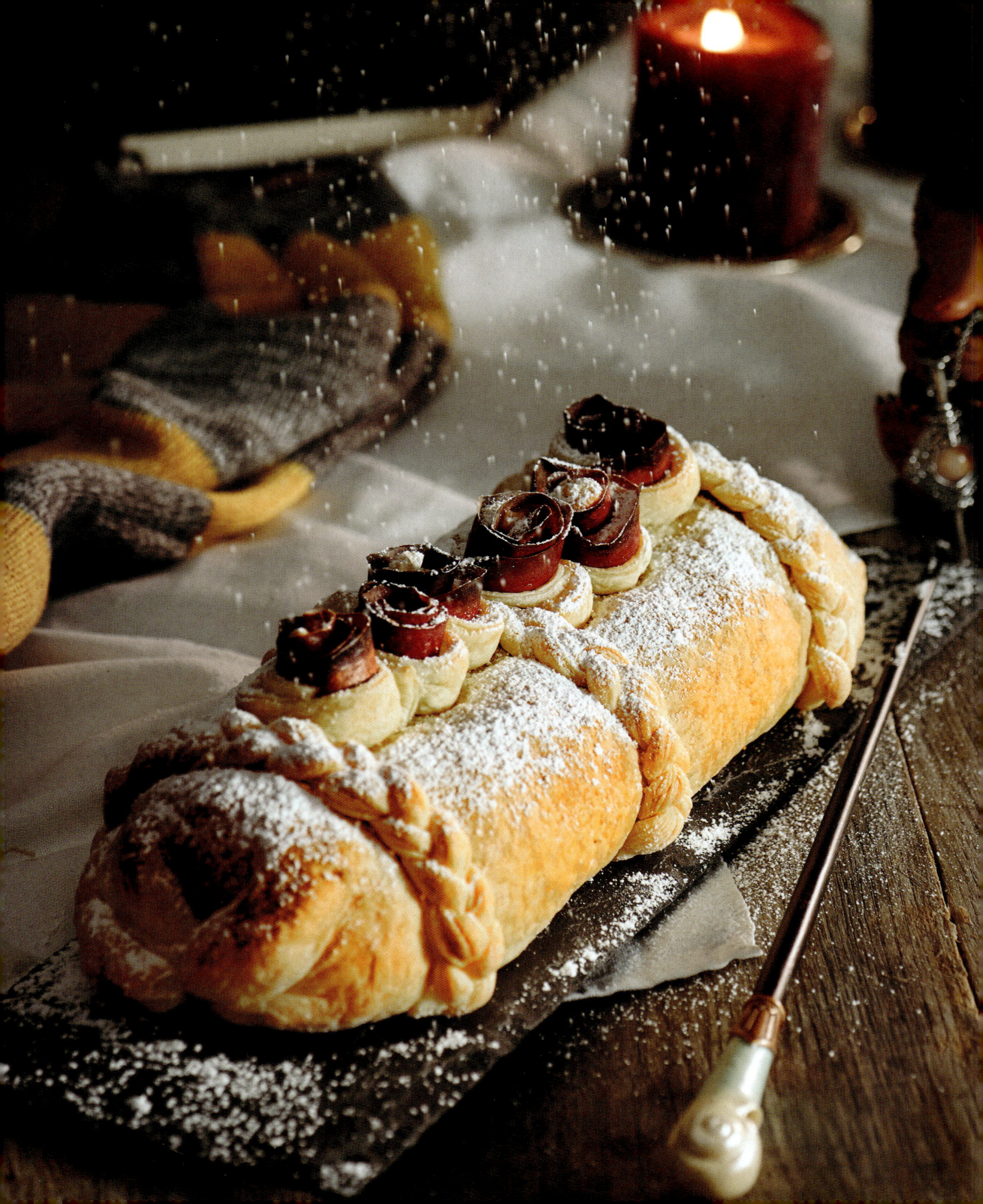

Enchanted Apple Strudel

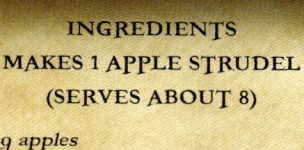

CONTAINS ALCOHOL

INGREDIENTS
MAKES 1 APPLE STRUDEL
(SERVES ABOUT 8)

- 5 cooking apples
- 3½ tbsp butter
- ¾ cup raisins
- 1¼ cup soft oatmeal
- ½ cup sugar
- 1 tbsp cinnamon
- 1 shot of rum
- 2 sheets of frozen puff pastry
- icing sugar, for dusting

1. Wash and dry the apples and carefully peel them with an asparagus peeler so that as much of the peel as possible comes off in one piece (ideally in a spiral). Set the peel aside and cut the apples into small pieces.

2. Preheat the oven to 375°F (fan).

3. Put the butter and raisins in a pan over a low heat and toss well. Once the butter has melted, add the oatmeal, sugar, and cinnamon. Then add the apple chunks and rum to the pan, mix everything together well, and cook for a few minutes.

4. Meanwhile, roll out the puff pastry. Roll out the first sheet and set it aside; use the second to create decorative braids and rosettes. To do this, cut the sheet into four strips of equal size (about 1-1 ½ in. wide), parallel to the long edge.

5. Remove the apple and raisin mixture from the pan and spread it in an even ridge down the first strip of pastry. Now fold the dough along both of the long sides and at the ends, and press down to seal the roll tightly.

6. Make braided bands from three of the four strips of pastry. To do this, cut the three strips into three thinner strips and then plait them to form a braid. Carefully wrap the braided bands around the strudel and press them down with slightly moistened fingers.

7. Now cut the fourth strip of dough into three narrower strips, and then cut each of those in half lengthwise, so that you end up with six strips of equal size. Lay a piece of apple peel along each of these strips, then roll them into small rosettes and place them at regular intervals along the strudel. Bake the decorated strudel in the preheated oven for about 20 minutes until the pastry is golden brown. Take it out of the oven, dust with icing sugar, and be sure to leave it to stand for 30 minutes before cutting it into slices!

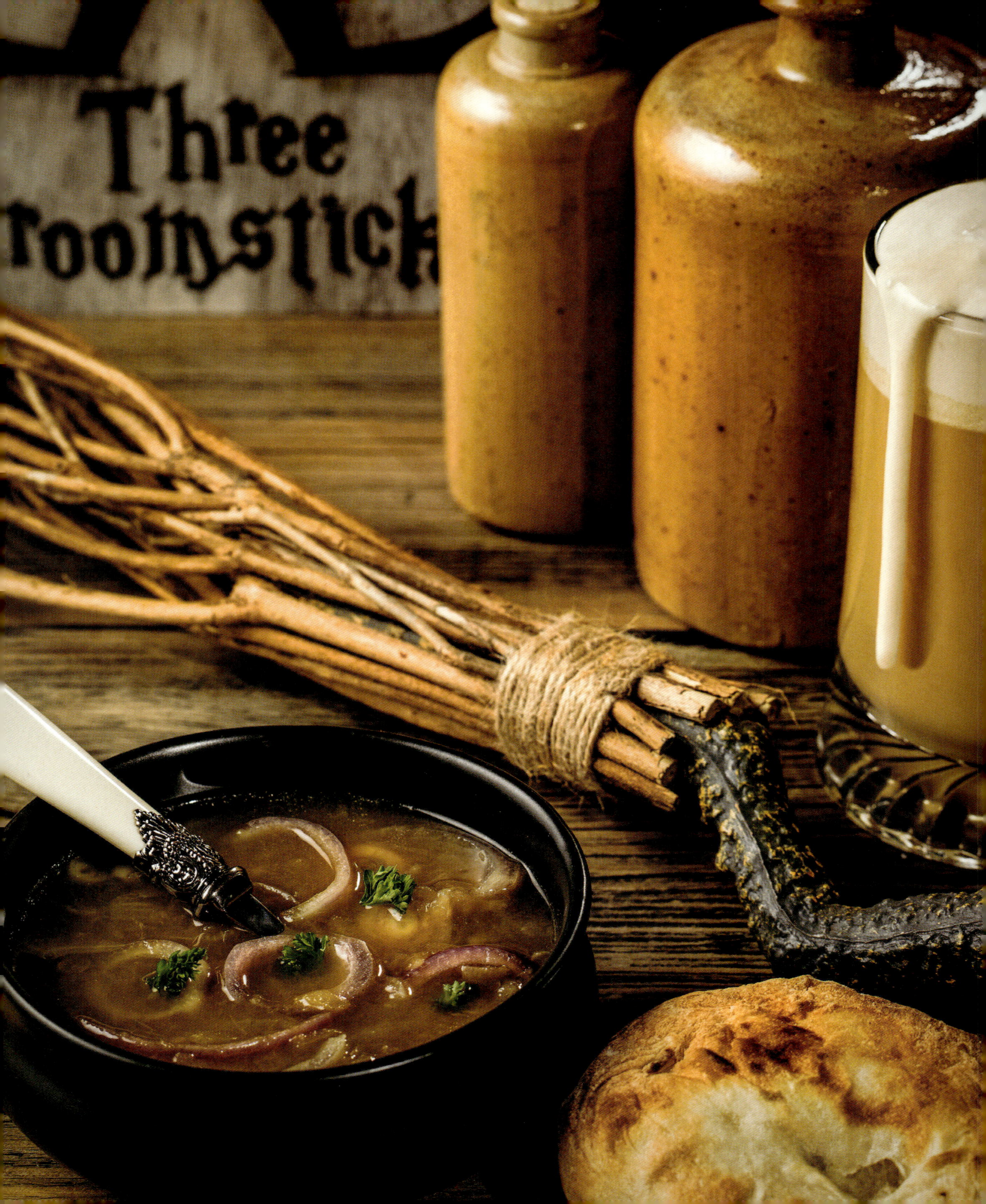
Three
roomstick

Kreacher's Onion Soup

INGREDIENTS
SERVES 4

zest of 1 lemon
½ bunch of parsley, finely chopped
3 tbsp clarified butter
2 lb onions, sliced into fine rings
4 garlic cloves, finely chopped
5 sprigs of thyme
1 bay leaf
1 tbsp cane sugar
4 cups vegetable stock
1¼ cups white wine
salt, freshly ground black pepper

1. Mix the lemon zest with the parsley in a small bowl, then set aside.

2. Melt the clarified butter in a large pot over a high heat. Add the onions and sauté, stirring constantly, until the onions are translucent and smell fragrant. Turn the heat down to medium, add the garlic and sauté it briefly. Now stir in the thyme, bay leaf, and cane sugar, pour in the vegetable stock and the white wine, and simmer gently for about 30 minutes.

3. Season the soup with salt and pepper, ladle it out into bowls, and scatter over the lemon and parsley mixture. Serve with toasted French bread.

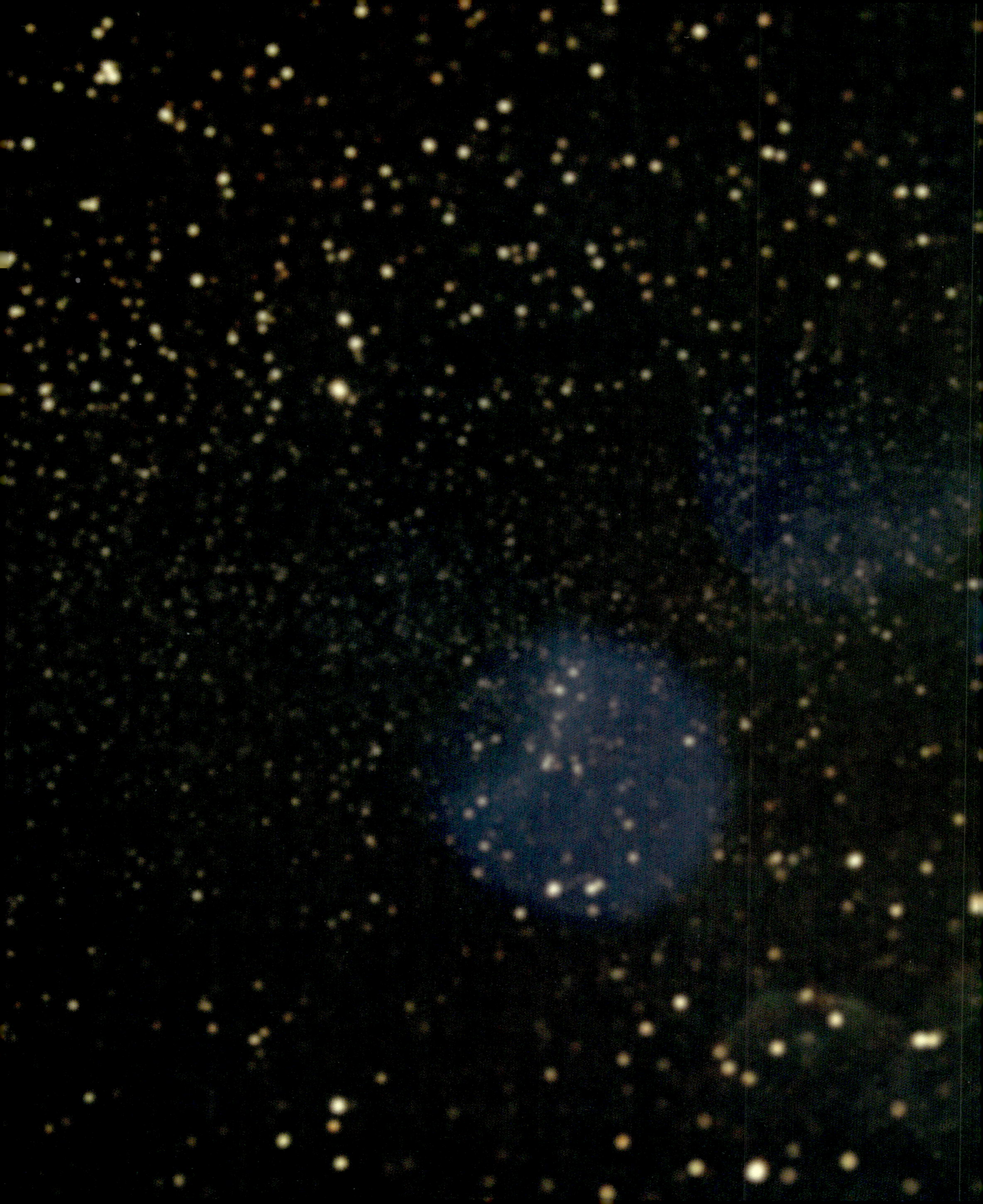

Classics from the Three Broomsticks

The *Three Broomsticks* tavern is on Hogsmeade's main street and has been run by Madam Rosmerta since time immemorial. Harry's father James and his Uncle Sirius enjoyed their very first butterbeer at Madam Rosmerta's back when they were students at Hogwarts. Despite her advanced age, the landlady is still so pretty that Ron regularly goes red about the ears when he has to order a drink from her. The *Three Broomsticks* is always full of people—not just students and teachers from the school of witchcraft and wizardry, but members of the wider magical community, too, including goblins and hags. Indeed, Minister for Magic Cornelius Fudge is a regular here, which isn't surprising when you consider that this pub has the best choice of drinks for miles around.

GULP & GUFFAW!
SIP & SHRIEK!
Pinnock's
GIGGLE WATER
AMERICA'S FAVORITE MERRYMAKING MELANGE
"LIQUID GLEE"
Produce of U.S.A

Gigglewater

CONTAINS ALCOHOL

INGREDIENTS
MAKES 6 SHOTS

3 fl oz Bourbon
1 fl oz butterscotch liqueur
2 fl oz apple juice
3 fl oz Champagne or dry sparkling wine
crushed ice

1. Pour the Bourbon, butterscotch liqueur, and apple juice into a shaker with a little crushed ice and shake vigorously for 30 seconds.
2. Strain into six shot glasses without the ice, then pour over champagne or dry sparkling wine.
3. drink a shot…
4. …and wait to get the giggles!

DOBBY THE HOUSE-ELF'S TIP: Butterscotch liqueur is easy to buy online, if you're of legal drinking age. If you're not, I'm afraid an ageing potion can't help you!

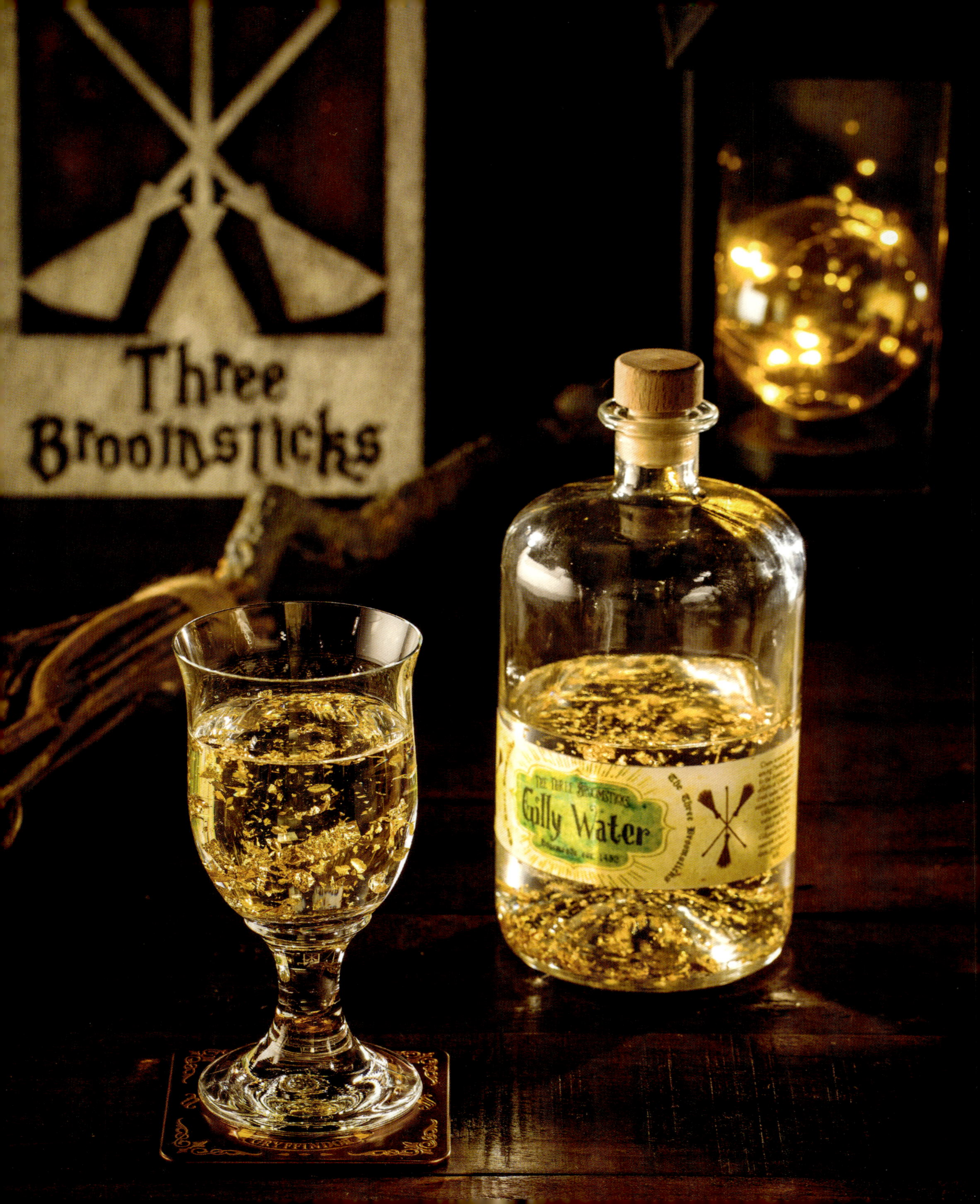
Three Broomsticks
Gilly Water

Gillywater

CONTAINS ALCOHOL

INGREDIENTS
MAKES 1 DRINK

1½ fl oz apricot juice

2 tsp apricot brandy

a few ice cubes

3 fl oz sparkling wine, dry or medium dry, ice-cold

edible gold leaf, finely shredded

1. Pour the apricot juice and apricot brandy into a shaker along with a few ice cubes, and shake vigorously.

2. Sieve the mixture through a bar strainer into a large cocktail glass, pour over ice-cold sparkling wine, and stir in some pieces of edible gold leaf for a touch of drama.

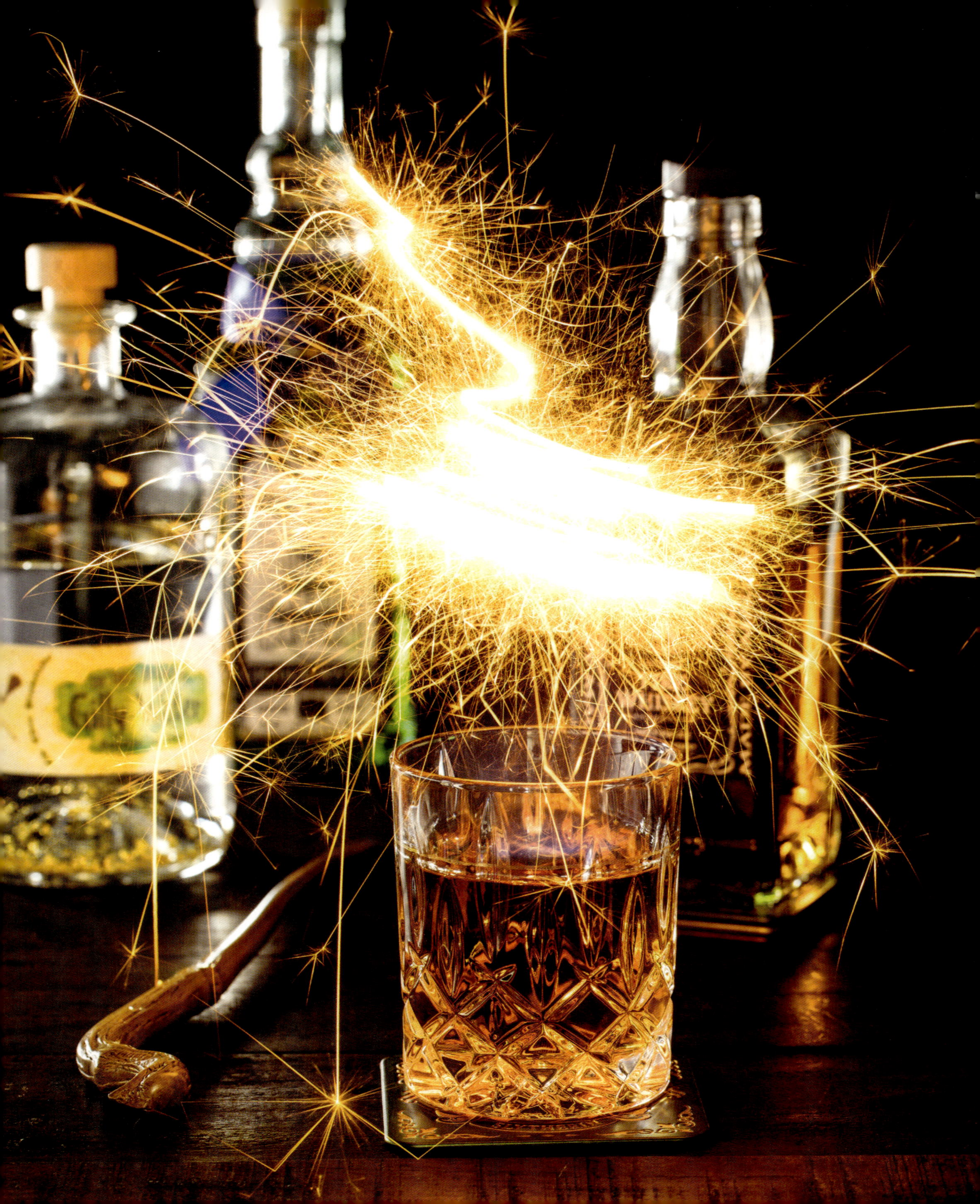

Old Firewhisky

CONTAINS ALCOHOL

INGREDIENTS
MAKE 2 DRINKS

juice and peel of 1 lemon
1 cinnamon stick
4 cloves
3½ fl oz Scotch whisky
2 tbsp honey
1 pinch of nutmeg
1 cup boiling water

1. Put the lemon peel, cinnamon stick, and cloves into a large pitcher. Pour in the lemon juice and whisky and add the honey and nutmeg. Fill up the pitcher with boiling water and stir with a long spoon until the honey has completely dissolved. Add more honey and lemon juice for flavor if necessary.

2. Strain the mixture through a sieve into two heat-resistant glasses and serve hot.

Mulled Mead
SHIPPED AND BOTTLED IN LONDON
BY WIZARD BREWERIES

Mulled mead

INGREDIENTS
MAKES ABOUT 6 PINTS MEAD

3 cups apple juice (naturally cloudy)
½ tsp cultured yeast
10½ cups water, boiled
4½ cups honey
2½ tablets of yeast nutrient
10 tbsp St John's wort
6 tbsp meadowsweet
5 tsp verbena
½ teaspoon Kieselsol (from a drugstore)

Plus:
Demijohn (about 10 pints) with fermenting essay and rubber stopper, thermometer, and bottles (for filling up)

1. First, sterilize the demijohn and all of the other equipment as thoroughly as possible, either by boiling them in water for 10 minutes (if you have a pot big enough) or rinsing them meticulously with a food-safe disinfectant, such as a soda solution. Don't forget to rinse them carefully with clean water afterwards!

2. Prepare the yeast culture. To do this, pour 250 ml apple juice into a sterile jar, carefully stir in the yeast, cover, and leave to stand in a warm place for about 1½ hours.

3. Meanwhile, boil the water in a large pot, then make sure that it cools down to below 75°F, as the yeast cannot survive higher temperature than that. Now put the water, honey, the rest of the apple juice, and the yeast nutrient salt into a container of sufficient size and mix thoroughly. Then fold in the yeast culture, ideally pouring it into the sterile demijohn via a funnel. Add the St John's wort, meadowsweet, and verbena. Seal the demijohn with the rubber stopper and leave to ferment in a warm place for 4 weeks. During this time, swirl the demijohn at least once a day so that the yeast doesn't settle.

4. Then leave to ferment for another 4 weeks, but do not swirl it during this time! You will be able to tell when the fermentation process is over because you won't see any more bubbles rising up into the fermentation lock. ONLY NOW (under no circumstance before!) should you open the demijohn and add the Kieselsol, which clears the yeast and makes it sink to the bottom. Leave to ferment for another week, then strain the mead into the sterilized bottles through a fine-mesh sieve. If kept sealed and airtight, the mead will keep for about 3 months.

5. Before serving, heat the mead in a pot over a low heat, stirring constantly. Pour into heat-resistant glasses or mugs and serve immediately!

Acknowledgements

According to Gamp's Law of Elemental Transfiguration, you can't conjure up good food and drink from thin air, and so too would it be impossible for anyone—Muggle or magician—to create a cookbook like this all on their own. (Indeed, that might well be another of the five exceptions to Gamp's Law.) In fact, many incredibly talented people have been working absolute wonders for months, without the slightest sorcery, to make it possible for you to hold this book in your hands right now.

They are (in no particular order): Jo Löffler & Holger "Holle" Wiest, my "Dinos", without whom nothing would have turned out quite as it has; Roberts "Rob" Urlovskis, who zapped away most of the technical problems that arose as if by magic, time and time again; Thomas Gießl, who's always there when you need him; Angelos "I'll do it in 3D" Tsirigotis, my trusty Swabian Greek (or Greek Swabian, whichever); Oskar "Ossi" Böhm & Annelies Haubold; the K-Clan, featuring Tobi, Andrea, Finja & Lea; Katharina "the only true cat" Böhm; my "brother from another mother" Thomas B. plus family, for many unforgettable moments; Ulrich "the pest" Peste, for the same reasons; Dimitrie Harder, who became a proper buddy over many, many hours spent in the photo studio; Thomas Stamm and his wonderful wife Alexandra for their esteem, support, and friendship; Karin Michelberger, Helge Wittkopp, Franz-Christoph Heel, and the charming Hannah Kwella, who tolerated my sporadic floods of emails with stoic fortitude; and, last but not least, my wonderful family, who once again gave me the time, freedom, and strength to embark on the amazing adventure that this has been.

Everything that you like about this book is down to these people. For any shortcomings in the content, odd wording, incorrect quantities, and excessive celery salt, you are welcome to point the finger of blame at me, ideally via the following social media channels:

Tom Grimm

Follow me at

@tom.grimm.autor

@tom.grimm.autor

@tom_grimm_autor

www.grinningcat.de

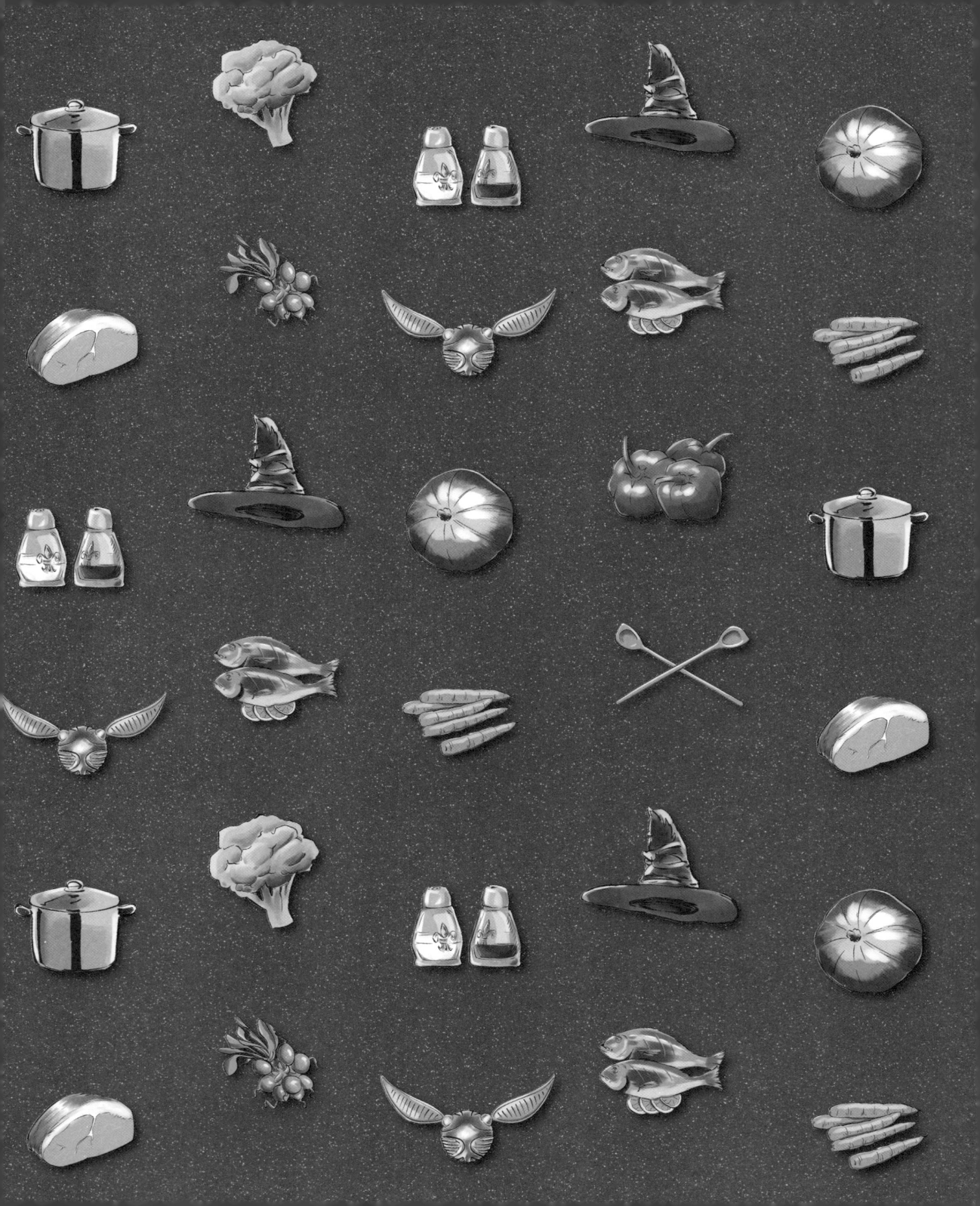